THE HIP-HOP UNDERGROUND AND AFRICAN AMERICAN CULTURE

THE HIP-HOP UNDERGROUND AND AFRICAN AMERICAN CULTURE

BENEATH THE SURFACE

James Braxton Peterson

First published in 2014 by
PALGRAVE MACMILLAN®
in the United States—a division of St. Martin's Press LLC,
175 Fifth Avenue, New York, NY 10010.

Where this book is distributed in the UK, Europe and the rest of the world,
this is by Palgrave Macmillan, a division of Macmillan Publishers Limited,
registered in England, company number 785998, of Houndmills,
Basingstoke, Hampshire RG21 6XS.

Palgrave Macmillan is the global academic imprint of the above companies
and has companies and representatives throughout the world.

Palgrave® and Macmillan® are registered trademarks in the United States,
the United Kingdom, Europe and other countries.

ISBN 978-1-349-45480-8   ISBN 978-1-137-30525-1
DOI 10.1057/9781137305251

Library of Congress Cataloging-in-Publication Data

Peterson, James Braxton, 1971–
    The hip-hop underground and African American culture : beneath
the surface / James Braxton Peterson.
        pages cm
    Summary: "In the Hip Hop Underground and African American
Culture, Peterson explores a variety of 'underground' concepts at
the intersections of African American literature and Hip Hop Culture.
From the Underground Railroad to black holes or from kiln holes to
solitary confinement, this project makes meaningful connections
across multiple iterations of Black concepts of the underground.
Since socially conscious Hip Hop music inherits much of its
socio-political and figurative significance from the Black
underground it functions as a logical recurring subject matter
for this study—situated at Black cultural and conceptual
crossroads"—Provided by publisher.
    Includes bibliographical references and index.

    1. Hip-hop—United States. 2. Subculture—United States.
3. Counterculture—United States. 4. American literature—
African American authors—History and criticism. 5. Literature and
society—United States. 6. African Americans—Intellectual life.
7. African Americans—Race identity. 8. African American youth—
Social conditions. 9. African Americans—Social conditions—1975–
I. Title.

E185.86.P525 2014
305.896'073—dc23   2014010010

A catalogue record for the book is available from the British Library.

Design by Newgen Knowledge Works (P) Ltd., Chennai, India.

First edition: September 2014

10 9 8 7 6 5 4 3 2 1

This book is dedicated to my Dad,
Iver A. Peterson Sr.
Thank you for teaching me how to excavate

CONTENTS

TABLES

ACKNOWLEDGMENTS

A project this long in the making requires quite a bit of acknowledgment. The germ for "Beneath the Surface" originated in my work for a graduate course at the University of Pennsylvania, taught by Dr. Farah Griffin. Professor Griffin's mastery of the interface between Black literature and Black music was absolutely inspiring to me then and continues to be so now. She also introduced me to one of my most formative mentors, James G. Spady. Spady is an organic intellectual whose indefatigable commitment to critiquing and chronicling hip-hop culture remains (for me) an unattainably ideal model. Brother Spady and Prof. Griffin provided me with the substantive sense that a project about various concepts of the underground in Black culture could be viable as a literary dissertation. I also owe a debt of gratitude to my original dissertation advisor, Dr. Houston Baker. Dr. Baker's guidance early on directly shaped the theoretical foundations upon which the dissertation ultimately rested. When Professor Baker moved on to a new institutional home, my work on the dissertation faltered and in some ways I lost sight of the goal of completing my work in a timely manner. Into that malaise stepped Dr. Herman Beavers. Dr. Beavers salvaged this project (and my academic career) at a critical moment. His guidance, input, editorial suggestions, and his enthusiasm for my work were indispensable assets in my professional development. Doc is a beacon for all of his students but I am extraordinarily proud to be his first PhD student at the University of Pennsylvania. He has continued to be one of my greatest supporters, and I am happy to count him among my dearest friends. Dr. Marcylieana Morgan and Dr. Guy Ramsey completed my dissertation committee. Given what Professors Morgan and Ramsey have accomplished since they both so graciously served on my dissertation committee, the bar has been set high for someone like myself who has benefited immensely from their mentorship and the models of their work ethic and scholarly productivity. Thank you.

That said, *The Hip Hop Underground and African American Culture* bares little resemblance to the dissertation project from which it was spawned. Several chapters have appeared in previous publications. Portions of chapter 3, "The Hip-Hop Underground and African American Culture: The Deep Structure of Black Identity in American Literature," originally appeared as "Linguistic Identity and Community in American Literature," in *Language in the USA: Themes for the Twenty-first Century*, edited by Edward Finegan and John R. Rickford, Copyright © 2004 Cambridge University Press. It is reprinted with permission. Chapter 7 is reprinted from "The Depth of the Hole: Intertextuality and Tom Waits's 'Way Down in the Hole'" in *Criticism: A Quarterly for Literature and the Arts*, vol. 52, nos. 3&4 (Summer & Fall 2010), Copyright © 2011 Wayne State University Press. Used with the permission of Wayne State University Press. And a version of the Epilogue, "The Ironies Underground..." originally appeared as "Re(tele)vising a Revolution: Commercial Basketball and a Chat with Gil Scott-Heron," in *Basketball Jones*, edited by Todd Boyd and Kenneth Shropsire (New York: New York University Press, November 2001). I am grateful for all of the professional work conducted by these editors and colleagues, especially Todd Boyd, Ken Shropshire, John Rickford, Ed Finegan, and Paul Farber. Chapter 6 of this book, "Tears for the Departed..." was greatly enhanced by input from members of the Africana Studies Program at Lehigh University during the inaugural session of the William R. Scott brown bag lunch lecture series. Comments and suggestions from Bill Scott, Monica Miller, Seth Moglen, and Berrisford Boothe were extremely helpful in my sense of the Black visual underground.

So many of my students, friends, and family have offered encouragement and input throughout the long process of writing and revising and rewriting this project. My mom and dad (Barbara Peterson and Iver Peterson Sr.), my siblings, IVA, Iver, Scott, Rob, Eunice, Elnora, and Barbara, who only offer love and encouragement even when the work keeps me away from family. Several people have been my eyes and ears in the underground over the long haul of researching and writing this project. Thank you Chris Norwood, Willie Frank Taylor, Erik Smith, and Raymond Brockington. To all of the students who have heard me talk about these ideas in the classroom and who have been inspired by them—Nicholas James, Ted Chung, Michelle Watson Taylor, Aaron Jones, Tanji Gilliam, Wilfredo Gomez, Cynthia Estremera, Sara Mikulasko, Mahdi Woodard, Bronwen Durocher,

Andrew Yaspan, Nadia Sasso, Justin DeSenso, Samina Ali, and so many more—Thank You!

This project would not be possible without the direction, support, and intellectual acumen of Dr. Mark Anthony Neal. Again, and like others mentioned here, Brother MAN's work ethic, scholarly productivity, and his commitment to mentoring me (and scores of other students) have been instrumental in my professional development and in the publication of this book. The influence of certain scholars should be readily apparent in my work and in the pages of this project. There are too many to list here, but some shout-outs on this matter are necessary. Dr. Salamishah Tillet, Dr. Imani Perry, Dr. Joseph Schloss, Adam Mansbach, Dr. Tricia Rose, Dr. Jeffrey Ogbar, Dr. Murray Foreman, Dr. Elaine Richardson, Dr. Priya Parmar, Dr. H. Samy Alim, Dr. Geneva Smitherman, and Dr. David Herman have all consistently encouraged me to get my work done (and out) even as their own work has inspired me to do so. My ideal intellectual interlocutor is Michael Eric Dyson. Dr. Dyson is the most generous scholar that I have ever had the opportunity to work with; his mentorship is an immeasurable contribution to my professional career, and his support for this work and for my career has been both insistent and consistent for well over a decade now. Thanks Doc!!!

For all of the brilliance reflected in the genius scholarship and generous mentorship of those mentioned here (and anyone I may have regrettably left out), all of the shortcomings, intellectual limitations, mistakes, absences, and anything at all wrong with this book is solely ascribable to me. I would also like to thank my editorial team at Palgrave (Robyn Curtis and Erica Buchman) for their inordinate patience and for allowing me to write the book that I wanted to write. By the way, I am not the easiest person to live with when I am writing. I am moody, manic, silent, and sometimes standoffish. I am so grateful for my family—ALL of the Petersons, and for my family, my children, Breanna and James Peterson; and my life partner, the love of my life, Belinda Monique Waller Peterson. Thank you for everything!

CHAPTER 1

ROOTS, RHYMES, AND RHIZOMES:
AN INTRODUCTION TO CONCEPTS OF
THE UNDERGROUND IN BLACK CULTURE

The Black underground is a rhizome, a diffuse root that projects its multifaceted conceptualizations throughout African American culture. It spreads its root-like tentacles through the fabric of history, manifesting at continuous points in reality and in cultural production. In the book, I attempt to trace some of these tentacles, mapping the conceptual pathways left in the wake of certain manifestations of the Black underground as an artistic or political movement, visual culture, an aesthetic quality or a literary trope. In this introduction to the book, I have culled discursive and meta-discursive texts from a variety of media including music, television, literature, and art. The undergirding guide, this book's patron saint and muse, can be captured in the multitude of meanings assigned to the homological pairing of roots/routes. In this pairing, the phonological rendering of the word captures its homological masking of underground metaphors. The rhizomorphic qualities of roots/routes are useful introductory symbols to the various concepts of the Black underground. I don't employ the adjectival form of "rhizome" here to initiate an in-depth analysis of, and/or theoretical engagement with, the works of Deleuze and Guattari. The rhizome simply lends itself to a conceptual understanding of how the Black underground achieves its many meanings and manifestations in African American culture—particularly its extraordinary valence with politics, genealogy, history, language, and, most especially, hip-hop culture. According to Deleuze and Guattari, "a rhizome has no beginning or end; it is always in the middle, between things, interbeing, intermezzo. The tree is filiation, but the rhizome is alliance, uniquely alliance."[1]

There are too many alliances of the concepts of the underground in human culture for me to delineate them all in these pages. I have attempted to detail a few of these concepts in the chapters and pages that follow. I adopt several strategic and/or stylistic approaches that will become apparent throughout the book, but a description of some methodology is appropriate here. This book required the language of literary studies as much as it did a small set of ethnographic investigative experiences and journalistic work. It required as much of my own cultural immersion in hip-hop here at home and abroad as it did of my immersion in various academic disciplines, including linguistics, Africana Studies, and narratology. Due to the various disciplines and approaches available to me, I have resisted, wherever possible, the laborious language of traditional literary theory. Instead of neatly packaged theses and litanies of supporting examples, I attempt to construct discourses around/through the concepts of the underground as they have manifested themselves in hip-hop and African American cultures. I think of these discursive constructions as rhyming (at the discursive level) through repetition with a signifying difference. In this sense, you might consider me an emcee of the concepts of the underground in Black culture.

The chronological range of this book roughly extends from the nineteenth century (slavery and the Underground Railroad) to the twenty-first century (including underground moments in Black literature and the underground constitutions of hip-hop). In the interest of representing the complexity of this scope/range, I deploy the term "roots" in order to explicate and allude to several of my discursive points. Roots are the formative concept of the underground. Not only because they are the term that represents things underground, but also because they represent the human connections to history and genealogy. Roots are literally underground and figuratively emblematic of an individual's connection to his/her history and culture. The term functions in this introductory chapter as a sociolinguistic rubric through which the listener/reader can explore the concepts of the underground in Black culture. The debut of the *Roots* miniseries in 1977 presents an opportune initial example, especially in certain literary discourses that previewed the impact of the television version of this series on American society. On September 26, 1976, James Baldwin published "A Review of *Roots*" in the *New York*

Times. Here Baldwin actually reviews Alex Haley's literary text of the same name. He situates the book review in a political context at the outset of his discussion. He notes the bicentennial year and suggests the ironic invisibility of Alex Haley whom he heralds as "the first genuine black Westerner." Baldwin establishes the critical political context of Haley's hiddenness as being in the midst of Republican and Democratic conventions, presidential hopefuls, and "a carefully muffled pain and panic in the nation."[2] For Baldwin, Haley's narrative is a compassionate testament to a systematically forgotten Black history. "The world of Alex Haley's book begins in Gambia, West Africa in 1750. . . . In the re-creation of this time and place, Haley succeeds beautifully where many have failed." Some of the more striking elements of this little review become apparent when it is put into conversation with another one of Baldwin's classic essays and the inescapable fact that Baldwin's praise of *Roots* prophetically anticipates its extraordinary impact on television and the collective consciousness of an essentially pre-cable television American viewing audience. In "Alas, Poor Richard," Baldwin comes to terms with one of his literary mentors and artistic antagonists, Richard Wright. Through conversational reconstruction, Baldwin invites readers to participate in one of the most exclusive literary cliques of all time: that of himself, Chester Himes, and Richard Wright and his attendant French intellectuals. Baldwin vehemently disliked Wright's French intellectual friends, suggesting that for all of their mental might, these great French thinkers, including Jean-Paul Sartre, had no conception of or appreciation for Wright's complex personality. In order to rectify his legendary critique of Richard Wright's Bigger Thomas figure, Baldwin posits an underlying thesis regarding the Bigger archetype as well as other instances of blatant, unresolvable violence in Wright's work. "This violence, as in so much of Wright's work, is gratuitous and compulsive. It is one of the severest criticisms that can be leveled against his work. The violence is gratuitous and compulsive because the *root* of the violence is never examined. The *root* is rage. [my emphasis]"[3] These roots of rage are grounded in the autobiographical experiences of Wright from his upbringing chronicled in *Black Boy* to his uncanny portrayal of Bigger Thomas on film. Baldwin traces these experiences even as he critiques the Black artist in exile who experiences a constant "rootlessness." According to Baldwin, discussions about the roots of Black culture would invariably draw a negative response from Richard Wright. "'Roots,' Richard would snort, 'what—roots! Next thing you'll be telling me is that all colored folks have rhythm."[4] The irony for Baldwin in these conversational exchanges is that he considered Wright to be at the center of his literary genealogy, the roots of his artistic development, if you will.

The roots in Baldwin's discourse coalesce around his ultimate judgments about Black writers. According to Baldwin, Bigger Thomas's signal failure is his inability to see his own humanity. Almost via extension, he interprets Wright as an author frozen in the era of his life, only eventually able to realize that he and his work could become obsolete. For Baldwin, Bigger simply is not representative. By a comparable Baldwinian metric, Haley's Kunta Kinte is nearly Bigger's antithesis. The nuanced depictions of African culture and Black humanity in the face of White depravity suggest a watershed moment in American history for Black and White folk alike. Here was the "truth" about the roots of American culture. And where Baldwin critically shuns Wright and *Native Son*, he champions Haley and *Roots* as a defining moment in the sociopolitical fabric of American life. "*Roots* is a study of continuities, of consequences, of how people perpetuate themselves, how each generation helps to doom, or helps to liberate, the coming one...."[5] In a sense, where Baldwin denies the crown of the Black literary genealogy to Wright, he anoints Alex Haley as an author of all of our Black roots.

Returning to and re-viewing *Roots* in 2014 masks the impact it had on American popular culture in 1977. In 1977 nearly 130 million people tuned in to watch television's first successful consecutive-night miniseries. *Roots* appeared on television just years before cable television and VCRS completely fragmented the television-viewing audience. Thus nearly half the country watched the most comprehensive portrayal of American history and slavery produced in an audiovisual format to date. For the twenty-fifth anniversary of its broadcast, many of the actors/actresses, the executive producers, scholars, and various cultural critics commented on the significance of this television epic. In response to several well-publicized challenges to the authorial integrity of Alex Haley's narrative, Dr. Alvin Poussaint, Harvard psychiatrist, noted, "There was a larger truth that he captured: That we were brought here against our will, we were mistreated, we progressed, we had survived, we were a strong people who could keep going on, despite this experience, and become part of America." At least, according to Dr. Poussaint, *Roots*, the television series, fulfilled the promise of Haley's critically acclaimed genealogy. Again here,

Baldwin's sense of this significance is revealed through his intercourse with Richard Wright. Baldwin believed that Richard Wright's enormous popularity made the Bigger figure all the more dangerous to race relations in America. Bigger represents no one's roots. Haley's genealogy even with all of its inaccuracies—or more aptly described, samples of other histories—represents an important popular attempt at a cinematic, Afrocentric genealogy for a critical mass of Black folk living and working in a mid-1970s America. In a sense, Haley's *Roots* expands the geographic and Black underground spaces when compared to Wright's diagrams of ethnic and economic oppression in the South and in Chicago.

More Roots

Romare Bearden crafted a *Roots*-inspired television guide cover for the 1977 premier of the miniseries. The cover art simply and visually captures the signal issues held forth in the literary and televisual texts of *Roots*. The most poignant of these issues is the rhizomorphic geneaology of Black folk in America. The American-flag body and the Black (mask-like) head are juxtaposed with and in confrontation with the visual iconography of middle passage, a too-often overlooked historical experience in the discourses on slavery. The whiteness of the ship encases the mortally captured slaves in the hull of the ship, which in its near entirety, appears to be below sea level. I first encountered this image at a University of Pennsylvania exhibit in the fall of 1996 titled, "A Graphic Odyssey: Romare Bearden as Printmaker." I was only six years old when *Roots* aired, so although I have memories of it and its discursive impact, I did not recall the television guide cover art. This *Roots* image is remarkable for its aforementioned visual contemplation of Black American history. But it also represents a mass communication from an artist, whose creative roots reside in the multifaceted production of a postmodern visual art: collage and printmaking. Romare Bearden's art figures significantly into the formal aspects of underground concepts explored in this book in at least three ways. First, he deliberately chose to be a printmaker because he knew that making multiple copies of his work would allow his message to be disseminated more pervasively than if he simply painted originals. Note here also that printmaking is a collaborative effort. Second, Bearden favored the collage in his artistic production. His prints that are often imported parts of other cultural products (magazine images, ads, etc.) are also layered with colors, prints, and collage-like distortions of images. And finally, Bearden, layered his work with multiple techniques and styles. One image may be produced in three stages, each with an additional printmaking process to slightly alter the appearance of the original.

Bearden's 1975 painting titled "The Family" was also a part of the "Odyssey" exhibit. Bearden combined the techniques of Aquatint and photoengraving to render this piece. Much of Bearden's artwork during this era combined various artistic techniques including lithography, photolithography, and etching, among others. The reference to "The Family" is only to put into relief the "stripped-down" quality of his "Roots" drawing/painting. The *Roots* image was distinct from every other piece in this particular exhibit because it did not appear to employ as many layers or artistic techniques in its visage. However, this image is conceptually layered with the contested and forgotten history of slavery. The layering of American, African, white, and Black identities reflects Bearden's artistic penchant for sampling and collage. Finally, this semiotic portrait of a signal moment in American televised history also situates a Black visual artist, popularly exploding, on the cover of a mainstream print medium that is ushering in the multimedia emergence of television and the proliferation of channels (and texts) that television will soon feature.

The triumph of Romare Bearden's *TV Guide* cover art should be recognized as the realization of his own philosophical approach to art production and art dissemination. He was genuinely committed to the affordability of creativity and the accessibility of art for the masses. Whether or not this *TV Guide* cover or the airing of *Roots* on national television had any tangible effects on equal opportunity, police brutality, or other social ills in America that plagued African Americans is impossible to prove or disprove. The plausible impact on the cultural imaginary is suggestive but the rendering of this urtext in one of this century's most powerful emergent media clearly had affects on the up-and-coming generation of African American cultural producers. There are several contemporaries of Romare Bearden and Alex Haley who contend with the multivalent conceptualizations of roots as I have tried to detail them thus far (Baldwin and Toni Morrison, among others). Yet there are literary moments that precede this initial wrestling with the rhizomorphic roots of Black American cultural production. Frederick Douglass and Ralph Ellison's *Invisible Man* provide this introductory reflection with inspired complex scenes of cultural identification through the symbol of the root. In each of the following literary scenes, the botanical root functions as a placebo for existential connections to the roots of culture and humanity for the perspective protagonists. These placebo roots are important tangents in the rhizomorphic cartography of the concepts of the underground in Black culture because through these episodes we can begin to sketch the literary dimensions of the underground imagery manifested in roots.

The root in Frederick Douglass' 1845 *Narrative of the Life of Frederick Douglass, an American Slave,* is nearly unremarkable within the narrative structure of the text. Poet and literary critic Kevin Young astutely defines the root in Douglass's narrative as a fetish, "meaning a physical, visual, even private totem that provides power to its carrier."[6] After being hired out to a notoriously cruel, "nigger-breaking" slave master and "trainer" named Covey, Douglass quickly falls in contentious favor with him. Fearing his life, Douglass hides out in the woods surrounding Covey's plantation. He ventures a return, but he is turned back by a cowhide-wielding Covey. Tired, hungry, and out of options, Douglass turns to an associate of his, named Sandy, who happens to be a rootworker or conjure man. Sandy is married to a free Black woman and claims that he has not been beaten by a White man since he has carried a particular root in his right pocket. Douglass is immediately skeptical of the power of this root. "I at first rejected the idea, that the simple carrying of a root in my pocket would have any such effect as he had said...."[7] When Douglass returns to Covey's plantation, he initially reconsiders the powers of the root as he is not immediately set upon by Mr. Covey. But eventually Covey challenges him and Douglass rises to this challenge with inspiring results. "The battle with Mr. Covey was the turning point in my career as a slave. It rekindled the few expiring embers of freedom, and revived within me a sense of my own manhood."[8] Douglass's skepticism regarding the power of the root taps into the rational undertones of his narrative voice throughout the text. Yet the root "works" insofar as he is never again beaten by a White slave master. According to Young, "the root serves to empower Douglass: its mere possession allows him to no longer be a possession."[9] The root is a pivotal placebo against the fears and ills of slavery and its debilitating effects on Douglass's sense of his own humanity. Douglass's rejection of its powers and his simultaneous acceptance of these same powers (he *does* take the root with him when he leaves Sandy) symbolically reflect the complex relationships between an American slave and his/her

African roots. Those roots exist and are powerful, but a slave's ability to believe in the elusive and complex epistemology of African and/or Afrocentric cultures is limited by a rationalist Western indoctrination. Some of these tensions will be revisited throughout this book as they mirror a signal tension in American culture between underground and mainstream cultural products (music, literature, political movements, and language itself).[10]

Ellison's protagonist in the classic novel *Invisible Man* navigates his way through a geographic maze of rural and urban terrains, Black and White worlds in the north and south regions of mid-twentieth-century America. According to literary scholar Kimberly Bentson, *Invisible Man* is "a novel that is very much about the responsibilities to roots, to the past of oneself and one's blood."[11] During the midsection of the novel, an experience with Invisible Man's roots develops in a canny exchange with a yam vendor. This exchange takes place moments before Invisible Man (IM) witnesses the eviction of an elderly Black couple. The eviction episode is a turning point in IM's narrative as he returns to his valedictorian form and seizes the opportunity to speak publicly again (this time in service of Black resistance as opposed to his earlier valedictorian speech in service of White supremacy). It is at this impromptu speech that IM is discovered by the Brotherhood, an organization loosely modeled after the American Communist Party, and eventually funneled into his next identity as speechmaker for the same. The connection of this chain of events initiates in the exchange between IM and the yam vendor. Even as IM smells "the odor of baking yams," he is struck by nostalgia.[12] He remembers his home in the south and his childhood: he and his friends hiding behind geography textbooks and secretly eating yams. After IM reluctantly buys a yam for a dime, he embarks on an interior rant about the vagaries of food-identifiable stereotypes. He fantasizes about utterly embarrassing his mentor-turned-nemesis, Bledsoe, by publicly accusing him of being a chitterlings lover. This is IM's way of mentally grappling with his own shame about desiring and eating a yam, which is an archetypal (and publicly visible, as it were) connection to his southern roots. As he realizes the absurdity of his shame, he projects his realizations onto the figure he despises most at this time, Bledsoe. He imagines that the caption over his picture in the newspaper would read: "Prominent Educator Reverts to Field-Niggerism!" Eventually, IM exonerates himself from the shame of relishing one's cultural roots, no matter how they might be viewed in public, in the north, or in front of White folks. "To hell with being ashamed of what you liked. No more of that for me. I am what I am!"[13] He goes on to claim the yams as his "birthmark. . . . I yam what I am."[14] IM's reclamation of his southern roots through a public reconciliation with a yam presents multiple reflections of a root iconography. Of course, the yam is in fact a root, in botanical terms. It is categorized in the genus *Discorea*, and is the tuberous root of several tropical plants. Because it thrives in the tropics it is also a staple food in many African countries/cultures. Thus Ellison subtly portrays a dense and complex existential contemplation where IM comes to grips with an oppressive value system that has pushed him to ignore and/or shun his roots. His consumption of the yam is the most visceral means through which he can internalize a connection to his southern roots and by extension his historical connection to the continent of Africa. Similar to the aforementioned quote, IM's identification with the yam creates the opportunity for him to affirm himself by saying "I am." Of course, the trajectory is not that neat. For even as Douglass questions the power of his conjure root, when IM returns to the vendor for a second and third helping of these delectable yams he finds that his second yam is frost bitten and he throws it into the streets.

This yam episode in Ellison's *Invisible Man* quickly shifts into the eviction episode where IM attempts to assuage an enraged mob of Black folk who collectively witness the violently-made-public lives of an elderly couple named Mr. and Mrs. Primus Provo. Through IM's discourse and the relentless actions of the evicting officials, the gathering crowd collectively comes to understand the futility of a lifelong laborer's material reality. As IM scans over the paltry possessions of the Provos laid bare in the streets of Harlem, he recognizes an old newspaper clipping detailing the deportation of Marcus Garvey and an even older document that appears to be the freedom papers of some not-so-distant enslaved ancestor of Primus Provo. The entire scene draws IM closer to his roots than he has been in the novel up to this point. He is moved to speak to the crowd in this episode through his connection to the Provos and their tragic circumstances. As the elderly woman cries, he likens the effects (on him) of her sobbing to that of a child witnessing his parents crying and subsequently feeling the impulse to cry. This genealogical connection is all the more poignant for IM since it is a portal through which he will claim his penultimate identity in the novel; that of rhetorician/speaker/recruiter for the Harlem Chapter of the Brotherhood.

Thus far I have briefly detailed how the term "roots"—a synecdoche for the concepts of the underground—signifies in historical and literary figures as well as how it figured in the medium of television. The final frontier for the range of discourses in this book then is that of music. Much of the music of topical and figurative import for this book derives from the culture of hip-hop. Surely it is critical to understand the connection between the impact of the television program *Roots* in 1977 and the development of hip-hop culture during the same time.[15] The pervasive, mainstream media exposure of an archetypal genealogy for African Americans that traces Black culture to its historical roots in Africa affected all modes of African American cultural production in the mainstream media as well as the consumers of that media. Considering the content and theme of images already in circulation by the late 1970s, The *Roots* miniseries must have been refreshing and/or startling for an American television-viewing audience. According to scholar Mark Anthony Neal, "African American dysfunction was mass mediated and commodified for mass consumption via network news programs, Hollywood films like *Fort Apache*, and television programs like 'Starsky and Hutch' and 'Beretta'.... The commodification of the black poor or underclass as human spectacle became a standard trope of mass culture parlaying a clear sense of social difference from blackness...." Neal also notes that this mass-mediated exploitation (of racially and class-oriented tensions) affects both Whites and a growing Black middle class.[16] These mass multimedia interactions constitute a discourse in the Foucaultian sense. Discourse is language practice, used by various constituencies (the law, the government, the church, the state, or the media) to control power relationships between people. The language of influence here is television, but the discursive impulse was not limited to television media, and, eventually, other media proved to be more popularly accessible and more profoundly influential.

It is not at all coincidental that hip-hop explodes onto the postindustrial landscapes of the United States on the cusp of an electronics media explosion (VCRs, belt-driven turntables, Computers, Internet, and DVDs) and within two years of the debut of the televisual version of Alex Haley's *Roots*. Hip-hop culture's mass-mediated functionality lent itself thoroughly to a music born on the technological innovations and improvisations of DJs and the disenfranchised youth of inner cities.[17] In his philosophical fragment on Afro-American Popular Music, Cornel West asserts the following:

> Black rap music is more important than the crossover of jazz musicians to rhythm and blues, the rise of the "older" Michael Jackson, and the return of gospel music because, similar to bebop and technofunk, black rap music is emblematically symptomatic of a shift in sensibilities and moods in Afro-America. Black rap music indeed *Africanizes* Afro-American popular music—accenting syncopated polyrhythms, kinetic orality, and sensual energy in a refined form of raw expressiveness.... (my emphasis)[18]

This "shift in sensibilities and moods in Afro-America" derived from a complex valence between these sensibilities and the media images in mass circulation. What Professor West refers to as Black rap music is the most readily enterable form of discourse produced by/through hip-hop culture. The idea that the music enters a multimedia discourse and *Africanizes* popular forms in order to render itself, captures the complexity of Black culture in the public media. Rap music generally claims this Africanization through form although I will also suggest that the content of underground hip-hop wrestles with themes that speak specifically to a set of African American experiences. Still, hip-hop culture broadly conceived, engages in Africanization via its focus on oral traditions, and various Black diasporic influences on styles of dress, dance, and visual art.

One final addition to this short list of rhizomorphic roots-imagery is that of those hip-hop virtuosos, The Roots. In the late 1980s, if one were to venture to a lower (3rd or 4th) South Street corner in Philadelphia, one might find the early version of The Roots freestyling over a set of makeshift drums on that corner for the love of hip-hop. This image might be difficult to summon given the fact that The Roots were the house band for Jimmy Fallon's popular late night show—and have now become the "Tonight Show Band," as Fallon took over for Jay Leno in February 2014. The Roots are Questlove (Ahmir Thompson, drums), Black Thought (Tariq Trotter, lead vocalist/emcee), Kamal (keyboards), Leonard Hubbard (bass), James Poyser (writer/producer), and in the past they have featured either/both Rahzel and/or Scratch as verbal percussionists, a skill most often referred to as the human beat box. Although they won a Grammy for their 1999 single, "You Got Me" (featuring Erykah Badu and cowritten by Jill Scott) and now appear regularly on late night network television, The Roots have never been impressive in terms of their numbers of actual records sold in the marketplace—by contemporary music industry standards. They have consistently existed in an underground chamber of hip-hop culture and of mainstream super-popular rap music. To all indications they have done this willfully and purposefully. Having interviewed various members, attended multiple shows, and listened to each album numerous times, I submit them as an important manifestation in hip-hop of the concepts of the underground detailed in this book.

The Roots's first record, aptly titled *Organix*, was recorded (in the early 1990s) just before they embarked on their first European tour with jazz bassist Jamaldeen Tacuma. When they returned to the United States, they had several offers from record labels. Some scholars, journalists, and hip-hop aficionados would argue that by virtue of their contracts with so-called major labels, The Roots cannot lay claim to underground status within hip-hop culture. I do not necessarily agree with these claims or this limited definition of underground hip-hop, an argument/discussion that will be taken up more directly in chapter 4. The Roots' second and third albums, titled *Do You Want More?* and *Illadelph Half-life*, were received well critically, but neither reached the music industry's coveted, gold designation (500,000 units sold) within a reasonable time of their initial release. Their third album, *Things Fall Apart*, is named in homage to Chinua Achebe's novel of the same name, which is named after the line in the first stanza of William Butler Yeats's poem "The Second Coming." According to Yeats's poem, when things fall apart, the center cannot hold.

Achebe's protagonist, Okonkwo, grounds himself in a culture of violent, rarely emotional, masculinity, complemented by cultural conservatism and preservation most often practiced to ensure his social status within the Igbo community of his village. He attains success through his frugal, hardworking, stoic ways, but disrespects his late father for being lazy, effeminate, and unsuccessful, and his son, for exhibiting traits of his father. He beats his wives, sometimes to the point of death, and he murders his surrogate son in order not to appear weak before the male members of his community. The ultimate conflict of the novel stems from the colonial missionaries whose culture and religion slowly erode the Igbo traditions in the communities of Lower Nigeria. Okonkwo ultimately loses faith in his clan because of their inability to prevent the White government's messengers from escaping the village. The tragedy of Achebe's message is that Okonkwo's perceptions of masculinity, violence, and tradition were just as detrimental to the stability of Igbo cultural life as the missionaries and Christianity. The Roots' *Things Fall Apart* echoes similar conflicts for the constituents of hip-hop culture. In the opening skit of the album, a sample from Spike Lee's *Mo' Better Blues* features Denzel Washington's character questioning the vitality of jazz music in the face of dwindling African American support. Through *Things Fall Apart*, the Roots pose a question: Do you reach an audience by playing to its expectations, or by raising them to a new level? Throughout much of their career, they have produced art as if the challenge has been to raise those expectations to new levels. This is at least partially why the Roots can claim a common plight with the characters of Achebe's classic novel. As musicians they are committed to the roots and traditions of Black music. As hip-hop artists they are committed to producing quality music that reflects the culture's aesthetics without recklessly exploiting the art forms for material gain. But they are constantly battling colonizing forces within and external to hip-hop culture, including consumerism, violence, notions of masculinity, and tensions between change and maintaining tradition (some of the conflicts faced by Okonkwo). Their primary challenge has been to demonstrate the vitality of live instrumentation (the "organix," if you will) in hip-hop music where technology readily substitutes for musical instrumentation. Thus they are the vanguard of a stylistically trendy musical culture, but they "stay ahead of the game" through their insistent reliance on innovative hip-hop productions derived from the much more traditional live instrumentation. The Roots are at the center of poetics and live instrumentation in hip-hop. Their vibe has musically touched the careers of Ursula Rucker, Erykah Badu, Bilal, Kindred, Jill Scott, Jazzyfatnastees, Musiq Soulchild, Jay Z, Common, D'Angelo, Eve, Beanie Sigel, Cody Scott, The Philadelphia Experiment, and many many others. But they have created a musical extension of hip-hop that counters mainstream pop-cultural sentiments and musical trends and they have been able to establish an extraordinary array of influences on and collaborations with other artists through a commitment to their own musical roots.

On a more recent record, 2012's *Undun*, The Roots continue their artistically underground efforts in a powerful concept album that unfolds in a reverse chronology. *Undun* opens with an audible flat line, signaling the death of the album's main character, a mid-level drug dealer, whose pursuit of material gain is predicated on a capitalist sensibility equivalent to Malcolm X's rhetorical statement: "by any means necessary." The flat line in the opening track, "Dun," is haunted by a baby's cries and screams. Depending upon the listener's interpretation, the crying baby might indicate a child's response to the loss of a parent or relative or it may signal a baby's cry in the immediate moments following birth. Either of these interpretations (there may be many more) indicate the conflict and anguish that accompanies life (and loss of life) associated with an individual's experience navigating an urban underground economy: limited occupational options and the dangerous consequences inevitably linked to the illicit drug trade. The audible flat line and the baby's cry (in tandem) also represent both sides of the life/death divide. A baby's cry represents life aboveground just as the audible flat line signals death and an immanent eternity buried underground. These opening sounds outline the conceptual structure of *Undun*, a title that plays on the finality of one's life being "done" and the album's reverse chronology. The term "dun" has also been a part of the lexicon of African American Vernacular English (AAVE), functioning as a male referential term similar to "dude," "duke," "son," or "man"—informal, colloquial ways of greeting individuals (e.g., "what up, dun?").

The order and thematic structure of *Undun* distinguish it as an important concept album, but its lyrical content, designed to critically engage the prevailing messaging in mainstream popular hip-hop, reflects certain conceptualizations of underground themes in hip-hop music. "Tip the Scale," a song that comes late in the album and that reflects themes and concerns of the album's protagonist prior to his murder, delves into the ways in which the criminal justice system exploits the limited socioeconomic opportunities for too many poor Black and brown youth. The refrain suggests that homicide or suicide, living well or "a living hell" are life options as arbitrary as a coin flip. The narrators of the song understand the ruse of equity in our society and in the criminal justice system; they are therefore discovering ways to tip the scales (of justice) in their favor. The song's plodding melancholic tonalities suggest the limited viability of this particular option. That is, tipping the scales in favor of the album's protagonist requires a willingness to risk one's life and/or take the lives of others in order to strive for socioeconomic justice. In the second verse of "Tip the Scale," featured MC, Dice Raw previews his upcoming solo album, *Jimmy's Back*, based upon Michelle Alexander's *The New Jim Crow*. As the narrator of the second verse laments the probabilities of incarceration,

he claims that many "niggas" go to jail but not many (or any) of them
come out in the manner that Malcolm X emerged from prison—as a
revolutionary activist and thinker. Malcolm X's autobiographical narrative is one of the most formative texts within hip-hop culture—often
referenced and widely regarded as one of the most important prison
narratives relevant to the hip-hop generation. But his is a narrative
that is severed from the common prison narratives of the late twentieth
and early twenty-first century, a time period plagued by the privatization of the prison system, extraordinarily high recidivism rates, and
the institutionally racist implications of the so-called War on Drugs.
Ultimately, according to Dice Raw's narration, the scales of justice are
not equal in weight and, as a consequence, there are only two options
for Black and brown youth: digging tunnels or digging graves.[19] These
underground options—digging tunnels in order to carry out secret
drug trafficking across borders or digging graves for those who die in
urban American underground economies—really proffer no options
at all for *Undun*'s protagonist. They serve as a portrait of the alienated
urban protagonist on the precipice of a Black underground that presents as a life or death—an economic liberty or death option, but in fact
the only option is the social and/or real death that the dearth of viable
opportunities presents to too many poor young people of color in the
twenty-first century.

Concepts of the Underground

These various roots represent the rhizomorphic potential of this collection of essays and writings about hip-hop culture, African American
literature, and various concepts of the underground. Standard notions
of roots, Alex Haley's *Roots*, James Baldwin's reflections on *Roots*,
Frederick Douglass's mystical root, Invisible Man's yam, and The
Roots of hip-hop lore, all together constitute a segment or stanza
in my own version of academic verse on these themes. When I consider how hip-hop most directly influences my scholarship, this style
of discursive rhyming through repetition (with a difference) reflects
the aesthetic impulses of hip-hop toward bricolage, collage, sampling,
remixing, etc. This rhyming through discursive repetition with a difference is a process of identifying the semblances and the patterns of
underground signification, especially at the intersection of hip-hop
music and African American culture. One of the most regularly referenced and critically engaged concepts of Henry Louis Gates's work

is "signifyin(g)" or repetition with a difference. He effectively argues that the act of repetition is differential in African American culture at least in part because meanings are dictated by context. The distinction between semantics (the study of truth-conditional meaning) and pragmatics (the study of non-truth conditional meaning) collapses when the linguistic sign can readily be disassociated from its appropriate signified (e.g., the use of Railroad language to signify the Underground Railroad or the vast array of meanings generated by and through the concept of the underground itself). Another component to this argument derives from artistic notions of creativity. Gates (and others) suggest that African American art often relies on repetition and repurposing in the form of collage. The collage is both significantly repetitive and artistically collaborative—an art form with properties wholly consistent with some of the ways in which hip-hop music is created. In some collage and in much of the hip-hop music discussed in this book, the significance of repetition derives from the new sum of the old collected parts. Think of this book as a collage of various concepts, theories, disciplines, and academic approaches. The underground is a conceptual theme and in each chapter I depict a different snapshot of this theme as it manifests in a particular concept or constellation of concepts.

Chapter 2 analyzes the role of verbal and spatial masking in conceptualizing the underground. Working chronologically backward, from hip-hop producer DJ Premier to Frederick Douglass, and then chronologically forward, from Paul Laurence Dunbar to the Fugees, I construct a discursive parallelogram of masking as the subversive tool of choice in and of underground situations. My signal example of the ways in which dialect functions as a mask is a sociolinguistic analysis of the term "wilding," a concept circulated by a racially biased media in the immediate aftermath of the Central Park Jogger case. Once these forms of masking are detailed/unveiled, I briefly explore communicative and sociolinguistic contexts of the Underground Railroad and its uncanny connection to the world's first subway system, the London Underground, and other points/examples in the constellation of underground concepts.

Chapter 3 briefly explores linguistic identity in African American literature. After providing a parochial rubric for analyzing identity through linguistic and discursive c(l)ues, I interpret several scenes or passages in African American literature. Through a discussion of linguistic identity in African American literature, I attempt to define and employ the notion of deep structure in linguistics as an underground metaphor for literary interpretations of linguistic identity.

In chapter 4, I attempt to define the concept of the underground in hip-hop culture. Taking cues from the music and writings of Saul Williams, I explore hip-hop underground narratives of mythology and history. Many scholars have defined the hip-hop underground via particular performance venues (Morgan), and/or regional spaces/ affiliations (Harrison), and many have concluded that underground hip-hop should be defined by its relationship to the marketplace. While I acknowledge the important work of these scholars I also attempt to make space for thinking through an underground in hip-hop that centers on themes significant to the African American experience. Finally, I offer some examples of the ways in which hip-hop artists have engaged the concept of the underground in/through their lyrics.

Chapter 5 is titled "The Cipher of the Underground in Black Culture." The cipher is the movement of voice to/through various participants in a particular discourse (similar to discourse turns). So, for example, a group of emcees rhyme in a cipher about things in their immediate environment, usually to highlight spontaneous freestyling ability (lyrical improvisation). Sometimes the content or themes are connected, other times the form of the ritual, (the cipher) itself establishes the social space for the creative expression to occur. As I will detail in this chapter, the cipher is a fundamental concept in hip-hop culture. It identifies a ritualistic discourse amongst emcees. As a scholar of hip-hop culture (and Black literature), my sense of the African American literary discourse informed and expressed through tropes of the underground is that various artists and literary theorists are engaged in a tropological discourse that demonstrates the conceptual potency of the cipher in hip-hop culture. The concepts of the underground figure in Black cultural discourse in many ways. The discursive connections between Richard Wright, Ralph Ellison, Amiri Baraka, Thelonious Monk, Dr. Houston Baker, and KRS One construct a metaphorical cipher of the underground. Dr. Baker theorizes the Black (w)hole; Thelonious Monk provides a striking visual "underground" image; KRS One makes his contribution orally in the form of a storied rap titled Hol(d); and Wright, Ellison, and Baraka, all figure the trope of the underground in literature. Richard Wright's work functions as a literary "bridge" since his short story corpus connects the literature of the Underground Railroad to Black modernistic concepts of the underground in the mid-twentieth century. As a central theoretical formulation of my work this cipher showcases a vast artistic repertoire fully engaged with the concepts of the underground, many of which are treated in this chapter.

Chapter 6, "Tears for the Departed: See(k)ing a Black Visual Underground in Hip-Hop and African American Cultures," provides some cursory analysis of how concepts of the underground might be interpreted through visual media. Critical inquiry at the intersections of hip-hop music, African American literature, and Black visual culture inform a generative discourse for Black underground imagery within and across an array of interrelated texts. Through several pairings: Jonathan Green's "Seeking" and the Gravediggaz's "The Night the Earth Cried;" and Mos Def's "hip-hop" and Jeff Wall's "After Invisible Man," this chapter seeks to excavate a ritualistic intertextuality embedded in certain works that feature elements of what can tentatively be referred to as Black visual underground culture, a constellation of lyrics, images, and textual allusions that articulate an underground ethos present (if not readily audible/visible) in hip-hop culture.

Chapter 7, "The Depth of the Hole: Intertextuality and Tom Waits's 'Way Down in the Hole,'" turns to one of the most important television series for the hip-hop generational viewing audience. Through an in-depth analysis of HBO's *The Wire*'s theme song, I attempt to explore the underground imagery in the series and its powerful interactions with African American literature and a range of other concepts of the underground in this book. "Way Down in the Hole" is a Tom Waits's tune that is performed by four additional groups/artists, from a variety of musical genres, and all of them have a distinct "take" on the song. What emerges from these readings and hearings is a complex sense of the institutional expansiveness of *The Wire* as a series and its signal importance to discussions about underground economies and the African American experience in the late twentieth century.

Finally, I conclude with an epilogue that features excerpts from my interview with the late Gil Scott Heron and some brief reflections on nostalgia and critical memory in the public sphere. The epilogue is more a reflection than a conclusion as it seeks to consider the role that nostalgia plays in our understanding of revolution as a concept of the underground. Here I begin to think about what it means that Gil Scott Heron's classic poem, "The Revolution Will Not Be Televised," has been remixed by hip-hop for commercial basketball culture. Ultimately, in this age of media and digital information, the revolution might be more televisual than we initially thought.

CHAPTER 2

VERBAL AND SPATIAL MASKS OF
THE UNDERGROUND

In an album skit, DJ Premier, one half of hip-hop's underground duo Gangstarr, explicitly warns "break-record cats" against revealing the secreted samples in his production. The most striking aspect about this skit, on Gangstarr's fifth album, titled *Moment of Truth*, is the actual voice of DJ Premier.[1] We are used to hearing Premo (as he is affectionately called in hip-hop parlance) ventriloquize his artistic voice through a collage of samples and memorable hip-hop voices, producing for hip-hop's greatest artists, including Biggie Smalls, Jay Z, Nas, M.O.P., Snoop Dogg, and many others. Hearing his voice is revealing in and of itself, but he also anticipates the cottage industry within/out hip-hop that would reveal rare recordings and/or riffs secreted through the production process. He tells them plainly and forcefully to knock it off. This gesture may appear to be economically motivated because Premo has to pay legal sampling fees if his production secrets are revealed. However, since this prophetic response to the exploitation of hip-hop production (the revealing of sampling secrets for money by those viewed by Premo as transgressing the rules of hip-hop culture), many hip-hop artists and producers have been profiled on compilations that reveal the original songs from which many hip-hop producers shamelessly borrow. DJ Premier would not deny this impulse to borrow from the best of the Black, blues, soul music tradition. But those who reveal the code are considered to be operating in violation of a hip-hop policy that protects the creative expression of traditional Black American artistry, represented here as sampling, but tapping into the Black tradition of repetition with a signifying difference.[2]

Sampling in hip-hop is based on using previous musical recordings as an artistic medium from which DJs pull fragments in order to update and/or reflect upon these fragments of recordings, usually revised with the timing and rhythms of hip-hop culture and rap music. According to Joseph Schloss, the classic underlying beat structure in sample-based hip-hop is the loop or process of looping. Schloss likens this to a form of Skip Gates's notion of signifyin'.[3] He briefly takes on Adorno's critique of repetition and mass production in popular music and refers to his informants to discuss the concept of "locking up," which is an intermediary production process where the producer comes to an auditory point that she/he realizes that the sounds have all come together. As arguably one of the most prolific producers in hip-hop, DJ Premier has a tremendous artistic career at stake in the conflict over the underground nature of his own sampling practices. His urgent gesture to insulate hip-hop craft from deconstructive revelation through rules inherent in hip-hop culture speaks to the central themes of this chapter. These discursive gestures reflect an impulse to mask the musical origins of hip-hop production. DJ Premier takes the act of revealing production secrets as a personal affront to him because his musical mask here is, by extension, his personal mask, which not only protects him from exorbitant sampling fees and unwanted attention from the legal community but also defines and protects his artistic signature from competitive copying/ competition.

More than most lyrics in rap music, DJ Premier's rant directly suggests the notion that "rap texts are the product of particular kinds of spatial relations and spatial histories, and they therefore feature a distinct spatial repertoire that characterizes the music, identifying it as a unique genre without essentializing its cultural meanings."[4] Rap texts transform the spaces that they inhabit and they also resist the terms of essentialism through the phenomenon of masking where wearing a mask is an important subversive aspect of the lived experience of Black folks, especially as it is expressed in the African American literary tradition. The spatial paradigm set up here by DJ Premier is beneath the surface and it suggests the cultural insulation and authenticity of the underground space versus other more mainstream/above ground spaces where people betray the culture, in this case, by revealing the encoded samples of hip-hop production. I am primarily interested in coming to terms with the relationship between verbal and spatial masking as they apply to or derive from the concepts of the underground in African American culture(s). In this case the concepts are limited to wearing the mask, the mask of Black vernacular speech, certain ephemeral notions of underground in hip-hop, the Underground Railroad in American slavery, and tangential connections to the world's first subway system, the London Underground. I have chosen this particular constellation of representations of the underground because they all provide opportunities to analyze verbal and spatial masking in juxtaposition with each other, yielding a deeper understanding of the connections and interrelations of the underground and certain types of masking.

"Of all the artifacts out of Africa it is indeed the mask that most compels.... [I]t is the mask that attracts us to blackness, and rightly so. For therein is contained, as well as reflected, a coded, secret, hermetic world, a world discovered only by the initiate." For DJ Premier this "secret, hermetic world" is the underground production world of hip-hop culture, an artistic space that is insulated from rampant consumerism and must defend itself against unmasking in the public sphere. Premier polices the boundaries of an underground that is encoded through sampling in hip-hop culture. In this instance, sampling is both a hip-hop innovation and an example of how hip-hop music innovates. As Houston Baker points out in *Black Studies, Rap and the Academy*: "The black urban beat goes on and on... The beat continues to provide sometimes stunning territorial confrontations between black expressivity and law and order."[5] In hip-hop culture, the underground can be a tenuously constituted figuration of authenticity. If you are from and/or sound like you are from certain ethnically and geographically underprivileged classes, then your voice is more readily accepted as valid. Still, the lyrical content of rap as well as the sampling and musical productions frequently consist of signifyin(g) exchanges between artists who employ various themes to assert their authenticity or realness. For some artists, "keepin' it real"—a dated if instructive hip-hop phrase—means rapping about being a killer and a drug dealer, for others it means wearing expensive clothing and driving expensive cars, and still for others it means critiquing and challenging the artists who think they must rhyme about being a criminal in order to be authentic. In the DJ Premier rant, "keeping it real" means maintaining the mask of secrecy with respect to the sampling selections in the production of the music. Rather than serve as an important narrative of protecting and secreting of the underground world of sample-based hip-hop production, Premier's diatribe actually signals the emergence of the entire cottage industry within the music industry that has developed since the 1990s. This "break-beat" industry began as a small group of relatively unknown producers/DJs arranging compilations of the songs and sometimes the rifts/breaks in songs sampled by well-respected hip-hop producers. Now, legendary hip-hop producers—like DJ Marley Marl or 9th Wonder, actually reveal their own secrets through online platforms, multimedia, web series, and television. The culture of sampling has a microcosmic relationship with hip-hop culture itself since it emerges from near obscurity, thrives aesthetically, and then ultimately it must confront or (be confronted) by market forces. Not only is this a limited sense of how an underground phenomenon might work, or even how conceptualizations of the underground unfold, but it also underscores the tenuous, fluid nature of the underground designation within hip-hop culture. Being underground (either as a rapper or a producer) is, at best, a temporary and always contested state of authenticity for hip-hop artists. The underground designation, in hip-hop terms, masks space through discursive confrontations much like the subject matter of the Gangstarr skit as well as certain territorial confrontations between "black expressivity and law and order." Many of these discourses invoke some notion of cultural authenticity even in the face of deliberate appropriation of previously recorded musical forms. Such is the case in the skit where DJ Premier is essentially defending his right to create through musical bricolage and other collage-like techniques. His desire to not have to endure the legal entanglements that present themselves whenever he is unmasked as a producer is in concert with his impulse to preserve the mask of the underground in hip-hop musical production.

This approach to an underground culture of hip-hop music production is reminiscent of Henry Louis Gates's concept of cultural privacy. The "element of privacy makes it possible for a culture to use language to *mask* its meanings from all but its own initiates (my emphasis)."[6] DJ Premier's warning is a shout-out to this sense of cultural privacy. The discourse of most hip-hop DJ/producers (the DJ designation in hip-hop also includes production and sampling) is inscribed in the records that they select for sampling. The originality of their music is limited by how much (or little) is taken from the original and/or what capacity the audience has to determine whether or not a recognizable original musical work has been borrowed from.[7] The fact that "break-record cats" can exploit this musical game of cat and mouse between hip-hop DJ/Producers and the listening audience alienates Premo to the point of verbal outburst. And again, it is worth noting that since this discursive instance, the phenomenon of DJ's revealing their production secrets has become a part of the mainstream music industry—usually extending or enhancing the careers of producers who are past their popular prime.

The media and the music industry exert control over hip-hop music—especially its lyrical content as the market or the music industry work to "sign," copy, or expose potentially popular underground acts/artists. Masking in sampling production is an important strategy to subvert these forces, but the lyrics of rap music also engage in masking. Tricia Rose explains the encoded-ness of hip-hop culture and the need to subvert market forces through masking in her discussion of rap music as a social transcript, a term borrowed from James Scott's *Domination and the Arts of Resistance.*

> Rap music is, in many ways, a hidden transcript. Among other things, it uses *cloaked speech* and *disguised* cultural codes to comment on and challenge aspects of current power inequalities. Not all rap transcripts directly critique all forms of domination; nonetheless, a large and significant element in rap's discursive territory is engaged in symbolic and ideological warfare with institutions and groups that symbolically, ideologically, and materially oppress African Americans...rap's social commentary enacts ideological insubordination.[8] (my emphasis)

In much the same way that the underground is a conceptual structure that can convey meanings about space, secrecy, authenticity, and encoded(ness), Black dialect, particularly in the ways in which it is rendered through standard English orthography, masks meaning and can encode or obscure sociolinguistic realities. Spatial and verbal masking operate (sometimes in tandem) on the mainstream, "aboveground," market-related forces designed to silence, contain, and compel conformity among the artisans and constituents of Black expressive culture.

Hip-hop music's expressive "ideological insubordination" compels a rethinking of discursive, public and private space, and an intense sociopolitical interest in the forms of countercultural representation. An interesting point from which to continue is a critical intersection of scholars, spaces, a peculiar lexical item, and the ever-present inside outside dynamic that predisposes hip-hop generational discourse participants to employ verbal and/or spatial masks. In *Black Noise*, Tricia

Rose catalogues the term "wilding" in her list of phrases that are appropriated by the media and socially and strategically constructed to portray members of the hip-hop community in a negative light.[9] Baker discusses this same term in his earlier work, *Black Studies, Rap and the Academy*.[10] He devotes much of his second chapter to a socio-political critique of the Central Park Jogger incident. He is primarily concerned with the privatization of Central Park and the boundaries around private-public spaces such as the park, and Black public spaces such as East Harlem (which borders the northern boundary of Central Park). For Baker, the park is a site where rap music breaches public and private boundaries by boldly claiming sonic-public spaces. "When young America (especially young, Black, urban America)—with gigantic, multi-decibel-capacity radios and tape decks—began to set up shop in American public spaces...the hue and cry, lamentation and gnashing of polemical teeth threatened to deafen us all."[11] Note well that Baker's assessment predates the iPod horizon, and the general individualization of the digital consumption of music. That said, this Central Park incident features a public hearing that becomes a euphemism for aural contestation or what Baker refers to as the territorial contestation between Black expressivity and law and order.

Central Park (particularly through Baker's reading of it) was a battleground for the ideological and discursive rights to express a hip-hop identity in public. From the boom box to the progenitors of hip-hop who siphoned public energy from lampposts in parks in order to throw some of the earliest public hip-hop "jams," the park is an archetypal site of contestation for the culture. Baker's discussion builds to a seminal critique of the media's misunderstanding of a Black vernacular term, "wilding," and how that misunderstanding created a public perception about urban youth. In the 20-plus years since the case itself and the publication of *Black Studies, Rap and the Academy*, many facts have been revealed regarding the Central Park Jogging incident, and there have been significant developments. In fact, Ken Burns's documentary film, *The Central Park Five*, chronicles the systemic rush to judgment inflamed and validated by the media. Antron McCray, Kevin Richardson, Yusef Salaam, Raymond Santana, and Korey Wise—the Central Park Five—were convicted and imprisoned for the brutal rape and assault of Trisha Meili—the Central Park jogger. In 2002, after each of the five had spent between 6–13 years in prison, the New York State Supreme Court vacated their convictions due to lack of sufficient evidence and the confession of a lone serial rapist.[12]

Trisha Meili herself has no recollection of the crime. At the time of this violent crime, members of the media reported on and promoted the idea that groups of young urban males were engaged in random violent rampages through New York City. New York City chief of detectives Robert Colangelo said: "the attack appeared unrelated to money, race, drugs or alcohol" and went on to say that some of the more than 30–40 youths involved in a general rampage through the park "told investigators that the crime spree was the product of a pastime called 'wilding'"[13] Baker notes here how the media latches on to this term "wilding" and how it subsequently informs media consumers of notions of wild urban youths ruthlessly raping and assaulting upstanding urban citizens. I have come across no better instance of how the dialect as verbal mask works against its speech communities especially when public misunderstanding proliferates across media. Baker is quick to challenge the detective's grasp on the origins (or lack thereof) of this term and the danger of vernacular terminology misheard and/or misunderstood by the media. The Ken Burns film does a masterful job of documenting the ways in which the media constructed the term "wilding" in order to publicly convict the Central Park five, and by extension all male Black and brown hip-hop generational youth. The media-feeding frenzy on the "wilding" pastime quickly helps to cement the public convictions of the Central Park Five who ultimately spend too many years of their lives in prison for a crime they did not commit. Baker, in unison with Terry Teachout (a columnist for *The Commentary*), offers Tone Loc's "Wild Thing" as the chorus-turned-diabolical-phrase employed by the young, suspected criminals, in celebratory fashion as they terrorized people in the park. So the detectives and the media "hear" the term "wilding" and the scholars and journalists who are critiquing the detectives and the media suggest that this term is actually the chorus from one of 1989's most popular rap songs, "Wild Thing," written by Young MC and performed by Tone Loc.

Surprisingly, no one seriously considered the vernacular dialect of these youth—the evidence of which is on full display in the Ken Burns film. Unfortunately, the Black vernacular language of the accused youth functioned as a mask that was misheard/read by the detectives, journalists, the media, and finally, by scholars of African American Studies. No one engaged in the discourse surrounding this term considered the notions of dialectal, verbal maskings. A cursory review of any of a number of studies that have been done on African American

Vernacular English (AAVE or AAE) will yield a complicated-sounding linguistic feature described as consonant cluster reduction. This case of the doubly misheard "wilding—wild thing" could be a simple case of intervocalic consonant cluster reduction. In many dialects and vernaculars, particularly those that derive from African American variants of Standard English, consonant cluster reduction (the pronunciation of two adjacent consonants as one) occurs word initially (dat for that), word finally (tes for test), or intervocalicly (wiling for wilding). Thus the alleged assailants could have said they were wilin' rather than wilding or doing Tone Loc's "Wild Thing." The term "wiling" engenders an orthographic mask once it is transcribed from an interview onto a detective's notepad and subsequently printed in media. Since there is no spelling system that accounts for vernacular variants in speech, the entire mania created around this alleged pastime could have been based on a sociolinguistic misunderstanding. "Wilin" can be loosely defined as acting crazy, having a good time, or other colloquial phrasings such as "buggin" out. Insider/initiate knowledge is not necessary to access what should be basic reading for scholars/journalists who engage in discourses about hip-hop culture and rap music, cultural forms that showcase African American vernacular speech. When the production of this form is called into question and intersection with the constituency of the vernacular-speaking community, it would have been helpful to understand some of the basic linguistic structures. If one has knowledge of consonant cluster reduction as a formal component of AAVE then one need not know the meaning of "wilin" to know that the standard mainstream orthography for a vernacular lexical item such as "wilin" would generally be wilding.

The aforementioned discussion further suggests the importance of Gates's thesis concerning AAVE or Black dialects as a mask. The valence of public and private spaces with the vernacular complexity of the "wilin" episode begins to suggest a complex underground relationship between verbal and spatial masking. This relationship is hinted at in the discourse of DJ Premier, fleshed out in the "wilin" episode and is reified in the life and legacy of the poet who crystalized the concept of African American masking, Paul Laurence Dunbar. Paul Laurence Dunbar was one of the first African American poets to receive national critical acclaim. He was born in Dayton, Ohio, in 1872, to parents from Kentucky who were both born slaves—his father escaped and his mother was emancipated. Dunbar's upbringing was economically meager, but he was supported in his literary endeavors by his mother, and began writing poetry at the age of six. Dunbar authored a large body of dialect poems, Standard English poems, essays, novels, and short stories before he died at the age of 33. His work often addresses the difficulties encountered by African Americans and the efforts of African Americans to achieve equality in America. He was praised both by the prominent literary critics of his time and his literary contemporaries. After meeting Frederick Douglass at the 1893 world's fair, Douglass remarked that Dunbar was "the most promising young colored man in America."[14] Indeed, he was promising, but his most famous and most widely anthologized poem, "We Wear the Mask," was unfortunately a critical gloss on one of the more painful conflicts in his career as a poet. What Gates and other Dunbar scholars glean from this masterpiece is a seminal insight into a time bomb dilemma of linguistic masking for Dunbar and its effects on his ability to be acknowledged as a poet. In the introduction to *Lyrics of Lowly Life* (published in 1896, combining his first two volumes of poetry), W. D. Howells patronizes Dunbar in his attempts to free him from the trappings of racist and classist categorizations.

> I think I should scarcely trouble the reader with a special appeal in behalf of this book, if it had not specially appealed to me for reasons apart from the author's race, origin, and condition. The world is too old now, and I find myself too much of its mood, to care for the work of a poet because he is black, because his father and mother were slaves, because he was, before and after he began to write poems, an elevator-boy.[15]

Howell continues in this vein, attempting to situate Dunbar in a discourse on American Letters. For Howell, Dunbar represents his discovery of the basic humanity of the Black race achieved through literature. This, of course, sounds absurd now, but in 1896, this kind of justification was considered to be progressive. Still, Howell does not hesitate to relegate Dunbar to writing about his race in dialect.

> Yet it appeared to me then, and it appears to me now, that there is a precious difference of temperament between the races which it would be a great pity ever to lose, and that this is best preserved and most charmingly suggested by Mr. Dunbar in those pieces of his where he studies the moods and traits of his race in its own accent of our English. We call such pieces dialect pieces for want of some closer phrase, but they are really not dialect so much as delightful personal attempts and failures for the written and spoken language.[16]

Gates suggests that when Dunbar used dialect successfully, he managed to contain a musicality inherent in the form itself, significantly an oral form, within a stylized, literate, written form. Dunbar did not write music in dialect; dialect conveyed musicality in Dunbar's best poetry.[17] This is a critical distinction that reveals the interactivity of Black vernacular speech and Black musical traditions. Due to the success and popularity of Dunbar's dialect poetry, his Standard English poems and other writings were often overshadowed. Like Howells in the introduction to *Lyrics of Lowly Life*, Dunbar's audience identified with the verbal mask of blackness in his popular dialect poems. It is therefore ironic that "We Wear the Mask" has enjoyed such staying power in the anthologies of American Literature and Poetry. Dunbar would have been proud that one of his Standard English poems has etched itself into the American canon, but that mask of which Dunbar speaks troubled his short literary career and continues to be relevant for poets of the twentieth and twenty-first centuries.

In 1996, some 100 years after the publication of *Lyrics of Lowly Life*, The Fugees released their second album, *The Score*. *The Score* was a resounding success, critically, artistically, and economically (selling over 15 million records worldwide). In a track titled "The Mask," The Fugees capture Paul Laurence Dunbar's poem with a variation of Robin Kelley's reading of that same poem intact. Kelley names the first section of *Race Rebels* after Dunbar's poem and proceeds to describe the collective masks that were worn by southern working-class men and women. Kelley suggests that employers were almost totally unaware of a complex system of subversion among Black workers.[18] In The Fugees' version of "The Mask," the first narrator (Wyclef Jean) must contend with his Burger King manager who believes that he can entice his employee into spying on other workers. Wyclef's rapped narration rejects the offer to be spy/traitor and suggests that employees are actually being spied upon by management. Although the narrator escapes the oppression of surveillance at his menial job he ultimately ends up working "underground" for the government, making missiles for World War III. The second narrator (Lauryn Hill) contemplates the constraints of space for a woman in a local nightclub. She dances with "Tariq from off the street" who does not respect her personal space on the dance floor. After the narrator slaps him for grabbing her around the waistline, his girlfriend gets in her (the narrator's) face. Hill's narrator promptly and directly checks her and claims that Tariq is acting out. The chorus to this revision of Dunbar's classic spells out the word "mask" and claims that the narrators wear the mask everyday for a variety of subversive reasons. For the Fugees, wearing the mask assists their narrators in the daily navigation of public spaces. In the work place and on the social scene, these characters must wear the mask in order to interact with people whom they do not trust. They camouflage their identities, and according to the chorus this practice is nearly universal. In the chorus, the narrators ultimately pose the question of how long people will have to wear the mask—a question that resonates resoundingly with the fact that this is an update on a theme at least 100 years old in African American culture.

The mask, in both its verbal-vernacular incarnations as well as in its spatial configurations, also resides in the histories of the Underground Railroad and in the uncanny development of the world's first subway system. The stakes may have been somewhat higher in these historical moments than those of the late-nineteenth-century poet (Dunbar) or for the narrative characters in the Fugees' remake. For the Underground Railroad, verbal masking is a revolution in communications, and the contestation over space often meant the difference between life and death. The underground deterritorializes mainstream conceptions (i.e., standards) of space through an unabated desire for freedom and an extraordinary ability to use the encodedness of language. In Chapter Four of Ben Sidran's *Black Talk*, titled "The Evolution of the Black Underground: 1930–1947," he suggests that the "nature of the 'underground' was cultural rather than political, a '*communications revolution*' that preceded the political revolution.[19] For my purposes, a communications revolution describes a linguistically conscious phenomenon that occurred when Black fugitives and White and Black abolitionists co-opted *railroad language* to describe the Underground Railroad, or, when Amiri Baraka, Richard Wright, and Ralph Ellison engage in what reads like a dialogue centering around the *underground* as a Black, unsettling trope. The relationships between music and literature in African American history suggest that linguistic assertions upon musically, or literally, discursive spaces, *can be political acts in and of themselves*. For example, in *Black Music*, Baraka discusses a communications revolution in Bebop: "Bop also carried with it a *distinct element of social protest*, not only in the sense that it was music that seemed antagonistically nonconformist, but also that the musicians who played it were loudly outspoken about who they thought they were. (my emphasis)"[20] Bebop and early Rhythm and

Blues (R&B) musicians deliberately posited themselves as constituents of a cultural underground, one encrypted against easy detection or entry by mainstream White or Black Americans. According to Eric Lott, in his essay titled "Bebop's Politics of Style," Bebop was "brilliantly outside, bebop was intimately if indirectly related to the militancy of its moment. Militancy and music were undergirded by the same social facts; the music attempted to resolve at the level of style what the militancy fought out in the streets."[21] The subtle connections between Bebop and hip-hop include the conceptualization of the underground in Black culture. In fact, the hip-hop underground inherits its "politics of style" from the range of black oral and expressive forms that precede it.

The underground tropes in literature and rap music or hip-hop culture have not yet been connected to each other through a conceptual lineage. Moreover, the connections between these undergrounds and the signs, symbols, and themes that string them together through Black history have not been systematically studied and/or described. For example, one of the most important physical/tangible symbols connected to the Underground Railroad is the train and the train's most important theme or function: movement. Various Underground Railroad scholars and documentarians, including William Still, Henrietta Buckmaster, and others claim that the Underground Road was named so by the owner of a fugitive slave named Tice Davids.

It came about, according to those who were best informed, around 1831. A fugitive named Tice Davids crossed the river at Ripley (Ohio) under the expert guidance of those river operators who worked within sight of slavery. He was escaping from his Kentucky master, who followed so closely on his heels that Tice Davids had no alternative when he reached the river, but to swim. His master spent a little time searching for a skiff, but he never lost sight of his slave, bobbing about in the water. He kept him in sight all the way across the river and soon his skiff closing the distance between them. He saw Tice Davids wade into shore, and then—he never saw him again. He searched everywhere, he asked everyone, he combed the slavery-hating town of Ripley....Baffled and frustrated, he returned to Kentucky, and with wide eyes and shakings of the head he gave the only explanation possible for a sane man, "He must have gone on an underground road."

"The phrase spread like a wind. And the friends of the fugitives completed the name in honor of the steam trains that were nine-day marvels in the country. . . ."[22] The language used to describe the "nine-day marvels" was refigured for the vernacular of the Underground Railroad. Thus, conductors, stations, depots, and the term "train" itself became signified variations of their standard counterparts. This phenomenon signaled the communications revolution that was already taking place in order for the Underground Railroad to operate at all. But for my purposes it also points to the importance of real-life occur-rences in understanding figurative spaces such as the underground and the languages or vernaculars that constitute them.

"One of the inexplicable and dismaying characteristics of slaves which lent strength to the Underground Railroad (UR), was their grapevine, their telepathy, their intercommunication, call it what you will."[23] Henrietta Buckmaster here hints at the "unknowability" of the black slaves' communicative means of establishing and/or maintaining an *invisible* underground mobility out of bondage. Technology ironi-cally converges with invisibility since the phrase, "underground rail-road" spread like a wind,[24] at least in part because it signified around the language of recently constructed railways in America. Charles Blockson, the chairperson of the Underground Railroad Advisory Committee (URAC) insists that the success of the Underground Railroad relied primarily on the communicative network established among free and enslaved Black people.

> Slaves are too often portrayed as passive victims waiting to be led out of slavery. But long before the invisible Underground Railroad was organized, slaves in colonial America had frequently esaped alone or with others from their owners to seek freedom. Their routes were many and varied, they often traveled in disguise, through woods and farms, by wagon, boat and train, hiding in stables and attics and store-rooms, and fleeing through secret passages; but the destination they sought was always freedom.[25]

The actual Underground Railroad's communications revolution geographically spans most of the antebellum United States and has been officially commemorated through the Underground Railroad Advisory Committee's recent studies and projects directed toward a geographically disseminated National Park:

> In 1990 Congress directed the National Park Service to study how to best interpret and commemorate the Underground Railroad, empha-sizing the approximate routes taken by slaves escaping to freedom

before the Civil War. This study was completed in cooperation with an advisory committee (The Underground Railroad Advisory Committee, URAC) representing experts in historic preservation, African American History, United States History, and members of the general public with special interest and experience in the Underground Railroad.[26]

While collecting experiences and conducting research in London, the name, mass transit functionality and pervasive semiological presence of the Underground was intellectually engaging, but a secondary interest of mine was to uncover any relationship between the London Underground(s)—the world's first subway system and the undergrounds in hip-hop and African American cultures. The impulse to locate a literal underground had already yielded important conceptual connections between distinct ideas in my research, such as figuration and movement, freedom trains and subways, and most importantly, between literature or art and reality or what some scholars call "mimesis." In reality, the London Underground was opened for business on January 10, 1863. In literature, one of the world's most popular novels documenting the Underground Railroad was published on March 20, 1852, in America. This novel is Harriet Beecher Stowe's *Uncle Tom's Cabin*. Normally, the literary critic engaged in mimetic readings of literature studies literature that reflects reality. In this case, what emerges is an alternative mimetic relationship between the literature of the Underground Railroad (of which Stowe's text is a mainstream paragon) and the reality of the London Underground transportation system.

First, we should understand that as scholar John William Ward suggests: "Stowe organized her fiction around one of the universal motifs in human experience, the story of a journey that metamorphoses itself into a symbolic quest, a search for the meaning of life itself. As one stands back from *Uncle Tom's Cabin* and regards it whole, one sees how deeply the novel is characterized by movement, how pervasively it presents a world of people in constant motion" (Ward 485). "Movement" and "people in constant motion" automatically brings to mind mass transit and/or migration, but this novel is also about slavery. And the signal spatial movements in this novel are the flight North of Eliza, George, and young Harry and the "forced transportation of Tom South to physical degradation and death...." The former takes place on the Underground Railroad. This Underground

Railroad narrative embedded in *Uncle Tom's Cabin* reaches the pinnacle of its circulation just prior to the development of the London Underground transportation system.

"In England, because Mrs. Stowe had no copyright there, pirated editions began to appear and from April to December, 1852, according to one authority, twelve different editions appeared; before the public was satisfied, eighteen different London publishers turned out forty different editions and sold about a million and a half copies" (Ward 480). This was in 1852. "In 1855, a Parliamentary Select Committee had been set up to consider how to combat the congestion [in London]. It was estimated that over 750,000 people were entering London everyday, whether by main line railway, or by road, and the streets were being blocked by a variety of...vehicles" (Glover 8). So in 1855, just 3 years after a proliferation of pirated, underground versions of *Uncle Tom's Cabin* are dispersed throughout London and the rest of England, a Parliamentary committee begins the urban planning, which leads to the opening of the London Underground in 1863. Thus a London underground railroad is constructed in reality reflecting the extremely popular Underground Railroad figured in literature from the real-life figurative concept in pre–civil war America. Today, the London Underground is a major business with three million passenger journeys made a day, serving 275 stations over (253 miles) of railway. The London Underground subway system is all about movement and maps. And the beauty of it is its simplicity. You can move around the city quickly and efficiently. This book, like this mode of travel, is about the presence and re(con)figuration of the underground as a concept in African American cultural production, the presence of the sign of the underground at the intersection of hip-hop and African American literary cultures. One of the more striking aspects of the Underground in London is its pervasive semiology. There are signs everywhere. This pervasiveness is a pragmatic result of urban planning. People can navigate the city of London (speaking a variety of languages and hailing from all over the world) with relative ease as a result of this pervasive semiotics of the underground. The signature of the underground is simple and easily recognizable from significant distances. Again, it is also the first subway system, and this book employs aesthetics of hip-hop culture, where the importance of the subway is apparent, not only as a muse for rap artists, but also as the original disseminator of hip-hop's language of art (or graffiti).[27]

Both the subway and the Underground Railroad use transit and transportational qualities to communicate and disseminate language (in the case of the subway as art/graffiti) in the figurative and literal underground. The subway's role as muse and artistic communicator linguistically (and historically) connects it to the communicative power of the Underground Railroad. The evolution of graffiti and the subway's role in it, reflect the "grapevine" of the Underground Railroad (UR) and the community that facilitated it. This UR community put into motion a communications revolution that vehemently challenged the American slavocracy then, and now historically reenters the underground via music (jazz-bebop, rap), literature (Ellison, Wright, and Baraka), and art. Yet what lurks beneath the surface, of many of these examples—DJ Premier's warning, cultural privacy, transcribing AAVE, wearing the mask and certain communications revolutions—is a slippery sense of Black authenticity.

Authenticity Underground

The verbal and spatial concepts of the underground briefly glossed in this chapter provide interesting coordinates for the construction of models that analytically address a myriad of issues central to the discourse on notions of the underground within hip-hop culture as well as an important set of ideological dilemmas that emerge from the enormous popularity of rap music and hip-hop culture throughout the world. This set of dilemmas includes contemplations of racial and or musical authenticity in hip-hop culture that are complex and can be limited depending on how the discourse is framed. Following Perry (2004), Jackson (2005), and Jeffries (2011), a key distinction in the discourse lies between racial authenticity (in this case in hip-hop culture) and musical or artistic authenticity. Jeffries's important research among constituents of hip-hop culture finds "that there is a robust set of standards for what makes a good MC, and listeners' evaluations of rap music are not clearly organized along race and class lines. Instead, a culture community of hip-hop fans emerges, and these aestheticians prioritize lyrical content, technique (flow), and signifying (layered meaning) as the principles that are important to rap music."[28] Signifying in and through rap lyrics is an abiding aspect of the collection of underground hip-hop music that I focus on in this book. These are verbal/dialectal masks that are meant to be decoded so that listeners become more conscious of the debates on authenticity within the communities of hip-hop culture. The fact that the concept of the underground is a trope through which emcees/hip-hop artists signify on mainstream rap music and market forces becomes a powerful contribution to the discourses on authenticity.[29] To critically engage the texts, musical and literary, that I am primarily concerned with is to (almost by default) consider issues of Black authentic experiences. At the same time, racial authenticity cannot be dominant in my discussions of the hip-hop underground and African American literary culture. The crux of the problem, or system of problems, lies (at least partially) in the fact that American blackness is a fluid category. Moreover, the distinctive historical relationship between Black cultural production and American mainstream appropriation and commodification forces the discussion into a type of stasis that perpetuates the notion that the most oppressed Black people (the folk or vernacular culture) are always already the most authentic Black people. Literary, cultural studies scholars and social scientists from W. E. B. Du Bois and Hurston, to Kwame Toure and Charles Hamilton, to Joyce Joyce, Houston Baker, Skip Gates, to Imani Perry, John L. Jackson, and Michael P. Jeffries are for the most part consistently insistent on the limitations of authenticity discourses and racial identity. In some ways definitions of authenticity in music/art are less convoluted than those definitions that attempt to arrive at some form of authentic Blackness.

Imani Perry deftly argues that notions of "the real," in the aesthetics of hip-hop culture, are "an authenticating device responding to the removal of rap music from the organic relationship with the communities creating it."[30] Here is where the confluence of Black concepts of the underground, racial, and artistic authenticity can become a generative discourse about how discernment shapes a collective, constitutive sense of the intersections between underground hip-hop and African American literary culture. And it is the technical nature of "the real" discourses—what allows them to function as a device to parse these critical issues—that underwrites the tentative relationship between the underground, community, hip-hop culture, and authenticity.

John L. Jackson (2005), Michael Jeffries (2011), and others "consider authenticity [to be] not something located in one object or another but instead [it is] a socially constructed quality arising from performers' ability to manufacture a sincere connection with audience members."[31] One way of thinking about the discussions centered on issues of authenticity (artistic and racial) is what I will simply define as *notions* of movement—with an understanding that these notions of movement inform certain concepts of the underground, are relatable to Perry's "the real" discourses in praxis, and reflect John Jackson's sense of the strategic maneuvers that performers make in order to establish sincere connections with their audiences (Jackson 2005). Early African American writers—Chesnutt, W. E. B. Du Bois, Toomer, and Hurston—located authentic Black experiences in the south, where African American communities were perceived to be organic, particularly in a geographical/regional sense. As African Americans migrated to modern, northern, industrial cities, this locus of authenticity shifted to the north in the collective consciousness of America.[32] Richard Wright eloquently, if heavy handedly, chronicles this shift in an assortment of short stories, novels, and autobiographical narratives (many of these authors/narratives are subject to literary analysis in other chapters of this book). In the early hip-hop era, the Black authentic experience was lived in the postindustrial city. This locus of authenticity within hip-hop culture shifted to the West coast gang-oriented postindustrial city and finally shifted again to the south as rappers such as Scarface, Master P, and Outkast reminded us that oppression of poor and working-class Black people is not peculiar to any one quadrant of the United States. Hip-hop culture celebrates this type of movement intrinsically. In fact, I still have hope for artistic visions of hip-hop culture as a new underground railroad of sorts, where communication about oppression and how to overcome and resist it is encoded in texts as diverse as quilts, films, photographs, paintings, music videos, Christian spirituals, and astrology (i.e., follow[ing] the north star) or, in this case, especially, recorded music made for popular consumption.

Again, Perry's articulation of "the real" discourses stands out among the scholarly discourses on authenticity. Gestures toward authenticity in hip-hop culture often respond to, or more often, preempt the "removal" of the culture—especially its music—from the organic interface between the culture and the community that produced it. In this sense, migrations, geo-spatial relationships, and geographic shifts articulated through the literary history of African American and hip-hop cultural production rely on "the real" discourses in order to make sense of movement, region, identity, and authenticity. Although most people reading this would consider the phrase "keep it real" to be trite, another phrase is quietly just as integral to the Hip-Hop ethos: "keep it movin." Movement here, of course, is not limited to physical and geographic space (e.g., from below ground to above ground and or back or from the south to the north or from the east coast to the west coast, etc). In an essay on the mobility of hip-hop identity, Christopher Holmes Smith asserts that "rap in it's varying forms of mass-mediated ethereality, promotes symbolic forms of travel in ways that are often denied to physical bodies. This fluid movement across and through boundaries sparks a veritable insurrection of meaning that strikes at the very heart of the *inter/intracultural communicative process* which dominant social formations work so feverishly to regulate. (my emphasis)"[33] In a detailed analysis of abstract syntheses in African American identity formation, Smith decodes Method Man's (of the Wu-Tang Clan) classic lines referencing the Palestinian Liberation Organization (PLO), Buddhist monks, and White Owl cigars:

> Method Man [here] deftly relates his stage persona to the armed resistance of members of the Palestine Liberation Organization, the mystical wisdom and fraternal bonding of Buddhist Monks from the Pacific Rim, and couches both metaphors within a trademark of urban American drug culture, the White Owl brand cigar.[34]

This example (indicative of the symbolic movements encrypted in rap music) captures what I believe is a foundation for discussions of authenticity in hip-hop culture and an important context within which verbal and spatial masking operates. Symbolic forms of travel provide constituents of hip-hop culture with the means to envision an authentic self that is not defined, that is also unmasked and not delimited by the static notions of Blackness proffered in traditional discussions or depicted via mainstream media stereotypes. Being Black (or any other racially confined category) in hip-hop is not a closed set of attributes such as hairstyle, clothing, musical tastes, or being oppressed, but rather it is the subjective impulse toward sincerity and the psychological ability to define oneself through movements, geographically, spiritually, and linguistically.[35] "Black authentic narratives are prevalent in hip-hop not because they congeal to produce a single coherent discourse of authenticity but because performers strive to build sincere connections with the audience."[36]

I have not thoroughly fleshed this out here, but the role of language variation in Black speech communities, what sociolinguists alternately refer to as Ebonics or African American (Vernacular) English (in the US), functions as a discreet figurative movement that an individual and/or community can make away from oppressive standards (in this case Standard English in America) toward a sincere projection of self. A final component of my thoughts on Black authenticity in hip-hop comes from J. Martin Favor's *Authentic Blackness*.

> The ability to control aspects of African American identity assumes primary importance both for the performers and for those who study the discourse of identity. Those who can bend class and geographic position to their own purposes have the power to shape what "race" is. By reshaping race, they add to the complexity of the discourse of Black identity rather than impoverishing it with false notions. Of greatest import is the recognition that the control over, or performance of, certain aspects of racial identity points out the nonessential nature of racial categories.[37] (22)

While the dispensing or dispersal of racial categories is not an expressed goal of either verbal or spatial masking within contextualized concepts of the underground, the idea that "class and geographic position" can be bent to the purposes of artists or the market entities that manage, promote, and often exploit them is a significant factor in understanding the complexities of the intersections between underground hip-hop and African American literature and culture.

My strategy in opening this chapter with a comparative interpretation of DJ Premier's warning against hip-hop cultural violators who would reveal production secrets was to initiate a continuum/constellation of cultural discourses historically interconnected with a set of underground aesthetics that includes these discourses, as well as those of artistic practice, literature, cultural authenticity, and sociolinguistics. DJ Premier closes his skit with a powerful assertion that the "underground" is eternal; that the underground culture that he is defending and protecting will, in fact, live forever (Gangstarr's *Moment of Truth*, 1998). In Douglass's 1845 *Narrative of the Life of Frederick Douglass, an American Slave*, he plainly captures the critical significance of the codes protected by this type of cultural privacy insisted upon by DJ Premier. Here Douglass claims: "I have never approved of the very public manner in which some of our western friends have conducted what they call the underground railroad, but which, I think, by their open declarations, has been made most emphatically the upperground railroad...those open declarations are a positive evil to the slaves remaining who are seeking to escape."[38] For Douglass, public discourse that reveals the inner-workings of the Underground Railroad actually alerts slaveholders and slave catchers to the routes and escape plans or possibilities of perspective fugitives. It is an unmasking and in effect, Douglass is telling certain abolitionist writers to knock it off. He is speaking directly here to the prominence of several abolitionist writers whose literary exposures (at least in Douglass' opinion) were threatening the secrecy of the Underground Railroad. The striking discursive resemblance of DJ Premier's warning and Douglass's biting criticism stems from a common directive between the Black cultural moments of 1845 and 1998. This directive is to maintain cultural privacy (i.e., to strategically keep the verbal and/or spatial mask in place) particularly in the face of threats from an oppressive outsider. Language, discourse, and the imperative insulation of the under-ground community are the most important tools in accomplishing this directive.

CHAPTER 3

THE HIP-HOP UNDERGROUND AND
AFRICAN AMERICAN CULTURE:
THE DEEP STRUCTURE OF BLACK
IDENTITY IN AMERICAN LITERATURE

In as much as this book grapples with the underground in hip-hop culture, African American literature and music, language, particularly linguistic identity as it is represented in literature, tends to suggest the extensive role of African American Vernacular English (AAVE) in these discussions. In chapter 3, AAVE informs the verbal masking that often emerges among literary subjects, hip-hop artistic personas, and various individuals in a range of underground contexts. In this chapter I focus briefly on various African American/ethno-linguistic identities in literature, and the theorems herein that largely refer to and reflect the use of Black vernacular speech (or any Black variety of Standard English) in music and cultural production. Many of the ways in which writers present and represent social identity in American literature are not directly related to traditional linguistic analyses, yet many depend directly on language. The question we might ask of any novel (or poem, play, or other literary genre) is what do we know about the identity of the characters/actors in the particular text: who we are reading? This question has many possible answers, but for the student of literature and linguistics the answers can be limited to four modes for analyzing the social identity of a character. Whether or not the representation is authentic to the ethnicity, class, or sexual orientation, characteristics of "real-life" persons or community certainly haunts this discussion. The four modes explained and exemplified in this chapter address some of these concerns, while offering an efficient means of analyzing African American identity in literature and the roles language plays in constituting social (and racial) identity in American literature.

African American linguistic identity in literature is the primary focus here. How are African American identities (re)presented linguistically in American literature? Throughout this brief chapter, gender, class, and sexual orientation will be incidentally subsumed within the analyses of ethnic discussions, but the same analytical tools will be helpful in ferreting out other types of identities in literature and culture. What follows is a brief description of categories that facilitate the readers' capacity to excavate markers of identity from the sociolinguistic representations of race on the printed page.

Authors and the Theme of Identity

Linguistics, particularly sociolinguistics, has historically grappled with inside-outside dynamics with respect to collecting and confirming accurate linguistic data from communities. We do not want to be essentialist in our thinking here, but it is worthy of note that critically acclaimed representations of ethnic and gender identities in American literature have generally been written by authors whose ethnic or sexual identities correspond to those of their principal characters. Consider Alice Walker (b. 1944), Nobel Prize winner Toni Morrison (b. 1931), Ralph Ellison (1914–1994), and James Baldwin (1924–1987) for African American and lesbian and gay literature; Sherman Alexie (b. 1966) for Native American and working poor literature; Amy Tan (b. 1952) and Frank Chin (b. 1940) for women and men's Asian American literature; and Esmeralda Santiago (b. 1940), Richard Rodriguez (b. 1944), and Sandra Cisneros (b. 1954) for Latina/o American literature. The abilities of these authors and others to provide cogent sociolinguistic situations and representations of their perspective ethnic and gender backgrounds can at least partially be credited to their insider knowledge and autobiographical experiences. The identity of an author does not ensure an authentic rendering of character, of course, but the history of American literature suggests that misrepresentation and overdetermined linguistic techniques (think of Mark Twain's *Huck Finn*) have been resoundingly counter-represented in the works of the aforementioned nonwhite or nonheterosexual or non-middleclass authors and many of their contemporaries. These counter representations or counter-narratives develop comparable ethnic and linguistic

portraits of traditionally biased characterizations. In short, they proffer a competing frame of reference for nonstandard-speaking characters in American Literature.

Reenvisioning Stereotypes

Many times these same authors who have often charged themselves
as protectors of their particular cultures use the very same stereotypes
that have been circulated as tools of oppression against them and their
constituents. Of course, these stereotypes are often either turned on
their "heads" or otherwise subverted so that they reflect the ignorance
of the American Mainstream or the strength of the culture in question, as will be exemplified by Charles Chesnutt below. Stereotype
operates on many linguistic levels, including semantics and discourse.
You may note that the discursive relationships (who can speak and
when) in texts like Chesnutt's *The Conjure Woman* are informed by
stereotypical ethnic situations and they often have corresponding
oppressive/power relations.

Situational Contexts

Situational contexts form the pragmatic milieu for sociolinguistic variation. If a book is about slavery, we can expect that many of
the main characters are Black or Southern American and thus speak
African American English (AAE) or Southern American English. If
a novel is about life on an Indian reservation, we can expect Native
Americans as main characters. There are much more subtle instances
of situational contexts. Certain discursive situations (or speech events,
as ethnographers call them) lend themselves to specific identities.
Children playing "the dozens" are most likely African American children. In any number of Asian or Latina/Latino American texts there
are situations where a character is confronted with English as a second language. These moments are caste as linguistic epiphanies for
characters across the spectrum of American multicultural literatures
(e.g., Esmeralda Santiago's *Almost a Woman*). In certain situations,
readers can clearly discern the nuances of identity from the linguistic
contextual information. (Though the term may have become trite in
intellectual parlance, the meaning of *multicultural* as used in this chapter includes a complex cultural spectrum of identities organized into
speech communities that are components of every culture.)

The Politics of Orthography

The notion of politics in sociolinguistic representations in literature reveals the hegemonic relationship between Standard English spelling and the varieties of English (i.e., vernaculars) that have distinct systems but must conform to standard orthography. Politics also underscores the narrative interface between social biases such as racism or sexism and the plot including characters and their various ways of speaking. Furthermore, when speech in literature is represented through mis-spellings and the use of apostrophes and other diacritical marks—(dey be chillin')—the vernacular is always visually incorrect. This style of writing sociolinguistic variation in literature is referred to as eye dialect. Eye dialect is a term that linguists have traditionally used to describe techniques for orthographically representing the speech of characters who speak in vernaculars of American English. This is often the most subtle, but probably the most linguistically productive approach for ana-lyzing the representation of identity in American literature. Vernaculars of American English are as systematic and rule-governed as standard American English (SAE). In order to convey these vernaculars, authors regularly amalgamate standard English spelling into what sometimes appears as gibberish and almost always looks and reads like a form of language that is derived from and subordinate to SAE.

There are other, less visible ways of conveying vernacular speech in literature. Some of these rely on stereotypes and situational contexts (numbers 2 and 3 above) and still others on insider knowledge of the lexicon and developing sociolinguistic conventions of the vernacular in question (like the dozens in the works of Richard Wright and Zora Neale Hurston). They also rely on a thorough knowledge of its more subtle (i.e., less visible) features including, for example, copula dele-tion, regularization of verb patterns, and distinct lexical features, all of which will be illustrated below.[1]

More than modes of reading, these four ways of arriving at social identifications in literature function as an analytical model for apply-ing general linguistic concepts in literary criticism and critical think-ing about race, gender, class, sexual orientation, and other aspects of culture in American literature. Representations of identity (in this case in literature) provide critical opportunities for readers to apply linguistic and sociolinguistic concepts to their thinking and writing on race, gender, and/or class. A reader will often need to employ only a single investigative technique in order to recognize the identity of any character or set of characters in a novel. Beyond the deceptively simple identifying function, these modes reveal the continuous re-creation of identity throughout the text. They present identity's evolution in one respect or another, within the same narrative, code-switching within a few sentences or a paragraph. Although these categories appear to be simple, each of them has cultural and linguistic nuances beneath the surface. The following passages aim to create a general context for sociolinguistic, underground readings of identity in African American literature. Passages, concepts, and characters from popular texts within these subsets will demonstrate how authors linguistically key us into the identities of their characters.

Orthographic Masks

Applying the four analytical concepts described at the head of this chapter to the interpretation of African American literature presents some of the most fruitful analyses for understanding the myriad relationships between identity, linguistics, and literature. African American literature provides us with a substantive corpus of texts from which to make assessments and draw conclusions about the representation of identity in literature. African American literature (and representations of Black people speaking in literature) date back to the dawn of American literature. From the very start, however, the speech of slaves and later of ex-slaves, as expressed by even well-intentioned authors, has been orthographically contorted into what reads like ignorant approximations of Standard English. These orthographic challenges mirror the "wilding" transcription example mentioned earlier, but the problems of African American linguistic subjectivity represented via standard English orthography predates the Central Park incident by many decades.

In Mark Twain's *Huckleberry Finn*, Huck's sidekick, Jim, provides a prototypical example.

> "Goodness gracious, is dat you Huck? En you ain' dead—you ain' drownded—you's back ag'in?...Lemme look at you chile, lemme feel o' you. No, you ain' dead! You's back ag'in, 'live en soun', jis de same old Huck. (Twain, BEP version, p. 73)

Orthography overindulged (as in this example) is the least subtle way of conveying identity in literature and sometimes the most offensive. Traditionally, Twain has been lauded as an exceptional dialectologist; a southern scholar who traveled the American south thoroughly only to accurately represent the speech of his characters. This, of course, may be true, but literature limits the authenticity of vernacular speech in at least two ways. Unlike hip-hop music or vernacular speech, you cannot hear it, and vernaculars cannot be adequately represented using Standard English orthography.

By contrast with Twain and others, African American authors have made orthographic transitions away from eye dialect toward a textually invisible vernacular. These transitions initiate in the work of Richard Wright's *Uncle Tom's Children*.[2] If orthography is a way of representing language using letters and diacritics, then traditional literary attempts to represent AAVE tend to regularize Standard English orthography and limit the reader's understanding of the vernacular by representing AAVE as orthographic approximations to Standard English. An example from Chesnutt's *The Conjure Woman* (1899) bears this out. Here, Uncle Julius recounts a story to the wife of his future employer.

> De nex' mawnin' de man wuz foun' dead. Dey wuz a great 'miration made 'bout it, but Dan did'n say nuffin, en none er de yuther niggers had n' seed de fight, so dey wa'n't nuffin done 'bout it, en de cunjuh man come en tuk his son en kyared 'im 'way en buried 'im. (Chesnutt, 1969:172)

There is an extensive spectrum of representations of AAVE in literature, ranging from Harriet Beecher Stowe and Charles Chesnutt in the nineteenth century, to Jean Toomer (1894–1967) and Gloria Naylor (b. 1950) in the twentieth. It is Richard Wright (1908–1960), though, who, in *Uncle Tom's Children*, demonstrates a politically profound orthographic transition away from the earlier representation exhibited by Chesnutt.

> The white folks ain never gimme a chance! They ain never give no black man a chance! There ain nothin in yo whole life yuh kin keep from em! They take yo lan! They take yo freedom! They take yo women! N then they take yo life! (Wright, *Uncle Tom's Children*, 1938)

First, note the absence of the diacritical apostrophes excessively used in Chesnutt's orthography. The AAVE representation of Wright suggests that marking the standard orthographic absences (especially final consonants in final consonant clusters) is not necessary. The vernacular begins, orthographically, to stand on its own, as it stands

Table 3.1 Comparative orthography

Chesnutt's Orthography	Wright's Orthography	Comments
nex', foun'	lan	fewer diacritics
'im, mawnin'	em, nothin	illustrates fewer diacritics
nuffin	nothin, in yo	intervocalic consonant cluster variation 'ff' to 'th' and back
gimme	wuz, yuh, kin	standard pronunciations, deliberate eye dialect

on its own in everyday conversational interaction. Apparently, showing orthographically "less" can reveal *more* of the systematic and stylistically beautiful elements of AAVE. Table 3.1 might be helpful in detailing how the Chesnutt and Wright passages are alike and different.

Wright also employs distinctive ritualistic AAVE features such as the dozens. His first short story titled "Big Boy Leaves Home" begins with several young Black boys playing the dozens.

> Yo Mama don wear no drawers...
> Ah seena when she pulled em off...
> N she washed 'em in alcohol...
> N she hung 'em out in the hall... (Wright 17)

According to Smitherman, the dozens is "a verbal ritual of talking negatively about someone's mother...by coming up with outlandish, highly exaggerated, often sexually loaded, humorous 'insults'.... The term...is believed to have originated during enslavement, wherein slave auctioneers sold defective 'merchandise,' e.g. sick slaves or older slaves, in lots of a dozen; thus a slave who was part of a dozens group was 'inferior.'" Thus the dozens, a verbal ritual, has distinct roots in the lived experiences of the ancestors of African Americans. In his book-length study of the dozens, significantly subtitled "A History of Rap's Mama," Elijah Wald argues that "the dozens can be tricky, aggressive, offensive, clever, brutal, funny, inventive, stupid, violent, misogynistic, psychologically intricate, deliberately misleading—or all of that at once, wrapped in a single rhymed couplet."[3] Through the figurative language of AAVE in African American literature (including the dozens, sermons, and rapping), readers can begin to understand a more comprehensive, systematic approach to identifying Black speakers without the visible orthographic approximations found in the illustrative excerpts from Chesnutt's *The Conjure Woman* and Twain's *Huck Finn*. Wright's "dozens" passage is also distinguishable orthographically, but his commitment to detailing the ritual of playing the dozens represents an important addition to literary representations of Black speech.

Variations in orthographic strategies for representing Black speech in literature highlight political subtleties in how authors portray characters and, by extension, how readers perceive the real-life speech communities that these characters represent. An excerpt from Ralph Ellison's *Invisible Man* (1952) demonstrates how some of the less visible orthographic strategies play themselves out in literature.

> When I see Matty Lou stretched out there I think she's dead. Ain't no color in her face and she ain't hardly breathin'. She gray in the face. I tries to help her but I can't do no good and Kate won't speak to me nor look at me even; and I thinks maybe she plans to try to kill me agin, but she don't. I'm in such a daze I just sits there the whole time while she bundles up the younguns and takes 'em down the road to Will Nichols'. I can see but I caint do nothin'. (Ellison, *Invisible Man*, 65)

Although Ellison relies on apostrophes in his orthography (*'em, nothin'*), he also displays significant vernacular verbal regularization in Trueblood's speech (*I tries, I thinks, I just sits*), as well as deleted copulas (*She gray in the face*). These are AAVE features that are orthographically "invisible" in that they are not represented by "errors" in the standard spelling. Thus, they can convey the style and language of the vernacular without making AAVE appear as though it were orthographically derivative or inferior. Essential to the African American writer's work, this is *underground* signifying. Beneath the surface of Standard orthography lurks the verbal structure and vernacular dexterity of AAVE. In this sense, underground describes the encoded or hidden vernacular features versus more obvious eye dialectal representations.

Adjacent to this underground signifying in literature exists the linguistic concept of deep structure. "The notion of deep structure is an abstract, intuitive concept that may be said to be like your gut-level understanding of what somebody says, and it is based on your understanding and knowledge of your native language."[4] Our native language is African American. And although many linguists have various opinions about the status of AAE, which includes AAVE, most sociolinguistic/variationist scholars are clear on the fact that AAE has systemic qualities that distinguish it from SAE. The history of deep structure in sociolinguistics originates in the work of William Labov. In his landmark essay, "The Logic of Nonstandard English," originally published in Georgetown Monographs in Languages and Linguistics in 1969, Dr. Labov establishes an academic polemic against sociolinguistic ignorance in the humanities, most specifically in educational psychology.

> These notions (that black children are verbally deprived) are based upon the work of educational psychologists who know very little about language and even less about black children. The concept of verbal deprivation has no basis in social reality. In fact, black children in the urban ghettos receive a great deal of verbal stimulation, hear more well-formed sentences than middle-class children, and participate fully in a highly verbal culture.[5]

Labov directly contends with Carl Bereiter, Siegfried Engelmann, Mark Deutsch and Arthur Jensen, all of whom offered various racist interpretations of limited and mostly invalid data to ultimately suggest that Black children were either genetically inferior, suffering from permanent social ineptitude and/or verbally deprived. Most of them refer to any constellation of these anti-qualities as Verbal Deprivation Theory.[6]

Dr. Labov's charge of inauthentic data is well deserved. The interview formats used in several government programs (Operation Head Start for starters) were "asymmetrical" and by nature, unable to collect reliable sociolinguistic data. Interviews needed to be more conversational if they were going to be used to diagnose verbal ability. More importantly, the verbal ability that many test-givers were searching for was only available in the language of the children. In the cases in question here, that language was African American Vernacular English (AAVE) that for many of the informants was a language which was not acceptable in a contrived interview format. The sociolinguistic interview is designed to be more conversationally friendly.[7] Yet, even using the more appropriately formatted interview (which allows for culturally pertinent topics and narratives to be told), Labov suggests that asymmetry in age or race directly affects the type of data that can be collected from a sociolinguistic informant.[8]

After Labov successfully argues that the data of his chosen opponents is inauthentic he proceeds to uncover the logic in "nonstandard" English. He chooses the double negative form, or what he, in corrective tone, calls negative concord in his description of Black English Vernacular (BEV) features.

> If a nonstandard speaker wishes to say 'He does not know nothing', he does so by simply placing contrastive stress on both negatives…indicating that they are derived from two underlying negatives in the deep structure. But note that the middle class speaker does exactly the same thing when he wants to signal the existence of two underlying negatives: 'He doesn't know nothing'. The dialect difference, like most of the differences between the standard and nonstandard forms, is one of *surface* form, and has nothing to do with the *underlying* logic of the sentence. (my emphasis) (Labov 226)

In order to establish "logic" here Professor Labov argues that there is a shared, deep structure between AAVE and Standard American English (SAE).

The concept of deep structure is a signal concept of the underground in African American culture. Labov refers to deep structure as the "underlying logic" of language. In *Talkin and Testifyin*, Dr. Geneva Smitherman fleshes out the meaning of this concept. "Though abstract, deep structure is where the true meaning of a given language resides. Through ordered linguistic rules, deep structures of a language are transformed into surface structures. These are the concrete manifestations of the deep structures, that is, what actually gets expressed in speech or writing. Although each speaker of a language has his or her unique way of talking, the speakers all share common deep structures; otherwise, they could not understand one another and there would be no communication."[9] Certainly the obvious imagery of linguistic inner workings beneath the surface of expressed language lends itself to my connected conceptualizations of the underground in African American culture. But deep structure accounts for the variations in English and can be used to explain the arbitrary nature of standardization in linguistics. "Despite…differences in surface structures (in English vernaculars),…speakers of different states can understand one another, all are speaking the English language and they can all communicate because the various dialects have the same source of meaning: English deep structure."[10] If AAE shares its deep structure with all variants of English then we can readily understand that SAE is standard because of America's sociopolitical infrastructure.

The concept of deep structure in linguistics dates back to Noam Chomsky's extraordinarily influential work in *Aspects of the Theory of Syntax.* Chomsky revolutionizes the thrust and focus of the entire field of linguistics. Moreover he redeems the field of linguistics from empirical disintegration for what we think of as traditional scientific inquiry.[11] "They (the early Chomskyans) had, in a few short and feverish years, hammered out an elegant framework which accomplished the ultimate goal of all linguistic work from at least the time of the Stoics. They had formally linked sound and meaning."[12] That deep structure is the conceptual centerpiece of this revolution in the field of linguistics supports the redemptive underpinnings in this book from the Underground Railroad to Dr. Houston Baker's recuperation of Richard Wright with Black (W)hole Theory.[13] Moreover, the complexity of language and innovations in theories of linguistics underscored by and through Noam Chomsky's work reveal the importance of understanding AAE in critical analyses of Black expressive forms such as literature and music.

Analyzing deep structure, orthography and various individual vernacular features are not exclusive ways of reading linguistic identity in African American literature. Zora Neale Hurston's body of work provides an exceptional opportunity for readers to appreciate the relationship between literature, identity, and linguistics. Hurston (1903–1960) was a student of Franz Boas, called the father of American linguistics and a firm believer in an anthropological approach to linguistics, someone who led the field toward thoroughly empirical goals (Harris 1993:19). Hurston's life work was dedicated to collecting and representing the vernacular culture of southern Black people, particularly Black speech communities in her home state of Florida. More importantly, in her work Hurston represents the verbal virtuosity of Black women. Sociolinguists who studied Black speech after Hurston published her most famous novel, *Their Eyes Were Watching God* (1937), attributed much of the quantifiable data on African American Vernacular English to male speakers. Not only does Hurston present understudied female informants in her anthropological work, but in *Their Eyes Were Watching God* she also creates characters who advance a womanist agenda through vernacular speech, often in speaking situations dominated by males. In order fully to appreciate the worldview that Hurston affects through language and speech community, you must read the novel. Its protagonist, Janie, is "powerful, articulate, self-reliant, and radically different from any woman character [Black women readers] had ever before encountered in literature" (Gates 1998:xi). Her narrative is actually told by her friend Phoeby, and one literary critic has argued that "Janie's voice at the end of the novel is a communal one, that when she tells Phoeby to tell her story ('You can tell'em what Ah say if you wants to. Dat's just de same as me 'cause mah tongue is in mah friend's mouf') she is choosing a collective rather than an individual voice, demonstrating her closeness to the collective spirit of the African American Oral tradition."[14] The words "mah tongue is in mah friend's mouf" also speak directly to a bond between Phoeby and Janie. In Phoeby's mouth, Janie's life story is safe from misrepresentation.

Janie's journey toward her full-fledged identity begins in puberty and ends in tragedy. Along the way, she marries a politically ambitious dominating husband named Joe Starks. After years in an economically stable relationship, Janie's capacity for holding her tongue in verbally abusive interactions with Joe utterly diminishes. In a store that the couple owns and operates, several dozens-like exchanges with Joe in front of an audience of their friends (mostly men) involving "some good natured laughter at the expense of women" bring Janie to her boiling point.[15]

> Naw, Ah ain't no young gal no mo' but den Ah ain't no old woman neither. Ah reckon Ah looks mah age too. But Ah'm uh woman every inch of me, and Ah know it. Dat's uh whole lot more'n you kin say. You big-bellies round here and put out a lot of brag, but 'tain't nothin' to it but yo' big voice. Humph! Talkin' 'bout me lookin' old! When you pull down yo' britches, you look lak de change of life.[16]

Within weeks of this exchange (four pages in the novel), Joe Starks becomes fatally ill, and the narrative implies that he does not recover from having been put in his place verbally in front of his own speech community. On a symbolic level, Hurston is using this linguistic murder (if you will) to reflect Janie's development as a woman. After Joe's death, Janie takes over the store and eventually moves into the next phase in her development as a woman: a relationship in which she finds some spiritual and sexual satisfaction. "In *Their Eyes* Joe Starks's death terminates twenty years of oppressive wedlock for Janie and frees her to achieve mutual, conjugal pleasure with Tea Cake."[17] In her groundbreaking work on psychoanalysis and African American literature, the late Claudia Tate argues that most of Hurston's novels depend "on rhetorical and dramatic jest to construct textual meaning."[18] This is certainly an accurate assessment of this particular passage in *Their Eyes*, as the last signifying jest between Janie and Joe signals a liberating victory for Janie and the overall significance of rhetorical and linguistic prowess for the characters of Hurston's novels.

For the purposes of this book (and for the sake of at least one hip-hop intervention in this chapter), Janie's linguistic murder might also be couched within the cultural context of a fairly pervasive metaphor of lyrical (or rhetorical) murder in the competitive discourses of hip-hop performance. While many emcees embrace the language of murder as analogues for verbally destroying their adversaries, an apropos example of this lyrical move, one related to Janie's undressing of Joe Starks in *Their Eyes*, is an interlude recorded for Rah Digga's debut album— *Dirty Harriet*—released in 2000. The interlude, "Harriet Thugman," is a discrete distillation of major themes on Rah Digga's first major label release. In some ways, Rah Digga's career as a hip-hop artist is indicative of Tate's analysis of lyrical prowess in African American literature; that somehow Digga's presence (itself) in what is often (and rightly) characterized as a male-centered industry is the embodiment of rhetorical contestation replete with deeper constructions of textual meaning in and for hip-hop culture. Rah Digga exploits the full force of how an author (or in this case an emcee) can manipulate themes of identity in order for audiences to access deeper meanings with respect to her words/lyrics. According to Yvonne Bynoe, Rah Digga (nee Rashia Fisher) "has earned the respect of audiences and her male peers with rugged lyrics, a superior flow, and a take-no-prisoners attitude."[19] Her emcee moniker as well as the title and themes of her first album construct underground imagery directly alluding to the most well-known architect of the Underground Railroad—Harriet Tubman. "Given its clandestine nature, the UGRR [Underground Railroad] has left historians with few ways to re-create its activities or measure its extent. Yet this unique woman's career offers efficacious insight. Through sheer power of will and fierce determination, Harriet Tubman pursued her own road to freedom and in doing so, she led the way for others."[20] Tubman's work on the Underground Railroad is legendary and Rah Digga's allusions to her and that history mark her as an underground hip-hop artist right at the intersections of the narratives of an historical figure who also populates the literary histories depicting the Underground Railroad. In Ann Petry's treatment of Harriet Tubman's life, titled *Harriet Tubman: Conductor on the Underground Railroad*, she makes the following claim about Tubman's voice. "She sang when she was in the fields or working in the nearby woods. Her voice was unusual because of the faint huskiness.

Once having heard it, people remembered it."[21] Petry's description of the "faint huskiness" of Tubman's voice also serves as an accurate description of Rah Digga's artistic voice. Moreover, "according to Rah Digga...Harriet Tubman inspired the album's title. Rah Digga [has] stated that, like Harriet Tubman who led people to freedom, she is leading other female rap artists to realize that they can succeed using lyrical skills rather than their sexuality."[22] This sentiment elides Digga's important work to distinguish her voice in the male-centered space of hip-hop culture with a bifurcated view of how women might express themselves as emcees. This limitation does not undermine the underground significance of Rah Digga's allusions to Harriet Tubman or her moment as an embodied iteration of lyrical prowess in hip-hop culture.

"Harriet Thugman" is barely 90 seconds, the shortest track on the album. It is produced by Busta Rhymes and announces itself in the slightly husky voice of Rah Digga: "The Harriet Tubman of hip hop has returned...." She goes on to construct textually meaningful connections to African American history. She likens herself to a "house nigga" to indicate her commitment to working in recording studios; an analogy that requires some understanding of the kind of commitment that becoming a successful recording artist demands and the challenges of artist development for women within technological spaces often owned, operated, and managed by men. She refers to her "gritty lingo" and alludes to the fact that she is college educated. Her veiled threats to emcees—that worry her male counterparts—reflect her confidence and her willingness to verbally confront her male counterparts. Digga concludes her verse in a set of aspirational, if not utopian, musings—leading her "nation" to a place where people are not harassed by police, where marijuana is legal, where underground emcees are "primetime," where lyrics liberate people, and where "Black presidents" govern. Finally, she asserts that her verses are delivered by a literary visionary. Rah Digga's emphasis on the linguistic and the literary are liberating levers for her artistic presence within hip-hop culture. She claims the underground as a space of authenticity and embraces the historical mythos of Harriet Tubman in order to illustrate and strengthen her artistic claims. Ultimately, Rah Digga's Harriet Thugman/Harriet Tubman is a striking example of an intersection of underground concepts in hip-hop culture with concepts of the underground in African American literary history.

Sociolinguistic Transformations

Among the most extraordinary underground moments in African American literature with respect to linguistics and the identity of speech communities is one that occurs in Chesnutt's *The Conjure Woman* (1899). Above, we saw examples of the eye dialect Chesnutt (1858–1932) used to depict the speech of his main character, Julius, who recounts various tales of a surreal African American way of life that features root work and conjuring among slaves in Lumberton, North Carolina. Lumberton is a tri-dialectal community, including southern vernacular varieties of speech from Native Americans (the Lumbee), African Americans, and Southern White Americans. But that's not what is most striking about the use of language in *The Conjure Woman*.

Chesnutt is deliberate in distinguishing Julius's speech community from that of the northern White couple who take up residence on his former master's plantation. The couple speaks SAE. Julius speaks AAVE. Moreover, he tells his stories (he explains his reality) in the vernacular. But Julius does not actually relate his own narrative. We experience Julius's world through the eyes and mouth of his White employer. And this subtle conundrum unfolds in the philosophical discourses on transformations. Most of the folktale-like narratives of *The Conjure Woman* involve a metamorphosis or transformation. For instance, one woman turns her illegal husband (illegal because by law slaves could not marry) into a tree in an attempt to keep him close to her. The conjure woman turns another character into a humming bird so that he might find a loved one. A conjure man turns a slave into a donkey in another tale. In general, the northern White business-minded husband does not believe the surreal vernacular aspects of Julius's narratives. His wife, however, is somewhat more sympathetic to the fantastic tales. One day, before Julius is able to bend the wife's ear, her husband begins to read to her from a philosophy text.

> The difficulty of dealing with transformations so many-sided as those which all existences have undergone, or are undergoing, is such as to make a complete and deductive interpretation almost hopeless. So to grasp the total process of redistribution of matter and motion as to see simultaneously its several necessary results in their actual interdependence is scarcely possible. There is, however, a mode of rendering the process as a whole tolerably comprehensible. Though the genesis of the rearrangement of every evolving aggregate is in itself one, it presents to our intelligence. (Chesnutt 1969:163–4)

At this point, the husband is interrupted by his wife, who refers to his philosophy as nonsense. The husband thinks to himself: "I had never been able to interest my wife in the study of philosophy, even when presented in the simplest and most lucid form" (1969: 164). We can think of this episode as a complex case of sociolinguistic irony. The wife believes that the philosophical passage is nonsense, but upon close reading, this philosophy is grappling with a (Standard English) scientific explanation of the fantastic reality that Julius has so vividly described (in the vernacular) for the couple since they have moved south. The irony is further complicated by the fact that the husband critiques his wife as if he completely understood the philosophy he is reading. Yet he makes no connections between "transformations" or the "redistribution of matter" and the tales of metamorphosis that Julius tells. To the husband this *philosophy* is completely legitimate; by contrast, Julius's world is inauthentic fantasy. Yet the only "thing" that separates these two worldviews is a variation in language.

We can push the envelope of this interpretation a bit further by introducing the notion of linguistic transformations. In the 1950s and 1960s, transformational-generative grammar shifted some subfields of linguistic inquiry away from empiricism and closer to cognition. In fact Noam Chomsky developed syntax into an abstract formula that, through structure, began to account for meaning (i.e., semantics). The transformations are cognitive functions that transform underlying phrase markers (like noun phrases or verb phrases) and structure rules (the rules for creating phrases) into grammatical sentences. (For fuller expositions, see Harris 1993, Chomksy 1957). But such transformations seem absent from the linguistic processes of the husband and the wife in *Conjure Woman*. The surface sentences of the philosophical passage are incomprehensible to both of them.

Chesnutt's sense of transformation and its inherent function in language and the realities that are shaped or created by language are fleshed out in the narratives of Julius as well as this peculiar philosophical passage where transformation gets a standard overhaul, yet SAE speakers cannot grasp the totality of its meaning nor the meaning of Julius's vernacular world. This striking discursive confusion reflects the duality of Chesnutt's lived mulatto world at the turn of the twentieth century. It is an excellent example to thread through to the rubric established at the onset of this chapter because Chesnutt's life and this particular text can be thoroughly analyzed with the tools of this rubric, most notably the Politics of Orthography, but also

Re-envisioning Stereotypes (Julius ain't as dumb as he appears to be), and the Authors and the Theme of Identity.

The analysis of African American sociolinguistic identity presents a wide range of possible interpretive approaches to American Literature. Since the thrust of sociolinguistic analyses of American Literature require a scholastic search beneath the orthographic surface of the actual writing, I consider this study in Linguistic identity in literature as one of the key applications of the concepts of the underground detailed in this book. The cursory exemplification of linguistic identity in African American literature begins to suggest the far-reaching interpretive value of the hip-hop Underground and African American culture. The concept of deep structure is a fundamental link to my ideas about the underground and the ways in which sociolinguistic investigation produces meaningful interpretations and a complex understanding of the relationships between orthography, sociolinguistics, literature, and identity.

CHAPTER 4

DEFINING AN UNDERGROUND AT
THE INTERSECTIONS OF HIP-HOP AND
AFRICAN AMERICAN CULTURES

The narrator of Saul Williams's *Dead Emcee Scrolls* opens his collection of poems and essays with a story about a series of scrolls
that he discovered in the catacombs of the New York City subway
system. Williams narrates a story of how he descended into the underground and discovered cryptic scrolls encased in an aerosol paint can.
As the narrative unfolds, he enigmatically argues that these found
scrolls serve as the sui generis texts from which his spoken word, hip-
hop-oriented lyricism emerges. This is an instructive place to begin
the herculean task of defining a hip-hop underground, interstitially
linked to and with African American culture. This definitive process
is distinct from the extensive ethnographic, linguistic, and anthropological work done by Marcyliena Morgan (2009) and Anthony Kwame
Harrison (2009). Each of these major works on the underground of
hip-hop culture focuses on the rich tradition of underground hip-hop
music cultivated and circulated from and throughout the west coast
of the United States. Morgan's *The Real Hip-Hop* centers on a physical space/place—the historic Project Blowed located across the street
from Leimert Park in Los Angeles. Harrison's *Hip-Hop Underground*
also focuses on the west coast but Harrison centers his work on the Bay
area and the inimitable "Do-It-Yourself" (DIY) ethos that has thrived
in the Bay area for successive generations of underground hip-hop
aficionados. In addition to these under groundbreaking works, the
analysis in this chapter borrows Herman Gray's notion of *cultural
moves* (CM), elements of Salamishah Tillet's *Sites of Slavery* and Ray
Jackendoff's *conceptual structures* in order to elucidate the intersections

of underground hip-hop and certain aspects of African American culture. Gray's work investigates (and interrogates) the assumption that African American cultural production and the sociopolitical movements that accompany this production desire a particular form of national recognition—recognition usually in the form of subjective Black representation—in media, politics, business, etc. Jackendoff's conceptual structures are a theoretical framework through which an expansive prelinguistic sense of the concepts of the underground in African American culture can best be understood. And finally, since so much of the scholarship on the concept of the underground in hip-hop looks westward for various exegetical concerns/issues, here I take up an underground mixtape/playlist of my own making that seeks to balance this left coast-centered discussion with a range of artists and rap lyrics that "speak" to the locus of underground hip-hop and African American culture generally from regions/coasts heretofore overlooked in the scholarship.

Saul Stacey Williams was a signal artistic figure during the mainstream emergence of spoken word Poetry in the mid-late 1990s. He is featured in many of the major documentaries of spoken word competitions and contests that are often referred to as "slams." African American literature and poetry have always been thematically and stylistically intertwined with Black music. Spoken word is no exception. Spoken word Poetry borrows its proliferation of venues (of spaces and places) from the Jazz and Bebop traditions, its attitude and performance styles from hip-hop culture, and its potent lyrical content from the very best of the Black poetic traditions. Williams was born to Reverend Saul S. Williams and Juanita Sealy-Williams on February 29, 1972, in Albany, New York. He and his family (he has two older sisters) resided in Newburg, New York, which is approximately 60 miles north of New York City. Williams attended public school in Newburg. He began his elementary education at a magnet school for the gifted and talented called Horizons on the Hudson. He began writing and acting in the third grade. He attended Newburg Free Academy High School and in his junior year he studied abroad, in Brazil. From 1990 to 1994 he attended Morehouse College in Atlanta, Georgia, majoring in philosophy and drama. During his senior year in college, Williams began publishing his writing regularly in Morehouse's Red Clay Magazine. His content focused on social issues and it was through this writing experience that he began to recognize poetry as his most efficient mode of communication and expression. After Morehouse, Williams attended graduate school in New York and began performing at the famed Nuyorican Café where he won the Grand Slam in 1996. Williams received his Masters in acting (MFA) from New York University's Tisch School of the Arts in 1997.

During this same year he wrote *Slam* with Marc Levine and Sonya Sohn. They filmed *Slam* (which is fictional) during the summer of 1997. *Slam* is probably Williams's most popular work and to date the most popular film about the spoken word art form. The main character, played by Williams, is a small-time marijuana hustler/poet who is arrested and imprisoned for dealing. Once he is trapped inside the system, Williams's character befriends a grisly convict (played by urban journalist Bonz Malone) who is a veteran of the ways of the prison system. Bonz Malone's character is fascinated by Williams's ability to navigate the dangers of imprisonment, including impending violence, by speaking his poetry aloud to his potential adversaries. Ultimately Williams's character survives the experiences in the prison industrial complex and redeems himself through the artistry of spoken word. I rehearse Williams's biography briefly here in order to underscore his actual emergence as a poet and its important (aboveground) corollary relationship to the more underground mythological narrative presented in *The Dead Emcee Scrolls*.

The most compelling way to experience Saul Williams's artistry is live, but his audio recordings as well as his printed poems engage the listener/reader at many cultural, spiritual, and artistic levels.[1] A great deal of his work navigates the intersections between a range of conceptualizations of the underground and African American culture. In "Twice the First Time," a spiritual spoken word rap on the *Eargasms* compilation, he deconstructs the relationships between various forms of the Black oral tradition, including spirituals, chain gang work songs, and rap.[2] In traditional spiritual style he sings the chorus: "I will not rhyme over tracks. / Niggas on a chain gang used to do that a waaay back. / I will not rhyme on tracks. /Niggas on a chain gang use to do that a waay back." His verses flow like a traditional locomotive over well-lubricated tracks (i.e., sparse musical production), while the chorus simultaneously endorses the spoken word form and speaks to the complexities inherent in the historical trajectory of African American oral and folk forms. Chain gangs and prison work songs predate and inform the verbal and rhythmic acuity of rap music. Williams's poetic assertion that he will not be bound by "tracks" doubles as his own personal separation from the commercial musical production of popular rap music as well as an important reminder of the role of the prison system (historically) and the modern prison industrial complex in the developments of rap music. The move to separate his poetics from mainstream/commercial bondage—here in the form of rap's popular/commercial musical production—is what I would argue as a deliberate cultural move toward conceptualizations of the underground. According to Herman Gray, CM "question conventional assumptions about recognition and visibility, and especially, assumptions about African American investment in representation as a route to African American membership in national culture" (Gray 2). Gray's "cultural moves" function with the sense of "cultural privacy"—discussed in chapter 2.

Although this is difficult to pinpoint, Williams's break from musical "tracks" occurs as spoken word emerges (mid-1990s) and as underground hip-hop begins to establish itself, according to Anthony K. Harrison. "Against the commercial ascendance of Music Industry rap, during the mid-to-late nineties a specific subgenre known as 'underground hip hop' developed through networks of Do-It-Yourself (DIY) artists/entrepreneurs, home-based industries, and locally-focused collective movements" (Harrison 29). Harrison does not necessarily have Williams or spoken word artistry in mind in his work on the DIY underground communities on the west coast, but Williams's work, especially as it is exemplified in these lines about not rhyming on tracks, suggests both the critical positionality of underground hip-hop as it is defined by Harrison and the artistic interface of certain conceptualizations of underground hip-hop and African American culture. This initial example of Williams's lyrics also reveals the limitations of defining underground hip-hop exclusively as the Bay Area's DIY movement and/or the localized spaces in which underground hip-hop is performed—á la Morgan's in-depth ethnography on the underground hip-hop performance space—Project Blowed in Los Angeles. Morgan is specifically aware of the spatial limitations in unpacking the range of meanings inherent in the concepts of the underground in Black culture. "Through both commercial and underground media forms, the art, dance, music, and words of hip hop transcend language, neighborhoods, cities, and national boundaries…" (Morgan 48). Morgan charts this transcendence in order to explicate and briefly explore the spread of hip-hop culture around the globe. Many scholars (including Neate 2004) have tracked these developments and ethnographically documented the conceptual and affective transcendence of hip-hop music, especially as it relates to identity formation among youth. This transcendence also underscores the conceptual structures underpinning underground meanings in hip-hop culture and across the spectrum of African American experiences (i.e., from the Underground Railroad to Richard Wright's "Man Who Lived Underground" or Amiri Baraka's "Dutchman" to concepts of the underground in hip-hop culture). The underground in hip-hop can mean a specific location/space like the cellar for the Cella Dwellas, or the sewer for Das EFX, but these spaces also represent meanings beyond space—semantic systems constructed through the artistry of underground hip-hop that begin to take shape as deliberate CM toward an engagement with history that is not necessarily dictated by market forces (i.e., marketability) or other entrapments of mainstream success/acceptance (e.g., misogyny, materialism, and/or violence). The broadest range of conceptualizations of the underground in hip-hop extend from spatial references, literal allusions, and antimarket sentiments to figurative spatial constructs, notions of authenticity, and a bevy of concepts that emerge from the history of the Black experience in America.

Thus, in addition to Morgan's and Harrison's important assessments of hip-hop's cultural and geographic transcendence, underground hip-hop's places/spaces or underground hip-hop's "spotlighting [of] commercial rap music's inauthenticity..." a range of conceptual iterations especially in the content of certain rap lyrics must be considered in tandem and in conversation with these well-developed definitions. For example, in "Twice the First Time," Saul Williams works to defamiliarize the creative process (not rhyming over tracks) as well as the listening process. According to the narrator in "Twice the First Time," you haven't heard hip-hop until you've listened to Rakim (of Eric B and Rakim fame) on a Mountaintop or until you've heard Biz Markie's "Nobody Beats the Biz" in the forest. The call for a spatial reorientation in the rap music listening experience informs my suggestion that underground hip-hop can also be defined beyond any spatial constraints as a particular variation of Gray's CM, here defying convention by challenging the constituents of hip-hop to experience the music beyond the confines of the urban spaces where much of the music has been produced and engineered historically. Williams simultaneously suggests and promotes the concept of recontextualizing the listening experience. He accompanies himself throughout the song with his own rendition of a Human Beat Box—the oral (re)-production of percussive instrumentation considered by many to be a "lost" element of hip-hop culture. Williams rhymes over a track even as his chorus suggests otherwise. The track consists mostly of his own human beat box and some string arrangements, but the lyrical messages are clear and the aesthetics of the stripped-down, nonconventional, musical production underscore his artistic arguments/suggestions (as well as my assertions here) that defining a concept of the underground at the intersections of hip-hop and African American cultures require conceptual structures as much as it does lyrical content, space/place, and relationship to commerce and the popular rap music marketplace.

Ray Jackendoff's work in *Language, Consciousness, Culture: Essays on Mental Structure*, explores "the mental structures involved in a variety of cognitive domains: language, consciousness, complex action, theory of mind, and social/cultural cognition" (Jackendoff xvii). Jackendoff's arguments cohere linguistic processes with neuroscience in order to more accurately codify the combinatorial interactions between varying levels of linguistic function and cognition. Conceptual structures are mental, linguistic, and arguably prelinguistic phenomena that encode language at/on multiple levels—phonological, morphological, syntactic, and semantic. "Pre-linguistic phenomenona" are somewhat beyond the scope of this discussion, but the codification of conceptually repetitive "combinatorial interactions" reflects a structure for how concepts of the underground in African American culture and hip-hop can be generated. "Conceptual structure is a level of mental structure that is largely *autonomous* of language and *epistemologically prior* to it. The function of language in the ecology of the mind is to express conceptual structures overtly for purposes of communication. Language also serves, through the medium of verbal imagery, as a means of making thought consciously accessible" [emphasis in the original] (Jackendoff 193). At issue here are the ways in which the lyrical language of underground hip-hop reflects or outlines expressive (and expressible) examples of the conceptual structure of the underground itself. In this sense, underground is a conceptual structure informed by the cultural histories that drive the socially conscious artistic sensibilities of hip-hop artists who in turn lyrically perform, represent, allude to, or reflect upon the concept of the underground. The aforementioned example of lyrics alluding to chain gangs, railroad tracks, commerce, and bondage, more broadly conceived, suggest the range of the underground-as-conceptual-structure especially as it is related to the ways in which underground hip-hop is projected and perceived both as linguistic content and the cultural consciousness of a particular set of African American historical experiences. In this case, those experiences include (and regularly reference) the legacy of slavery in America, the symbolic power of railroads and the signified but lyrically unexpressed allusion to imagery of bondage, freedom, and commerce.

The opening chapter of Saul Williams's *Dead Emcee Scrolls* (titled "Confessions") references the modern and arguably literal model of the Underground Railroad—the New York City subway system. Williams's narrator journeys into the subway and finds his poetic voice.[3] Before he relates his subterranean journey, Williams's narrator waxes eloquently about the affective aspects of the hip-hop listening experience. "When the beat drops, people nod their heads, 'yes,' in the same way that they would in conversation with a loved one, a parent, professor, or minister" (Williams xi). According to the narrator, "music speaks directly to the subconscious" and "the consciously simplified beat of the hip hop drum speaks directly to the heart" (Williams xi). These affective assertions invite a conceptual-structural approach to defining underground hip-hop music—especially the underground hip-hop music listening experience. Williams's affective assertions ring true. Hip-hop music listeners respond kinesthetically to the percussive elements of the production. For Williams, this interaction with the music invokes the aesthetics of the drum and the Afrocentric narratives that traditionally attach to these allusions. But these points are also useful in understanding how conceptual structures of the underground—in this case the excavation of African percussive aesthetics (and kinesthetic responses)—inform the meanings of the underground concept in hip-hop culture. One of the conceptual structures of the underground in hip-hop then is the concept of an African heritage loosely defined and inextricably linked to hip-hop cultural subjectivity and creativity.

Throughout "Confessions," Williams's narrator goes on to explore the technological, musical, and cultural intersections responsible for the emergence of hip-hop music in American (and global) popular culture. The narrator questions the evolving influence of music (and lyrics) that operate in such affective ways. He also laments the market effects on the content of the music. Here, Williams recalls the late-1990s' shift in the lyrical content of hip-hop music that developed as the music became more and more popular—the idea that as hip-hop garnered its platinum status in the music industry it became more formulaic—featuring more materialism, violence, and misogyny as a staple of that content. He claims that "as the music grew more openly misogynistic and capitalistic, I found myself being a bit more picky about exactly what I would choose to nod my head to" (Williams xii). These reflections form the backdrop for Williams's narrative where he ventures underground and discovers the scrolls that inform his work.[4] They also serve as a narrative example (a story) for a central tension in the concept of the underground in hip-hop between commercial success, distribution, etc., and DIY and alternative market models. Williams's narrative/narratological approach to his own experiences with hip-hop culture also takes a participatory turn in that he relates (or laments) his participation in certain elements of the culture. He is most obviously an emcee/rapper/poet, but he also claims: "I never really tried to DJ, but I definitely tried my hand as a graffiti writer...I would try, but I sucked and I knew it. So usually, I just focused on writing rhymes" (Williams xiv). Note the juxtaposition of "writing rhymes" and being a "graffiti writer." The narrator's respect for graf writers derives from their craftsmanship, originality, and their penchant for encoded writing—acknowledging that graf writing is both visually (i.e., orthographically/calligraphically) encoded as well as linguistically/semantically encoded. This scriptocentric gesture is also an important precursor to Williams's underground narrative. "Flashlight in hand, we descended the platform and ventured into the darkness. The mazes we journeyed were womblike and seemed infinite" (Williams xv). Anthropologists and journalists who have studied the homeless (or houseless) that live in the New York Subway system suggest that "the underground networks are not only vast but chaotic" (Toth 44).[5] "New York's subway lines wind through 731 sprawling miles of New York's five boroughs, in tunnels that burrow down to eighteen stories below ground at 191st Street and Broadway in Manhattan....New York's subways constitute the largest urban railroad system in the world, with 6100 cars that carry a quarter of a million pounds of flesh and blood each day" (Toth 44). After some searching in the underground catacombs of the New York City subway system, Williams ultimately emerges with the "dead emcee scrolls" tightly coiled inside an aerosol spray paint can. The scrolls are so named in order to signify on the archaeological importance of the Dead Sea scrolls, their mid-twentieth century discovery in

underground caverns, and to symbolize the mythic underground origins of verbal hip-hop craft—that is writing and speaking/rapping.
   The narrative of Williams's journey into the subway is an archetypal representation of underground concepts in hip-hop culture. In
order to best explore how the conceptual structures of the underground operate within hip-hop, some additional definitions of the
terms may be useful. In Yvonne Bynoe's *Encyclopedia of Rap and Hip-
Hop Culture*, the underground is defined as "a term to describe rap
music that is not associated with a major record company, or that
reflects the more diverse and often socially aware rap music and hip-
hop culture developing around the United States but not usually
promoted by commercial entertainment outlets, including radio and
music video programs" (Bynoe 397). Bynoe's definition is consistent
with Morgan, Harrison, and others who suggest that underground
hip-hop has a resistant relationship to the mainstream music industry
market(s)—resistance that takes the form of what Harrison and others
refer to as a DIY approach to producing, promoting, selling, and cir-
culating the music. The definition then pivots to "more diverse" and
"socially aware" content (presumably) in the lyrics. One challenge in
defining a hip-hop underground or discerning what can and should
be considered underground hip-hop is to make some determina-
tions and provide some tools for evaluating generally what constitutes
diverse and/or "socially aware" content. In *The Hip-Hop Wars*, Tricia
Rose contributes some additional terms and concepts to this effort to
define the underground. "In the battle over the politics of hip-hop,
convention separates the commercial realm from conscious rap, with
the latter largely considered part of 'the underground'. The distinctions made between the two tend to revolve loosely around whether
or not a given artist has politically progressive content" (Rose 241).
Opposing commercial and conscious may present a bind; the terms
are not semantically opposites yet within the context of the discourses
on what constitutes underground hip-hop music, conscious content is
juxtaposed with and generally opposed to commercial music and content. In my list below there are several examples of songs that arguably
have conscious content, yet they are also commercial in the sense that
Bynoe suggests—that is, they are distributed by so-called major labels
and they are promoted by "commercial entertainment outlets." For
me this bind suggests a more symbiotic relationship between what is
generally considered commercial/mainstream versus what is generally
considered underground. Both Morgan and Harrison circumnavigate

this bind by focusing almost exclusively on underground music, venues, markets, and models on the west coast of the United States.

Another important aspect of Rose's discussion on these matters is her assertion that "politically progressive content" is a factor around which distinctions about underground versus mainstream/commercial hip-hop "revolve." This is an important litmus test, if you will, for the central approaches to defining underground hip-hop music beyond the scope of market forces and geographic locale—that is, defining underground hip-hop on its own terms—via conceptual structures, CM, and sites of slavery. "Politically progressive content" would be, generally speaking, those lyrics that made political statements and assertions, critiqued socioeconomic conditions, and/or directly embraced an ethos of social justice. While what constitutes politically progressive content has and will continue to be dependent on sociohistorical contexts, the heuristic devices of Jackendoff's Conceptual Structures (CS), Gray's Cultural Moves (CM), and Tillet's Sites of Slavery (SOS) offer some necessary approaches to determining (and conferring) underground status upon the set of songs/lyrics considered in this book as well as those briefly listed in this chapter. It goes without saying that the reduction of the critical theoretical work of Jackendoff, Tillet, and Gray is done so here in the spirit of full respect for these works and in the interest of critical applications of compelling ideas to the content listed below (table 4.1).

For the purposes of the following brief gloss of the underground hip-hop playlist detailed in table 4.1, Jackendoff's Conceptual Structures (CS), Gray's Cultural Moves (CM), and Tillet's Sites of Slavery (SOS) are the tools by/through which I have evaluated the rap songs (especially the songs' lyrics) listed in the table. The CS, CM, and SOS rubrics are not the holistic or sole determining factors in what can or does constitute underground-ness in hip-hop culture. Instead these categories serve to elucidate heretofore unannounced and somewhat underappreciated phenomena that additionally inform underground discourses with respect to hip-hop music especially, but not exclusively. Note also here that this list is NOT exhaustive; it deliberately attempts to focus on hip-hop music produced and recorded in places other than those that have been most discussed in the literature on underground hip-hop. That is, the list deliberately looks away from the West Coast and toward other regions—especially the East Coast—in order to cover some sense of the discourses on the concepts of the underground in Black culture. This playlist also flouts

Table 4.1 A hip-hop underground playlist

Song Title	Artist/Speaker	Year	CS	CM	SOS
"You Can't Hate the Roots…"	Malcolm X	1962	X	X	X
"Go Underground"	B.B. King	1970	X		
"Underground"	EPMD	1990	X		
"Funky Child"	Lords of the Underground	1993	X		
"Hold"/hole/whole	KRS ONE	1995	X	X	
"Underground Lockdown"	Hurricane G	1997	X	X	
"M.U.G."—Money Underground	O.C. fea. Freddie Foxxx	1997	X	X	
"In(Sense)"/*Beneath the Surface*	Onomatopoeia	1998		X	
"Nathaniel"	Outkast	1998			
"Liberation"	Cee-Lo/Outkast	1998		X	X
"Underground"	Thema Simone Bryant	1999	X	X	X
"Mathematics"	Mos Def	1999			
"Harriet Thugman"/*Dirty Harriet*	Rah Digga	2000			X
"Liberty"/*Underground Railroad*	Mastermind	2000	X	X	
"Africa Dream"	Talib Kweli	2000			X
"Something's Gotta Give"	V.I.Kings	2003		X	
"Still Ain't Good Enough"	Random	2006			
"Underground Kingz"	UGK-Underground Kingz	2007		X	
"Keep It Real"/*African Underground-Depths of Dakar*	Pato	2007	X		
"Bboy Underground"	Digikid84	2008	X		
"Underground"	Eminem	2009			
"The Grand Illusion (Circa 1973)"	Pharoahe Monch feat. Citizen Cope	2011	X	X	X
"Praying Man"/*Live from the Underground*	Big K.R.I.T. feat. B.B. King	2012	X	X	X

what I consider to be the porous boundaries between commercial/mainstream/aboveground hip-hop and underground hip-hop. Many of the songs/artists on the playlist have so-called mainstream music deals. Still others have released popular (i.e., pop) music and have not done so via traditional DIY methods. Not every song on this list can (or should) be considered "politically progressive," "socially aware," or conscious. Dispensing the commercial/conscious distinction or any of the other related binaries or binds that are sometimes present in the discourses on underground hip-hop is not the aim of this listing or of this chapter on the whole. Instead, the aim here is to expand the terms through which we define and/or discern underground hip-hop. Of the songs on the list, many of them ("Something's Gotta Give," "Still Ain't Good Enough," and "The Grand Illusion (Circa 1973)"—see table 4.1) could be categorized in models similar to those detailed and researched by Morgan and/or Harrison. These three songs are all recorded by "consensus" underground artists who essentially produce, market, and distribute their own music (in the case of Random and the V.I.Kings). Each of these songs has an expressed socioeconomic critique of society—"Something's Gotta Give" is a warning about how people might respond in dire socioeconomic situations; "Still Ain't Good Enough" is a critique of the public education system— especially No Child Left Behind; and "The Grand Illusion..." is a majestic critique of awareness/consciousness itself.

"The Grand Illusion (Circa 1973)" is one of only four selections from the playlist that warrants association with all three (CS, CM, and SOS) rubrics/tools used in this chapter to indicate the underground-ness of certain hip-hop songs. Since Pharoah Monch is an east coast artist that most journalists, critics, and constituents of hip-hop culture would consider to be underground, his presence on the list and some explication of how "The Grand Illusion..." can be identified with and through the three rubrics of underground-ness might illuminate how the playlist and its attendant categories operate within the discourse on the hip-hop underground and African American culture. According to H. Samy Alim, who interviewed and analyzed the poetics of Pharoahe Monch's body of work: "[he] is one of the most prominent and respected hip-hop artists within the global hip-hop community, yet, he remains largely unknown to the general public. He is but one example of the talent that lies just beyond the reach of the limelight of popular programs..." (Alim 138). Pharoahe Monch's talent, lack of mainstream popularity, and the fact that he has consis-tently worked with smaller record labels position him as an under-ground artist. Much of his earlier recorded work within Organized Konfusion—a rap duo including Monch and Prince Poetry—is con-sidered underground hip-hop and many of those songs could also be featured on this underground hip-hop playlist. But "The Grand Illusion..." stretches the consideration of the CS, CM, and SOS cat-egories to their interpretive limits and thereby strengthens them all as teleological attributes across a range of underground discourses. The song opens with the refrain performed by Citizen Cope: "You're just caught up in the mass confusion/Confused by the Grand Illusion." The song's refrain and overall themes have an expressed purpose of unveiling the illusion of our mass-confused reality—a reality depicted via "photo-shopped images," "pornography," and operating based upon a "child labor economy." Awakening to this reality almost requires the listener to "put away your hope," as Monch subtly critiques an Obama administration that in 2010 had the "same political policies" as the previous US presidential administrations. Getting beneath the surface of our socioeconomic and political realities and confronting the world's neoliberal delusion is the central aim of "The Grand Illusion...." It makes certain CM almost by default as it seeks to construct intellectual space for recognizing the socioeconomic and political fabric of our society; yet Monch is clearly not interested here in conventional recognition. Instead, his lyrics emphasize a desire for the nonconventional recognition that often attaches to conspiracy theories and theorists and the counterhegemonic forces at work against the so-called grand illusion.

He briefly gestures toward the conceptual structures of the underground in his opening line: "We were told that the Hell below was a fiery inferno." Monch challenges the conceptualization of Hell and subtly suggests a reordering of how his listeners conceptualize the underground. In "The Grand Illusion" almost anything that "we were told" represents those narratives designed to contain and control us, hegemonic narratives that obscure the real socioeconomic reality in which we live. Jennifer Toth, who historicizes concepts of the underground in order to properly detail the lived realities of New York City's subway tunnel-dwellers, makes the following claim about the underground-Hell interface. "Mostly, the underground has long been synonymous with hell, in the Bible and in its interpretations. Dante's rings descend downward for example. In the nineteenth century, writers used the underground as a metaphor for a people who lived on the surface but were doomed by crime and mutilating poverty" (Toth 170). Monch's opening line intimates the possibilities of a right here (and right now) hell on earth. And Toth's references to the underground being analogous to the lived realities of those that exist under the brutal conditions of poverty and crime abstractly inform Pharoahe Monch's conceptual suggestions with respect to the underground-hell interface.

While "The Grand Illusion's" CS and CM possibilities are readily conceivable in the aforementioned contexts, the song's site of slavery formulates the most taut stretch of the three categories on the underground hip-hop playlist. Salamish Tillet is quite clear in her definition of terms with respect to her theories on what actually constitutes a "site of slavery" in the post–civil rights era. These "texts, figures, or objects" must "formally remember African American slavery" and in the case of "The Grand Illusion..." there is no formal remembering or specific allusion to African American slavery (Tillet 4). On first pass, Pharoahe Monch's lines about an exploited slave majority reference a version of enslavement where the multimedia information age conscripts its denizens to powerful surveillance and digital technologies, but digital enslavement is distinct from any formal allusions to the enslavement of African Americans. Too many other selections on the list properly satisfy Tillet's articulation of the SOS rubric for me to make too many argumentative claims for "The Grand Illusion...." That said, I suggest that Tillet's theorization of sites of slavery is so integrally embedded in the shared experiences of conscious underground hip-hop aficionados that most listeners of an artist like Pharoahe Monch will naturally frame his allusion to a delusive modern construction of enslavement within the context of their knowledge (limited or otherwise) of African American slavery.

This underground hip-hop playlist is constructed in chronological order and many of the songs—some conspicuously so in their titles—engage various iterations of the underground-as-concept within hip-hop and (sometimes) African American culture. For any song featuring rap lyrics or titles that play on the underground conceptually, the "CS" column on the chart will be marked "X." (See table 4.1 for all references/descriptions mentioned in this section.) For example, EPMD's "Underground," released in 1990—prior to the timeframe that Harrison and others designate as the emergent moment for/of underground hip-hop—features the refrain: "coming straight from the underground!" EPMD's "Underground" was not one of the tracks on the album, *Business as Usual*, that was released as a single. The fact that "Underground" was considered an "album cut"—that is a song produced and recorded but not necessarily released as a single for popular consumption—nearly compels the cultural-move designation, but the song's preeminent connection to these discourses is through its actual conceptualization of the underground. Obviously in the refrain— "coming straight from the underground"—EPMD are not suggesting that they are literally emerging from a sewer, rising from the grave, or digging their way out of some cavernous mining tunnel—although all of these images are metaphorically useful for their listeners. They are making an authenticity claim for themselves as artists/emcees and as Black urbanites with a particular sense of their inner city New York world. *Business as Usual* marks an important and pivotal transition in EPMD's artistic career.[6] It was their first album released on Def Jam records—then a subsidiary of Sony/Columbia. The rap duo's first two albums were released on Fresh Records, a much smaller label and marketing entity within the music industry. Considering both Morgan and Harrison's work on underground hip-hop and the market forces of the music industry, this transitional moment in EPMD's career likely precipitated their desire to establish their underground bona fides through their very own "Underground." Understand that "coming straight from the underground" does not (and cannot) represent a trajectory with origins in some physical place or space, but rather projects a figurative space marked for its ability to convey authenticity upon those who can claim it. For EPMD, the aesthetic sense of "coming straight from the underground" also disrupts modern associations of enlightened progress, particularly those associations derived from conventional modernist discourses.[7] Claiming this particular conceptual structure of the underground was an important move for the group to make, especially as they became more successful in the music business and transitioned from a boutique label to a so-called major label for the marketing and distribution of their albums.

Other songs, especially certain artists (on certain albums), make underground CM that are distinctly designed to seek notoriety but they do so against the grain, beyond popular convention. For some, such as emcees, OC, and Freddie Foxxx in "M.U.G.," being "money underground" is about skills as much as it is about actually making money from battling rappers in competitive underground performance venues. This notoriety they seek is antithetical to the notoriety of the imagined popular rappers at whom their battle raps are targeted. The song is about its rap narrators making certain CM—rap battling in the underground—and the song itself makes CM in reflecting how underground fame is quite distinct from its popular counterpart. Last and most significant of this ongoing process of discerning and defining underground hip-hop are those songs that make specific allusion to the institution of slavery and/or the Transatlantic Slave Trade. There are many reasons why the "sites of slavery" designation becomes meaningful within the definitive discourses on underground hip-hop.

If "The Grand Illusion..." only makes a tentative abstract gesture toward Tillet's *Sites of Slavery* concepts, Talib Kweli's "Africa Dream" represents an alternative example that boldly and directly references the American institution of slavery in order to both commemorate and remember the institution in a manner that directly wrestles with concepts of citizenship in a racial democracy. "Africa Dream" opens with the sounds of an ocean, an African drum riff, and a Zimbabwean proverb—"If you can talk you can sing / If you can walk you can dance." The talk-sing portion of the proverb speaks directly to the forms of rap music. Rap forms exist somewhere between talking and singing, but Kweli's use of the proverb here also conceptually operates as an endorsement of the equal stature of rapping and singing—an argument for the artistic viability of rapping itself. The song also sports various "sites of slavery" as Kweli claims that "we outlasted the middle passage" and/or that "bastards try to treat us like cattle." But the most oft-quoted lines from this song and probably from Kweli's body of work are the following: "These cats drink champagne to toast death and pain / Like slaves on a ship talking about who got the flyest chain." All of "Africa Dream" is an address of sorts to mainstream rappers. For Kweli, mainstream rappers suffer from the "Grand Illusion..." articulated by Pharoahe Monch. One consequence of the delusion that popular/mainstream artists suffer from is that their lyrics and songs often grapple with reality in ways that allow them to celebrate conspicuous materiality without any conscious understanding of how human commodification in American Slavery is the predicate for the capital accumulation and material success in America that they seem to so readily and wantonly celebrate. Thus the lyric—of "toast[ing] death and pain like slaves on a ship talking about who got the flyest chain"—puts into bold and powerful relief the inherent irony of celebrated materialism in popular hip-hop music. Too many rappers (consider 2 Chainz for ready reference) actually rap about having the "flyest chains." According to Kweli's astute metaphorical formulation, a popular artist's love for gold chains cannot be interpreted outside of the memory of the chains that bound slaves during middle passage. The ends here overdetermine the artistic means; that is, slaves in chains served the same purposes of capital accumulation, human commodification, and denigration as the individualistic pursuit of material wealth and the ostentatious display of the objects of materialism in popular music and too often within hip-hop culture itself.

Although each track on this "Underground hip-hop playlist" warrants its own explication and a specific rendering of the ways in which it can (or cannot) be categorized within one to three of the rubrics in the table, I will not take the time to do that here. What must be said though is that with any play list or any project such as this that attempts to embrace lyrical texts as critical subject matter, the first charge for readers is to be listeners. Only by listening to an underground hip-hop playlist can the discussions herein be made plain and/ or the assertions about certain categories be clarified or debunked. That said, the list features a handful of what might be considered perplexing selections as they are not categorized as hip-hop music and one selection, Malcolm X's "You Can't Hate the Roots of a Tree..." is actually a speech. B. B. King's 1970 recording, "Go Underground," is one such selection. It is a blues tune where going underground is the equivalent of retreating from society. King's bluesy narrator goes underground in response to being jilted and rejected by a lover. While these themes are central to the Blues tradition, unrequited love is not as prevalent as an expressive interest among most hip-hop artists. "Go Underground" then functions more as a placeholder of sorts. It allows the list to tangentially account for the fact that other concepts of the underground existed within Black music prior to the emergence of hip-hop culture and it gestures to another selection, "Praying Man," performed by Big K.R.I.T. and featuring B.B. King that in my estimation functions as an archetype for underground hip-hop music.

A somewhat less-perplexing selection is Dr. Thema S. Bryant's spoken word recording titled "Underground." Bryant's "Underground" is directly inspired by ideas in *The hip-hop Underground and African American Culture*. Nowadays Dr. Bryant is a world-class psychologist who appears on reality television programs and television talk shows to make powerful interventions for those who are in need of her expertise. But in the late 1990s, she was (like myself) a graduate student. We had multiple conversations about each other's research and dissertation projects. I am honored to say that one result of those conversations is Dr. Bryant's brilliant "Underground." As a graduate student she wrote and recorded *Sky: An Upbeat Black Girl's Song* featuring poetry from her book *The Birthing of a Lioness*. Bryant's "Underground" plays like a 90-second primer for *The hip-hop Underground and African American Culture*, because for all intents and purposes it is just that. She references middle passage, the great migration, underground movements, secret societies, the encoded-ness of AAVE, the Underground Railroad, wearing the mask, and various quotes from the lyrics of hip-hop music. It is a more compelling introduction to this book than this book's written introduction.

Malcolm X's "You Can't Hate the Roots of Tree..." functions in a similar fashion with respect to the underground hip-hop playlist itself. The speech lays the groundwork, if you will, for the comprehension of the concepts of the underground in hip-hop culture. Malcolm X's thesis, that you can't hate Africa without hating yourself as an African American, challenges listeners to excavate an African (genealogical) history, to remember the American institution of slavery and all of its deleterious effects on Black existence, and to understand that conventional American forms of recognition are antithetical to a healthy embrace of Black folks' African ancestry. X claims: "We discovered that deep within the subconscious of the Black man in this country he's still more African than he is American...." This discovery deep within the subconscious of "the Black man" represents the CM toward (and within) the conceptual structures of the underground that by definition must feature certain sites of slavery. I also lead the list with this speech in order to mirror my opening salvo in this book where I attempt to use the term "roots" to illustrate the polysemous nature of the concepts of the underground in hip-hop and African American cultures.

Although Marcyliena Morgan's *Real Hiphop*...locates its ethnographic focus on Project Blowed and hip-hop culture in the Los Angeles underground scene, her work also wrestles with the polysemic nature of the underground especially (and conceptually) at the intersection of hip-hop and African American cultures.[8] Morgan claims: "In hiphop the term 'underground' is in reference to many symbols, all of which coalesce around flight, fight, and freedom. The underground simultaneously recalls the era of slavery, when a people summoned incredible desire and courage for a chance to exercise control over their own language and communication, creativity, body, culture, spiritual practice, and life itself....[The underground] is the ultimate space and place of humanity."[9] Morgan's conceptual claims about underground hip-hop articulate and inform the categorizations and the assignment of attributes on the list referenced in this chapter. The hip-hop underground's recollection of the era of slavery and Morgan's astute distillation of the allusions to "flight, fight, and freedom" are indicative of several of the selections on the list, especially those that warrant all of the attributes across the categories of the playlist.

The two selections that directly engage the concepts of freedom are Mastermind's "Liberty" and Outkast/Cee-Lo's "Liberation." Mastermind is a little known underground rap group whose sole release is titled *Underground Railroad*. Morgan argues that the (actual) Underground Railroad is "the most recognized underground movement in the United States, especially for the African American community."[10] In "Liberty," Mastermind lyrically fantasizes about violently dispensing with mainstream popular artists within hip-hop and among the artisans of mainstream popular musical culture. They refer to themselves as a "mainstream disaster," and define "underground liberty" as the capacity to determine themselves as underground hip-hop artists. In a much more serious approach to similar subject matter, Outkast's "Liberation" (featuring Cee-Lo) meditates on self-determination in an absolute sense—beyond the limitations of artistry and the music business. "Liberation" features very little rapping, relying more on the singing skills of Outkast (Andre 3000 and Big Boi), Cee-Lo, and Erykah Badu, as well as a spoken word piece by Big Rube, who like Cee-Lo is also a part of Goodie Mob. The themes of "Liberation" are about freedom from the limitations of fame and the kind of conceptual and subjective containment that fame in the hip-hop music industry produces. Big Rube's rap/spoken word piece makes allusions to "strong roots" and "picking cotton from the killing fields" as he closes "Liberation" with a diatribe against those people and those social forces that attempt to bind hip-hop artists to limited formulaic versions of themselves.

The final song on this list, "Praying Man" by Big K.R.I.T featuring B.B. King, is the selection without which this book, especially the underground playlist, would not be complete. "Praying Man" was recorded as a part of K.R.I.T.' s *Live from the Underground* album released in 2012. Although *Live from the Underground*, released by Def Jam—a major/mainstream label—takes the "underground" in its title, the album as a whole might not be categorized as an underground hip-hop record because of its mainstream distribution, major label backing, and the fact that many of the songs on the album tend toward common, mainstream themes in both hip-hop and popular cultures. However, Big K.R.I.T. (K.R.I.T. is an acronym for King Remembered In Time), whose given name is Justin Scott, hails from Meridian, Mississippi, and clearly through his lyrics and the themes of

"Praying Man," he is committed to a certain underground ethos especially as it relates to conceptual structures (of the underground), CM
(into and within the underground), and the illumination of sites of
slavery in underground contexts. As with all of the selections detailed
in this chapter there is no substitute for listening to them multiple
times. That said, one way to begin to engage "Praying Man" is to
consider its constitutive components. The song has an excerpt from a
classic "Negro" spiritual as its epigraph, three verses written and performed by Big K.R.I.T., and a refrain written and performed by B.B.
King. "Praying Man" opens with an excerpt from "Glory, Glory (Lay
My Burden Down)." Although the words are barely discernible—"All
my troubles will be over / When I lay my burden down."—the powerful spiritual tonalities of the sampled recording establish an underground theme for the entire song. "Glory, Glory (Lay My Burden
Down)" has been recorded/covered by many artists including Odetta
(1956) and Mississippi John Hurt (1966); it has been rendered in multiple genres of music as well, including gospel, rock, folk, and blues
music. One important aspect of the proliferation or the versioning of
the song is that its lyrical themes maintain across genres of music. This
fact is most important in terms of appreciating the relationships across
Black musical genres—especially here, the blues and the spirituals or
gospel music. B.B. King's refrain immediately follows the song's spiritual epigraph. King's classic guitar play accompanies his understated
potent vocals in a refrain that narrates the turning point in each of Big
K.R.I.T.'s three verses. B.B. King's subject is lost or left behind by his
"people" when he hears "a praying man coming." The juxtaposition
of the spiritual epigraph to the song and the bluesy hook/refrain puts
into some relief the tensions and connections between the spirituals
and the blues, the sacred and the secular in African American culture.
In tandem, the classic spiritual sampled in the song's epigraph and the
legendary voice and instrumentation of B.B. King on the hook work
together to establish the textured grounds of African American oral,
folk, and spiritual expression. Each aspect of "Praying Man" separately
establishes its "underground" bona fides but the opening sequences
also distinguish it as a paradigmatic example of how hip-hop, African
American culture, and music often intersect and interact.

Much like the opening line of B.B. King's refrain—"Guess I was
on the road..."—each of "Praying Man's" verses begins with a line
establishing the narrator's movement along a path, trajectory, or journey. The first verse finds the "Praying Man" stumbling along a path

where he encounters the narrator of the song. The listening audience arrives at the eighth line (fourth couplet) of the verse before K.R.I.T. ironically and cleverly reveals that he is hanging from a tree: "I'm not sure how long I've been swaying in the breeze / Tired of talking to the trees and you're the first praying man that I've seen." Here the praying man is the only passerby to notice the song's narrator who has presumably been lynched, hanging from a tree. Listeners only know this from the phrases: "swaying in the breeze," and "talking to the trees." Shades of Billie Holiday's "Strange Fruit" shadow Big K.R.I.T.'s signifying reveal of the lynching scene. Again, Justin Scott/Big K.R.I.T. comes of age in Mississippi. In the nineteenth and twentieth centuries, during the height of lynchings in the United States, Mississsppi had the highest number of lynchings, some 581 between 1882 and 1968. Mississippi is also the site where Emmett Till was kidnapped, brutally tortured, and murdered (Peterson 2013). Although lynching is not, technically speaking, a site of slavery, the racist logic, racialized injustice, and mob violence that inform the practice of lynching in America are all consequences of the institution of slavery. In fact, lynching was an intractably evil response to the end of the civil war and the abolition of the Peculiar Institution.

At the outset of the second verse, the praying man is "boating along the sea" and eventually discovers this verse's narrator walking along a beach in shackles. The narrator briefly recounts scenes from middle passage: "stacked on top of [his] folk" in the claustrophobic hull of a slave ship. He laments the role that his "own people" had in the transatlantic slave trade and alludes to the ways in which some enslaved Africans sought liberation through suicide and/or starvation during the long mortal journey to the New World that is often referred to as the middle passage. By most historical accounts, the mortality rates for the middle passage ranged between 10 and 20 percent. But it should also be noted here that the journey from the African interior to the African coasts from which the middle passage began, was even deadlier at approximately 50 percent. In short, Middle Passage and the routes through which enslaved Africans were forced to travel in order to be forced into chattel slavery in the so-called New World resulted in the deaths of millions of Africans. K.R.I.T. confronts the history of slavery as directly as any of his peers or predecessors in hip-hop culture. Middle Passage—the middle portion—of the multipart journey from Europe, to Africa, and back, is an historically original point from which to examine the brutality of slavery. The achievement of this verse lies in its capacity to condense the imagery of the Middle Passage into a few couplets. The imagery of the verse communicates powerful underground themes about violent oppression, containment, and ultimately, liberation.

The third verse of "Praying Man" opens as the praying man is "driving along the road." He discovers the narrator running in an attempt to escape from slavery. The narrator has just witnessed the murder of one of his "kinfolk" as they were working in the fields. The sound effects in this verse feature the haunting echoes of dog's barking as the narrator relates his tale to the praying man breathlessly: "I heard of this railroad that ventures underground / And takes my kind of people to a place that we can't be found." The narrator's literal sense of the Underground Railroad actually underscores its figurative meanings as pathway to liberation for enslaved people. Sadly the sense of the fugitive's existence communicated in K.R.I.T.'s lyrical delivery and this verse's sound effects point to the reality that the Underground Railroad was not always able to insulate its constituents from the brutal pursuit of slave catchers and other beneficiaries of the slave trade who often went to great lengths to pursue and capture fugitive slaves. This verse does not allude to the Underground Railroad; it explicitly narrates a scene that reflects the actual history of the Underground Railroad movement.

Again, each of the three verses opens as the praying man encounters the narrator along some kind of path, coastal beach or road. The opening of each verse symbolizes the routes from liberation to enslavement and/or from enslavement to liberation. Each verse itself reflects some aspects of the roots of African American history in the United States: lynching, Middle Passage, and the Underground Railroad. (I spent some time playing on the significance of the roots/routes concepts at the outset of this book.) Each verse also concludes in a moment of liberation. In verse one, the praying man cuts the narrator down from the tree; in verse two, the praying man picks the narrator up "from [his] oppressor"; and in the third verse he offers the narrator a ride, driving him "far away from [his] oppressor, forever." For all of the brutality inherent in each verse and in each site of slavery—lynching, Middle Passage, and the Underground Railroad—K.R.I.T. climaxes each verse in the liberating moment. Yet these moments are complicated by the mortality associated with each site of slavery. Is the narrator dead as he sways from the trees; has he been left for dead on the beach; has he already been captured and/or killed as he tries to find the railroad underground? Each listener might wrestle with these interpretive questions. Ultimately liberation in this world and liberation in an afterlife have both served as emancipatory themes in the literature, music, and film that document the institution of slavery in America. "Praying Man" offers the paradigm through which each entry on this Underground hip-hop playlist can be judged. Yet, ultimately this list cannot be comprehensive because the Underground of hip-hop culture is constantly unfolding. It is as James Spady has suggested in his ethnography of Philadelphia hip-hop culture, a conflagration of corrugated spaces—each unfolding at its own appropriate time and in its own unique manner.[11] The conceptual structures, CM, and allusions to sites of slavery that shape the lyrics of the songs in the playlist referenced in this chapter, all work to provide important interpretive tools for the best understandings of how underground hip-hop projects a progressive range of intellectual, historical, and cultural possibilities for the constituents of hip-hop culture and for any listening publics invested in the social force of hip-hop music at its best.

CHAPTER 5

A CIPHER OF THE UNDERGROUND
IN BLACK LITERARY CULTURE

In this chapter the concept of the cipher is an underground signifier for distinct discursive relationships in the works of Richard Wright, Ralph Ellison, Amiri Baraka, Thelonious Monk, Houston Baker, and KRS One. These discursive relationships center on tropological variations on the concept of the underground referenced in the work of the aforementioned artists as kiln holes, manhole/sewers, basements, the subway, hell, black holes, or the black (w)hole. The rich semantic content attributable to the word cipher in Standard English (SE) as well as in African American Vernacular English (AAVE) offers a unique way of reading the oft-cited genealogical conversation in Black Artistic production, which, in this case, converses/converges on the trope of the underground.[1] This interaction between Wright and others is discursive only in as much as one can discern the inner workings of distinct concepts of the underground as they are configured in the following texts: Richard Wright's "Big Boy Leaves Home" and "The Man Who Lived Underground," Ralph Ellison's *Invisible Man*, Amiri Baraka's *Dutchman* and *The System of Dante's Hell*, the grammy-award winning album cover art for Thelonious Monk's *Underground*, Houston Baker's "Black (W)hole" theory and KRS One's storied rap titled "Hol(d)."

The cipher models how these authors/artists are engaged in a tropological, artistic speech event that in fact reveals a figurative system of writing based on various concepts of the underground. A cipher has many meanings, standard and vernacular. The Standard English meanings are as follows: (1) The symbol 0, indicating a value of naught, zero; (2) a person or thing of no importance or value;

nonentity; (3) (a) a system of secret writing based on a key, or set of predetermined rules or symbols, (b) a message in such writing, and (c) the key to such a system; (4) an intricate weaving together of letters, as a monogram; (5) [now rare] to solve arithmetic problems; and (6) [rare] to express in secret writing.[2] The use of the term "cipher" in the vernacular is somewhat more difficult to pinpoint. From Alim (2006), we have this question: From where does the term cipher in hip-hop Nation Language derive? Emcees form a cipher when they stand in some semblance of a circle and take turns rhyming. An entire study could be done on hip-hop ciphers alone. Consider how the traditional hip-hop cipher builds upon notions of expression through closed communicative interactions, often encoded by/for the experiences of the emcee. Ciphers are mini speech communities. They are inviting, but they are also very challenging. They have become a litmus test for modern day griots. Ciphers are also the initiating format for battling among emcees. The ritual of rhyming is reinforced by the physical arrangement of hip-hop bodies into a form that powerfully indicates the inside-outside dynamic that makes hip-hop culture so popular with those infatuated with counterculture. The cipher has no center except space or possibly the voice rhyming in turn; it is also secretly encoded by its participants.

The vernacular use of the term "cipher" in hip-hop culture does not just appear linguistically out of language limbo and it does not directly derive itself from SE. Instead, I suggest it flows into the everyday language of hip-hop from and through the Five-Percent Nation, from the minds and mouths of those poor righteous teachers who view the cipher as encompassing 360 degrees of daily lived experiences.[3] In the mid-1980s, the use of the phrase "non-cipher" was popular among hip-hop heads in the northeast quadrant of the United States. It entered my speech community from friends and cousins who were deeply committed to the science of mathematics through the tenets of the Five-Percent Nation. Non-cipher means/meant: not affirmative. It was more complex than a simple no. It meant that whatever occurred or was said just prior to the utterance of non-cipher was a break or rupture in the 360 degrees of life-space from the vantage point of the speaker. Out of respect for things unknown and the boundaries sometimes violated by sacrilegious academics, I won't attempt to describe the philosophies of Islam or the Five-Percent Nation, but my point here is that the Five-Percent Nation, which developed through Noble Drew Ali, Clarence 13X, the teachings of

Islam, and the Nation of Islam, introduced terminology to hip-hop-speaking communities that deeply affected the foundation of hip-hop culture. In particular, the ritual of rhyming as practiced by emcees and wannabe emcees incorporated discreet inclinations and impressions regarding the cipher from within the rubric of Islam. The concept of the cipher then, is essential to hip-hop culture's sense of itself particularly as an oral culture with emcees as a fundamental component to its genesis. Finally, the cipher indicates an epistemology that is nonlinear (consider repetition as a figure in Black culture) and as a shape it physically represents the ritual of rhyming itself.

The cipher of the *underground* as a communications revolution in African American culture begins with the first fugitive slaves and the literature and histories describing the existence of networks aiding Black fugitives' liberation. Richard Wright initiates a literary reengagement with these concepts of the underground in his writing. "From a symbolic reading of characteristic fictions such as 'Big Boy Leaves Home' and 'The Man Who Lived Underground,' a critic should feel compelled to designate Wright as the very center of that dark (and powerfully invisible) area of Afro-American life that constitutes its underground expressive (w)holeness."[4] This claim, developed by Houston Baker in his study *Blues, Ideology, and Afro-American Literature: A Vernacular Theory* directly informs my theoretical understandings of the Black underground in African American literature. Baker's notion of the black [w]hole is embedded in his own vernacular theory of Afro-American literature in its relationship to an "economics of slavery" that is resoundingly articulated by and through Blues music:

> Transliterated in letters of Afro-America, the *black hole* assumes the subsurface force of the black underground. It graphs, that is to say, the subterranean hole where the trickster has his ludic, deconstructive being. Further, in the script of Afro-America, the hole is the domain of Wholeness, an achieved relationality of black community in which desire recollects experience and sends it forth as blues. To be Black and (W)hole is to escape incarcerating restraints of a white world (i.e. a black hole) and to engage the concentrated, underground singularity of experience that results in a blues desire's expressive fullness.[5]

Baker centers "Big Boy Leaves Home" and "The Man Who Lived Underground" in his theoretical apparatus for black (w)hole expressivity. He thus retrieves Wright's texts from the critical treatments advanced by Ralph Ellison and James Baldwin.[6] And in so doing, he institutes a black literary critical communications revolution of his own, tropologically reassessing "the very center of...Afro-American...underground expressive (w)holeness."[7]

Wright's short story, "Big Boy Leaves Home," connects the Black underground to origins conceived as "fugitive property" departing "home" for liberated geographies. Wright's short story, Big Boy, escapes certain death in the South by traveling an antebellum version of the Underground Railroad.[8] His family communicates with the Black community's elders. They devise a plan by which Big Boy will hide in a kiln hole awaiting the arrival of Will, a Black interstate driver from the community, making a run to Chicago. Big Boy's experiences, following his self-defense murder of a White soldier in the south, read like any of the various stories of the Underground Railroad; escape, brutal pursuit by mob enforced law, hiding, and freedom coordinated through geographically disperse community efforts. The kiln hole space functions as a microcosm for his life challenges here. While Big Boy awaits his "freedom train," and by nominative abstraction, his Will, he kills a snake, a dog, and he witnesses the brutal lynching of his friend and fellow fugitive, Bobo.

Although Wright's text is rife with symbols (Will, the struggles with snake and the dog, trains to keep time, etc.), the short story's key image is the underground space where Big Boy undergoes a murderous rites of passage. He is in a kiln. A kiln is "any of various ovens for hardening, burning, or drying substances, such as grain, meal, or clay, especially a brick-lined oven used to bake ceramics."[9] At the same moment that murderous hate, paralyzing fear, and unreasonable racism are being burned into the mind and soul of Wright's protagonist, his kiln experience is a proleptic literary influence on two of the most important figures in Afro-American letters: Bigger Thomas of Native Son (1940) and the narrator of Black Boy (1945).[10] Wright's literary creations, from the ground up, if you will, are essential for the Black expressive urban realism that, in time, sparked the urban underground of hip-hop culture.

Baker's discursive participation in the cipher of the underground is not unremarkable. Not only does he redeem Richard Wright by constructing a theoretical apparatus based on a philosophical physics of the black hole, but he renders his own voice within an artistically and scholarly dynamic conversation in Black letters. For Baker, black hole theory means that Wright's kiln hole in "Big Boy..." and the sewer dwellings of fred daniels in "The Man Who Lived Underground" are spaces of potential black wholeness. And in discursive turn, his black (w)hole theory is what creates space for audiences to appreciate this significant understanding of Richard Wright as an artist through his short stories: "Big Boy..." and "The Man Who Lived...."

Wright's protagonist in "The Man Who Lived Underground" spends the majority of this narrative tunneling through the underground caverns of the world in which he used to live. At various points he witnesses a dead baby floating in the sewer water, a church choir singing, moviegoers watching a film; he steals diamonds, money, and a typewriter. "He saw these items hovering before his eyes and felt that some dim meaning linked them together, that some magical relationship made them kin. He stared with vacant eyes, convinced that all of these images, with their tongueless reality, were striving to tell him something...."[11] This particular assortment of experiences and purloined objects strives to foretell of the impossibility of fred daniels returning to an aboveground way of life. As other scholars have remarked, once he sees the dead baby floating in the sewer water, mouth agape and fist clenched in protest, he is himself, dead, baby.[12] Perhaps the most memorable aspects of this story have to do with how fred daniels figures the space in which he dwells. In particular, he develops a countercultural relationship to the "aboveground" world that he has voyeuristically deconstructed in the timeless space of the underground. "In this underground world, he (fred daniels) comes to a new authentic consciousness of his own and society's essential condition."[13] Daniels exemplifies this "new authentic consciousness" by reconfiguring the interior of his underground.

> He swabbed all the dirt walls of the cave and pasted them with green bills; when he had finished *the walls blazed with a yellow green fire.* Yes this room would be his hideout; between him and the world that had branded him guilty would stand this mocking symbol. He had not stolen the money; he had simply picked it up, just as a man would pick up firewood in a forest. And that was how the aboveground world now seemed to him a wild forest filled with death.[14] (my emphasis)

The blaze of dollar bill wallpaper illuminates fred daniels's newfound consciousness. He now sees the "aboveground" world as a death-laden wilderness, a modern wasteland. His ability to transcend the conventional meaning of society's most materially valued things (money, jewelry, watches, etc.) marks his voice as a distinct contributor to the cipher of the underground in Black culture.

Richard Wright's two turns on/in the cipher of the underground requires that fred daniel's narrative differ in content and form from that of Wright's other voice in the cipher: Big Boy. Big Boy's horrifying experience in the kiln hole on the Underground Railroad ultimately transforms him into either Bigger Thomas or some character like him since we can only assume that beyond "Big Boy Leaves Home," Big Boy must struggle up north with many of the same challenges that he faces in the south: constricted space and minimal economic or educational opportunity. The fire that burns in Big Boy is a direct reflection of the fire that burns Bobo in the murderous lynching to which Big Boy is a witness. One of Wright's most striking scenes in "The Man Who Lived" features fred daniels's dollar bill wallpaper realization. The intellectually illuminating blaze of the dollar bill wallpaper marks the continuing progress of fred daniels into an underground consciousness with which he cannot survive in any aboveground society. The illuminated idea that dollar bills have no intrinsic value is one that rings true for the cipher of the underground in Black culture; making it all the more discursive (i.e., conversational) that most of these narrators face economic as well as racial challenges in their perspective narratives. The presence of the diamonds has underground valence here as well. He values the diamonds even less than the dollar bill wallpaper. At least the dollar bills have utility underground; the diamonds do not. Indeed, the idea that fred daniels is returning these previously mined "precious" stones to the underground puts into bold relief the countless migrant and underpaid workers who must have mined them (quite possibly from somewhere on the continent of Africa).

The protagonist in Ralph Ellison's *Invisible Man* resides in a basement with illuminating walls as well. In the prologue, Invisible Man tells the reader directly that he steals light from Monopolated Light and Power. With 1,369 light bulbs (and counting) Invisible Man triumphantly brags "I've illuminated the blackness of my invisibility—and vice versa. And so I play the invisible music of my isolation."[15] If invisibility is a quality that derives from a lack of social responsibility of the mainstream (i.e., those in power) to see certain people (in this case IM or fred daniels) as individual human beings, then the light bulbs are merely metaphors (much like fred daniels's dollar bills) for the functional, illuminating essence of the underground space, a space where blackness can be figured and powerfully articulated. Indeed, IM loves the light in his underground dwelling. It illuminates the blackness of invisibility. "The symbolic content of Afro-American expressive culture can thus be formulated in terms of the black hole conceived as a subcultural (underground, marginal, or liminal) region in which a dominant, White culture's representations are squeezed to zero volume, producing a new expressive order."[16] According to Baker, the underground is a space where dominant culture's representations are squeezed to zero volume. The idea that the volume of White/dominant culture is turned all the way down in the underground resonates with an oft-overlooked yet culturally potent scene in Invisible Man's underground.[17]

In his introductory narrative in the novel's prologue, IM discusses the existential force of multiple phonographs playing Louis Armstrong's "What Did I Do to Be So Black and Blue?" "Now I have one radio-phonograph; I plan to have five. There is a certain acoustical deadness in my hole, and when I have music I want to feel its vibration, not only with my ear but with my whole body. I'd like to here five recordings of Louis Armstrong playing and singing…all at the same time."[18] Playing five records at the same time will not produce aural renderings of simultaneous vocals or music. The subtle staggering of sounds on phonographs directly anticipates the integral artistic, creative role of the DJ, particularly those artisans who created and developed hip-hop culture.[19] The potential for this type of musical reification of the black body through lyrical and musical volume exists only in the underground space where Invisible Man dwells and existentially considers himself. The final words of the narrator are rendered in rhymed poetic verse:

> But only partially true: Being Invisible and without substance, a
>   disembodied voice, as it were, what else could I do?
> What else but try to tell you what was really happening when your eyes
>   were looking through?
> And it is this which frightens me: Who knows but that, on the lower
>   frequencies, I speak for you?

In some ways, Invisible Man does speak for the hip-hop generation and the advent of the originators of hip-hop culture. The discursive verse of IM suggests the form/structure of emcee/rapper's interaction with a live hip-hop audience. His prologue features a prophetic glimpse of the act of hip-hop DJ-ing and the epilogue concludes with a disembodied voice (not unlike an emcee/rapper on record or a DJ heard through the radio) speaking to and for us in rhymed verse. The aforementioned "lower frequencies" circuit the underground discourses in and through African American culture.[20]

Amiri Baraka's discursive contributions to the ever-troping Underground Cipher include his classic 1964 play, *Dutchman*, and discrete textual snapshots of his avant-garde novel, *The System of Dante's Hell*. Dutchman takes place on a subway "in the flying underbelly of the city—heaped in modern myth." For a subway drama, Dutchman (as title) references ships and black Atlantic currents as much as it reflects subterranean movement/containment of underground concepts of race/gender relations in modern America. "The myth or legend implicit in the title "Dutchman" is that of the ghost ship, the Flying Dutchman, which roamed the seas and added unwary ships to its phantom entourage. Africans were initially smuggled to North America in a Dutch Man-of-War."[21] This nominative connection to slavery reflects Paul Gilroy's suggestion that the desire of Black writers to draw literary and historical connections to the brutal terror of slavery resides in our collective association of the experience of slavery with reason, itself.[22] If the conclusions of *Dutchman* lack reason, then the title betrays the historical initiation of what has become an unending physical and sociopolitical race war; a war verbalized by *Dutchman*'s protagonist and perpetrated by its antagonist.

The initial imagery of *Dutchman* is of a moving subway featuring a racially and sexually potent dialogic interaction between the main characters: Lula and Clay. "Lula and Clay engage in what Jones sees as the true dialogue *underlying* race relations in America. (my emphasis)"[23] Many literary critics and artists have discussed the logistics of *Dutchman* and its urgent homicidal conclusions. Lula escorts Clay through a script of his own demise reflected in his overdetermined, middle-class value system, and the violent, ritualistic designs of his antagonist. But before he is brutally stabbed to death, he delivers a treatise on the relationship between Black artists and their White audiences.[24] Beneath the surface of the mask (artistic), Black people want to murder White people. "Crazy niggers turning their back on sanity. When all it needs is that simple act. Just Murder. Would make us all sane." In one of the more popular plays of the Black Arts Movement, Clay articulates a murderous reduction of the "volume" of White dominant culture.[25] Gilroy alludes to this phenomenon in *The Black Atlantic*. "Violence articulates blackness to a distinct mode of lived masculinity, but it is also a factor in what distinguishes blacks from whites."[26] According to Gilroy's description, Clay's murderous monologue defined his own masculinity while articulating or aspiring to an authentic racial status.

Interestingly enough, the forms of Baraka's poetry circa 1964 reflect another mode through which Baraka epitomizes concepts of the underground. "Baraka's poetry negated whiteness by replacing white avant-garde forms with black jazz forms, for example, replacing the quiet rhythms of the Beat poetry with the more frantic rhythms of bop...."[27] In his 1985 study titled *The Poetry and Poetics of Amiri Baraka*, William Harris also suggests that Baraka's art (particularly after the publication of *The Dead Lecturer*) is designed to incite the "potential killer, the revolutionary Bigger Thomas, in the submissive black."[28] The design to incite marks Baraka's voice as one of the more powerful and aurally accessible voices in the cipher of the underground. His art is intentionally archetypal with respect to sociopolitical concepts of the underground. Through the various black forms that he employs, and the characters and Black musical figurations that he experiments with, Baraka establishes tonal blueprints for black expression and American poetry in general. "As could also be said of hip-hop emcees, Baraka's art puts a premium on projecting his bad attitude."[29] Of course, emcees of hip-hop culture inherit these historical inclinations both directly and from the likes of Gil Scott Heron, The Watts Poets, The Last Poets, Nikki Giovanni, Sonia Sanchez, and others.[30]

The central Black Arts message from Clay is that "violence provides an escape from minstrelsy; the Black who is forbidden to express his pain becomes a potential killer."[31] The unfortunate twist on this dramatically rendered oracle of posthumous figures in hip-hop culture is that most Bigger Thomases end up killing other Bigger Thomases. The outcome of *Dutchman* makes the dire conclusion that even talking about violent reaction or resistance, in this case Clay's vocalizations of murderous revolt, only serves to reinscribe the reasoning behind Lula's genocidal ritual. In other words, "America symbolically comes full circle through Lula's—the Dutchman's—murderous actions."[32] His monologue about Black artists only needing to murder White people leads directly to his own murder at the hands of Lula who represents White America. Since the murder narrative recycles itself at the end of the play the audience understands that Clay was actually destined to die from the beginning of the drama.[33] Direct connections between the beginning and the ending of underground epics like *Invisible Man* (prologue/epilogue) and *Dutchman* refigure the image of the cipher. These connections suggest the cyclical aspect of the cipher and by extension they reveal the turns of voice in the cipher of the underground.

In *The System of Dante's Hell*, Baraka constructs an avante-garde idiomatic and idiosyncratic autobiographical voice that narrates "Hell in the head. The torture of being the unseen object, and, the constantly observed subject."[34] In *The System*..., Baraka unveils a collection of literary influences from Dante to Whitman to Eliot to Ellison, and the significance of the underground as concept is most potent in the particularized referencing of his Newark, New Jersey, life experiences. The novel moves from character sketches, to snapshots of parties in East Orange, to encounters with childhood friends and foes with a frenetic and insistent referencing of Baraka's Newark upbringing. Being born and raised in Newark, my reader response to this voice in the cipher of the underground is acute. The Hell-on-Earth imagery of Dante's *Inferno* with a Barakan, signifyin' difference overdetermines these autobiographical fragments as distinctly underground discourses. But the referential obscurity (consider allusionists such as T. S. Eliot in his classic "The Waste Land" or the deconstructive underpinnings of Ishmael Reed's *Mumbo Jumbo*) is deconstructed in my personal reading of *The System*.... That is, I know some of the references, but some of the experiences that he details resonate with me in ways that help me to also appreciate IM's suggestion about speaking on lower frequencies.

Unlike Dante's *Inferno*, Baraka's system of Hell places Heretics in the deepest section/part of Hell. "It is heresy, against one's own sources, running in terror, from one's deepest responses and insights...the denial of feeling...that I see as basest evil."[35] In Baraka's system, heresy mirrors the debates and discussions about authentic Black identity. Inner depth and insight are essential qualities without which people (Baraka offers himself as example) are considered evil and relegated to the veiled subjectivity inherent in modern notions of Blackness.[36] The ninth circle of Baraka's Hell includes and has sections/fragments titled: The Christians, Personators (alchemists), Falsifiers, The Treacherous, and finally, The Heretics, Those Who are not True to Their Own feelings. The setting of this, the only continuous prose section in the novel, is a sin city properly titled "The Bottom."[37] Note well here that "The Bottom" is a fairly common municipal moniker for African American neighborhoods (or towns in the case of Toni Morrion's *Sula*) that subsist at the socioeconomic bottom of American society and, as such, these neighborhoods often feature the underground economies of drug dealing, prostitution, and other forms of crime. In "The Heretics," the recently arrived main character must face various challenges to his sense of humanity, masculinity, and his blackness by the police, a prostitute named Peaches, and three southern thugs. The nameless character's affiliation with the Air Force coupled with his northeastern-inflected idiom mark him as outsider even in the hell that urban life has come to symbolize in Baraka's System. "When I spoke someone wd turn and stare, or laugh, and point me out. The quick new jersey speech, full of Italian idiom, and the invention of the jews. Quick to describe. Quicker to condemn."[38] The narrator is in a "jook joint" filled with shades, ghosts, and spooks. He is literally dragged out of the joint by an overbearing woman named Peaches. She eventually verbally and physically forces him to have sex with her. At one point he escapes, but the dangers and uncertainty of the urban inferno force him to return to her. Soon he accepts his fate with Peaches and he ventures out for groceries. When he returns he details an epiphany. "It was a light clap of thunder. No Lightning. And the sky greyed. Introitus. That word came in. . . ." The thunderous sound absent the visual image of lightning suggests the power of speech over orthographic writing. Since the term "introitus" often refers to the vaginal opening, Baraka is also wrestling with Peaches's sexual dominion over his own narrator. This power relationship is one that Baraka further explores in the penultimate scene of his hell system. After the introitus, the narrator decides to leave Peaches and the Bottom. He asks for directions and proceeds to walk up a hill where he encounters three Black men who ask him to borrow money as a pretense for mugging him and then proceed to mug him because he is a "slick city nigger...Mr. Half White-muthafucka."[39] After they orchestrate the signature knock-down, they beat him senseless and the narrative abruptly reveals that this went on in a cave.[40] Baraka's narrator navigates an underground structure with multiple levels and figurative and literal pitfalls. The cave wherein these final scenes take place is like a jook joint with music and "whores" dancing on tables, but curiously the narrator sits reading from a book aloud while "they" danced to his reading. The image of people dancing to the spoken word is formative for Baraka's body of work and his connections to spoken word artisans in hip-hop culture.[41] Yet the narrator finishes his performance and falls weeping to the floor where Black people pour whiskey on his clothes. He realizes that his apparent ability to move bodies with his words is a tortuous nightmare from which he is woken up to the sounds of White men screaming for

God to help him. Here, in the final scene of *The System of Dante's Hell*, Baraka provides the picture of conflicted artistic ability in the tortured soul of his main character.

Thus far we have proceeded chronologically in this description of the cipher of the underground. Baraka's contributions to the cipher were in 1963 and 1964. While he was finding and defining his voice, he was also articulating the immense significance of pre-mainstream Black Music to Black culture. He includes Thelonious Monk as one of his exemplars of one of the main points of *Blues People*: that Black Music is the most innovative and definitive force in Black and American culture. Thelonious Monk's 1968 release, *Underground*, is similar to the release of Baraka's *Dutchman*.[42] It is a conglomeration of his underground craftsmanship, American popular culture, and a willed resistance to mainstream appropriation. *Dutchman* and *Underground* both point to underground imagery that both symbolizes resistance and resists appropriations of Black Art forms.

The Grammy award-winning cover art of Monk's *Underground* serves as symbolic imagery of the Black modern underground couched in revolutionary playfulness with the avant-garde Black artisan as central focus. Note the downward cinematic angle from which we view Monk (in his stage-propped studio) in full revolutionary regalia with weapons of destruction and war at his immediate disposal. His most potent "weapon" is readily at hand as he keys the piano. Gil Mckean's liner notes provide the full ironic depiction of this image as representation of Monk's potency in the Jazz movement.

> Although the illustration on the album cover may seem a trifle bizarre to the uninitiated, knowing intimates of Monk will recognize the setting as that of his studio, an important part of his Manhattan apartment. In this atelier are the memorabilia of an adventurous and richly rewarding life. Most noticeable, perhaps is the Nazi storm trooper. As real as he looks, he is stuffed, a trophy of the famed FFI. With a cry of "Take that, you honkie Kraut!" Capitaine Monk shot him cleanly and truly through the heart. He weighed 187 pounds, dressed.
>
> Thelonious's only pet is the cow who answers to the name Jellyroll and has the run of the apartment. It is interesting to note that Capitaine Monk had access to a piano throughout the combat and would never go on a mission without warming up with some forty or fifty choruses of "Darkness on the Delta." The field telephone on the wall, a memento of Normandy, now serves as a direct line to Le Pavillion in the event he wishes to order a delivery of French soul food.

The rest of the objects are really almost self-explanatory—the Nazi battle flag he captured at Nuremburg, the dynamite he used so often on key objectives in Germany, the grenades, machine pistol, the .45 automatic—all of them bring tears of nostalgia to Monk's eyes as he thinks of action-packed years gone by. He was part of the underground then—for years in post-war America his piano was part of the underground of jazz. Now, and indeed for the past few years, this jazz giant is emerging as the great artist he has always been, one of the most inventive jazzmen in history.

Actually, the title of this album, UNDERGROUND is something of a misnomer—Monk surfaced long ago! He has been committing thelonius assaults on certain hidebound enclaves of jazz since the mid-forties, and the attacks are beginning to tell. Oh yes, about the girl with the firearm in the background. No explanation was asked, nor was one forthcoming.[43]

The liner notes attempt to depict a reflection of Monk's career in the imagery of the cover art. Monk struggled with his creative individuality in a jazz marketplace that generally favored the mainstreamed influence of big band music in the Swing era. He was misunderstood by his audience, critics, and his peers. He abated his anxieties about the mainstreaming and commercialization of Jazz by performing almost exclusively in clubs local to Harlem, the home of his signature style, Harlem Slide.[44] He did this despite harassment from the police regarding his club-card, a pass to perform professionally in New York City. The playful, revolutionary imagery of the cover art and its attendant narrative signifies on Monk's struggles as a jazz innovator. According to Robin D. G. Kelley, author of the definitive biography of Thelonious Monk, the marketing department at Columbia Records was keen on promoting *Underground* to a younger audience. "The jazz market was shrinking and Monk's sales were steadily declining, so they decided to take a different tack: remake Monk into an icon for a younger generation."[45] The record company hired Dick Mantel and John Berg to direct and stage the now iconic album cover photograph. "This spectacular photo punned on Monk's role in the jazz underground—though by then it was ancient history. It also tapped into contemporary images of revolutionary movements—the Black Panthers, the Revolutionary Youth Movement, etc....[46] These visual allusions to underground movements are in some ways offset by the fact that the photo was staged by a marketing department deliberately intent on selling *Underground* to a young (White) Rock music audience. As Kelley argues, the release, reception, and sales of *Underground* did not go at all as Columbia Records had planned. "That the 'rock generation' did not run out to buy *Underground* surprised no one save Columbia's marketing department....Monk fans and jazz lovers bought *Underground* not for the photo, but because he delivered four new compositions. And yet, while sales were respectable, the reviews were mixed."[47] The imaging of Monk in a contrived underground photograph (for the marketing of an album titled *Underground*) captures the complexities inherent in attentive discussions of the various concepts of the underground. The photograph almost belies the machinations behind (or beneath the surface) of its existence. Thelonious Monk established his bona fides as an underground innovator of jazz music long before this particular marketing project attempted to leverage Monk's artistic authenticity in order to sell more records in the waning moments of jazz music's mainstream popularity. Monk's contribution to the cipher of the underground is therefore, like other artists in this cipher, his unique, complex artistic career, especially as it is manifested and symbolized in the album cover art of *Underground*.

Each of the participants described in the cipher craft artistic and/or intellectual entries that represent a wide range of Black literary voices. Richard Wright contributes from the short story genre. Ralph Ellison speaks from the American novel. Amiri Baraka dramatizes his turn on the one hand (*Dutchman*), and innovates its conceptualization through blatant avant-garde techniques on the other (*The System of Dante's Hell*). And then, Thelonious Monk is mediated in the underground through photographic art and one of his popular recordings, the music of which remains true to his artistic vision even as the photograph itself exists as a marketing tool. Baker's contribution coheres his theoretical explorations into the Black (w)hole to the other texts in the cipher through philosophy and underground literary criticism. That said, this cipher could not be complete without a voice hailing directly from the culture that produced the concept of the cipher as it is employed in this chapter.

The hip-hop example in this constellation of underground discourses could come from countless lyrics and/or emcees who employ the underground as trope and/or reference the underground space as an authentic site for hip-hop culture.[48] Many of these songs/artists are discussed elsewhere in this volume. One particular song resonates with the Black literary interventions in the cipher of the underground, particularly in its subject matter and the ways in which its linguistic form extends the spectrum of discursive genres to include sociolinguistic analysis. KRS One's "Hol(d)" is a morphological treatise on the subtle complexities inherent in the variation of AAVE.[49] "Hol(d)" is an unheralded track on KRS One's self-titled album. The third verse uniquely captures the gist of the song's themes, narrating the socially invisible existence of a nameless protagonist, plagued by urban alienation that ultimately results in incarceration. The narrator in "Hol(d)" experiences the signature economic depression of other figures or characters who participate in the underground cipher. He is confronted with his own poverty and a society that seems either unequipped or unwilling to help him or to "see" his humanity. They keep him on "Hol(d)." The song has three settings. The first verse takes place in the interior of the narrator's mind as he contemplates his lack of money. As he focuses on the hole in his shoe he decides to use his .45 caliber gun to rob someone. The second verse takes place in the outside world, where the narrator has an Invisible Man-type encounter with someone in the streets.[50] His .45 takes over and he murders the man. This is a signifying revision of Ellison's encounter in the opening passages of the novel. The difference here is that KRS's narrator commits a murder. This scene combines themes from Clay in Baraka's *Dutchman* with visions of Ellison's *Invisible Man*. KRS's narrator is socially invisible and his turn to murder and theft reflect an impulsive resistance to his socioeconomic condition. Just as "Hol(d)'s" narrator takes 40 dollars from the wallet, he is discovered by the police. The setting of the third verse is an interior view of the narrator's mind after he is incarcerated. He kills another inmate in self-defense and he is placed in solitary confinement for two weeks. Solitary confinement in "the hole" is an iteration of the underground that signals the social justice issues in our mass incarceration system/Prison Industrial Complex. This "hole" is an underground space distinct from those theorized by Baker and depicted by Wright, Ellison, Monk, and Baraka. Yet it remains connected to these discourses since it also reflects the challenges of imprisonment, containment, liberation, and (lack of) movement. In "the hole," KRS ONE's narrator is confronted with his own physically enslaved interiority as he comes to realize that his alienation and confusion in life at least partially derive from inability to understand that his needs and his wants dictated his actions. And then in typical KRS ONE, didactic fashion, he moralizes about the distinction between needs and wants.

The settings and the content of "Hol(d)" find cross-references throughout the cipher of the underground. His realization in the hole of solitary confinement is similar to fred daniels's new understanding of aboveground society after he escapes down the manhole and reimagines the structures and institutions of mainstream (aboveground) America in the underground. The violent encounters resonate with Baraka's descriptions of fistfights and beatings in various urban (inferno) settings and the potential to read murderous responses as forms of resistance to socioeconomic oppression. However, the most unique contribution that KRS ONE makes to the cipher is his use of the term "hol(d)." I have placed the "d" of the final consonant cluster, "ld," in parentheses in order to represent the distinct articulation of KRS ONE's rhymed speech acts. He ends the line of each verse with some variation of the word "hold." At the end of each line in a verse he pronounces this word in the same manner regardless of the term's meaning. Employing a stock feature of AAVE, he reduces his annunciation of the final consonant cluster in the word "hold" so that it always sounds like "(w)hole." The phonetic articulations are aurally identical, but the meaning of the term changes according to the content and syntax of the line. In effect, KRS ONE posits "hol(d)" as a morphemic mask with important underground vernacular variations. The monorhyme scheme of "Hol(d)" is another example of the Black dialect (AAVE) functioning as a mask. Beneath the surface of "Hol(d)" lies a range of underground terms, including whole and hole. The confluence of meanings and terms embedded in "Hol(d)" are hidden via the AAVE phonetics of the single term—hold. The vernacular form of this rap then stresses the contingency of meaning upon pragmatic contexts. This message/content simultaneously references the naturalism of Richard Wright, the oppressive nature of solitary confinement, and the cipher's participants' universal reliance on the potency of Black vernacular art in its complex pragmatic renderings.

Scholar and cultural critic Kimberly Bentson has suggested that "all of Afro-American literature may be seen as one vast genealogical poem that attempts to restore continuity to the ruptures or discontinuities imposed by the history of Black presence in America."[51] This cipher of the underground is one distinct aspect of this vast genealogical poem. The discursive conceptual "exchange," briefly detailed in this chapter, deeply reflects a range of Black artisans grappling with the ruptures imposed by institutionalized racism and its terrible

legacy in Black American life—including slavery, cultural commodification, and mass incarceration. The concepts of the underground in
this cipher represent a discursive, literary fluidity between identity
construction, artistic practice, and various physical settings of the
underground, all manifested in several genres of Black artistic production. It also serves as yet another example of the powerful intersections of the concept of the underground in hip-hop culture and
African American literature.

CHAPTER 6

TEARS FOR THE DEPARTED: SEE(K)ING A BLACK
VISUAL UNDERGROUND IN HIP-HOP AND
AFRICAN AMERICAN CULTURES

Critical inquiry at the intersections of hip-hop music, African American literature, and Black visual culture inform a generative discourse for Black underground imagery within and across an array of interrelated texts. Through certain textual pairings—Jonathan Green's "Seeking" and the Gravediggaz's "The Night the Earth Cried"; or Mos Def's "hip-hop" and Jeff Wall's "After Invisible Man," (among others)—this chapter seeks to excavate a ritualistic inter-textuality imbedded in certain works that feature elements of what can tentatively be referred to as Black visual underground culture, a constellation of lyrics, images, and textual allusions that articulate an underground ethos present (if not readily audible/visible) in hip-hop culture. In *Practices of Looking...*, Marita Sturken and Lisa Cartwright argue that "visual culture encompasses many media forms ranging from fine art to popular film and television to advertising to visual data in fields such as the sciences, law and medicine."[1] The Black visual underground functions in much the same way except that the subject matter embraces blackness and the cultural, spiritual, and political markers of Black identity—especially here in contemporary popular culture. "When we have an experience with a particular visual medium we draw on associations with other media and other areas of our lives informed by visual images. . . . Our visual experiences do not take place in isolation; they are enriched by memories and images from many different aspects of our lives."[2] In the following examples of Black visual underground images/texts, African American and hip-hop cultural "associations" can be discerned across visual media, and each example is "enriched by memories and images" from Black life—particularly in this chapter, the lived experiences of African Americans.

In the opening scene of the music video, "The Night the Earth Cried," the Gravediggaz's second single from their sophomore album, *The Pick, the Sickle, and the Shovel*, two African martial artists battle for the entertainment of a relatively nondescript African (tribal) community.[3] The rapper and superproducer RZA (née Robert Diggs) is the ruler of this community and presides approvingly over this martial exchange. The opening scene suggests a particularly utopian and deliberately ancestral portrait of continental Africa in a moment immediately preceding the transatlantic slave trade. The music video, directed by RZA, is released exactly one month before the release of Steven Spielberg's *Amistad* (November 10, 1997, and December 10, 1997, respectively); it serves as a powerful visual precursor to the feature films that RZA will (later in his career) both score and direct.[4] The single's prescient/prophetic relationship to the feature film, *Amistad*, is (as far as I can determine) completely coincidental, but no viewer of this music video and (a month later) the film *Amistad* can ignore the intertextual connections between them.

"The Night the Earth Cried" shifts quickly and seamlessly from the martial arts entertainment scene into scenes that depict the infiltration of European slavers—donned in white wigs and uniform colonial attire for white-minstrel effects. The slavers' guns give them an unfair advantage over the mastered martial artistry of the community and they subdue and capture them all. What follows are various visual depictions of middle passage and a futile attempt by one enslaved African to revolt en route, during middle passage. He is murdered, of course, shot down by the same guns that give the slavers their initial advantage on the continent. The refrain of the song punctuates the resistor's fall to his death in the Atlantic Ocean—and in response the earth cries. The narrator of the song can hear these cries and wonders to himself how many "Black Gods" have to die. The encoded meanings of the refrain and of many of the lyrics of the song itself summon a critical admonishment proffered by Monica Miller, a scholar of religion studies and hip-hop culture. According to Miller, "the competition for spiritual and existential space masked under asymmetrical patterns of engagement contributes towards *grave* misunderstandings and misgivings about hip-hop culture writ large. (my emphasis)"[5] The "earth" referred to here claims its standard meaning—a reference that

I interpret as being suggestive for how the underground (itself) cries, shedding tears for the departed Black Gods—those countless resistors to systematic enslavement and oppression.[6] But that reading alone (according to Miller) would be considered asymmetrical. In order to access its encoded, figuratively underground meaning, listeners/viewers would have to be aware of some tenets of the Five-Percent Nation, a cultural and spiritual (not religious) offshoot from the Nation of Islam founded by Clarence 13X in the early 1960s.[7] One of the tenets of the Five-Percent Nation is that women are "earths" and that Black men are "gods." Although most scholars of the Five-Percent Nation agree that Clarence 13X was the founder of the Five Percenters, according to Felicia Miyakawa's *Five Percenter Rap: God's Music, Message, and Black Muslim Mission*, the philosophical doctrines of the organization predate 13X by decades and have often been traced in the scholarship to an enigmatic Black leader, known as Noble Drew Ali (née Timothy Drew), born in North Carolina in 1886. Ali established the Moorish Science Temple of America in Newark, New Jersey, in the early 1920s. Miyakawa claims that "Noble Drew Ali considered himself heir to Garvey's black nationalist mantle, but whereas Garvey preached a message of physical repatriation to Africa, Noble Drew Ali wanted the 'Asiatic Blackman' to gain full rights in American society rather than a new society in Africa. Thus for Noble Drew Ali, repatriation was not physical but spiritual and political in nature."[8] These bits of information might illuminate the prophetic nature of "The Night the Earth Cried," even as they provide additional meanings for earths, gods, and the powerful look back into Black diasporic history that the song—especially via its music video—attempts to make.

Of course, these meanings maintain simultaneously. The gods, men, and revolutionaries are in rebellious (and interchangeable) concert with the women, the earths, and the underground. The distinction between Ali's philosophy and that of Garvey's is an important element of several claims that I hope to make here: (1) the notion that repatriation, that is, going back/returning to Africa can be both spiritual and political in nature; and (2) full citizenship rights must be attained right here in the United States. Part of seeing (and seeking) a Black visual underground, then, requires both the capacity to decode the visual and lyrical allusions to (again) what Salamishah Tillet refers to as "sites of slavery" and to come to terms with the ways in which the Black visual underground excavates narratives of resistance in order to ritualistically gesture toward Black diasporic identity/experiences. Tillet argues that "sites of slavery [are] the objects, texts, figures, places, and narratives from the American past that provide tangible links between present-day Americans and American chattel slavery" (5). She also suggests that "post-civil rights African American representations of slavery provide interiority and agency for enslaved African Americans [thereby writing] them into the national narrative" (5). More so than the song itself, the music video for "The Night the Earth Cried" introduces visual interiority and agency (via the martial artistry) while its depiction of resistance during the middle passage injects some modicum of agency into the national corpus of slave narrativity.

The imagery of the earth's tears shed during middle passage and captured in the Atlantic Ocean underscores the underground impulses of the group's moniker, the Gravediggaz, as well as the album's title— *The Pick, the Sickle, and the Shovel.* These traditional tools of actual grave diggers image the mortality of the peculiar institution and sharpen the group's metaphorical connections to excavation as a tactic for representing Black visual underground sensibilities. The lyrics of the song (somewhat disassociated from the visuals of the video) especially through Five-Percenter terms such as 360 degrees, the cipher, etc., are designed to both encode the song and invite potential initiates to the organization itself. And it is this invitation, in conjunction with the imagery of the grave digger, and the visual/spiritual/political return to an African ancestry on the cusp of the transatlantic slave trade, that together and in turn allude to an African American (Gullah) ritual known as "Seeking."

Gullah or Geechee communities are located on/in a series of islands located mostly, off the coasts of South Carolina and Georgia. These communities have long been the subjects of sociolinguistic and anthropological studies, mostly as a result of certain academic claims that the region's geography allowed it to be insulated from mainland America and thereby afforded its enslaved Africans distinct opportunities to preserve unsyncretized components of West African culture. In *Gullah Cultural Legacies*, Emory Campbell defines seeking as "a traditional ritual [that one follows] to become a member of the church: To meditate for a period of time during which nightly dreams are recalled and told to a spiritual leader for interpretation, [in] a sacred place in the forest [which] is visited three times daily...determining eligibility for Baptism and subsequently church membership."[9] Note well here that "seeking" is a syncretic "socioreligious" African

American ritual.[10] The term "seeking" was adopted (and adapted) by the Gullah speech communities from the plantation/slave owner class in "Low Country" South Carolina who were mostly practitioners of the Methodist religion. Near the conclusion of nineteenth-century Methodist church services in this region, the minister would ask congregants: "Who is seeking Jesus?" (Creel 1988). Gullahs interpolated this call and response ritual and used it to name the ritualistic practice of becoming initiated into the Gullah religious community. In *Peculiar People...*, Margaret Washington Creel (a well-cited religion studies scholar on the Gullah Community) describes at least three phases of the seeking rite/ritual. The first phase is precipitated by overt community pressure to become an autonomous/accountable member of the religion. The second phase involves some kind of commune/communication with the ancestors. In the third phase the initiate goes into the woods to seek God. The term seek/seeking in the Gullah dialect also means to pray (Campbell 2008). Margaret Creel also suggests that "solitude and meditation were essential features of the seeking period. Approved and unapproved night vigils were common. Such places as the *graveyard*, normally an absolute taboo for Gullahs...were favorite praying grounds for seekers. (my emphasis)"[11] In this third phase, the initiate fasts and shares his/her dreams with a spiritual elder in the church who often will interpret them. After a period of time (seven days and seven nights, according to some scholars, but with auxiliary phases that might extend the ritual over the course of three months), the initiate returns to the community and is embraced in the religion. In "The Gullah Seeker's Journey..." Elizabeth McNeil argues that "as would be proper for the seeker, the sequential critical junctures in the...initiation...concern her confronting the dead and gaining wisdom from those meetings."[12]

In 2006, Gullah/African American painter/artist Jonathan Green completed his work titled "Seeking" with generous support from the Monks at Mepkin Abbey in South Carolina. Mepkin Abbey was formerly known as Mepkin Plantation. Throughout the latter half of the eighteenth Century, Henry Laurens, whose letters about slavery revealed some conflicting views on the peculiar institution, owned scores of slaves between the 1760s and 1792 when he died. Not too long after the Monks acquired the plantation, they discovered an African American slave burial ground. It was their desire to properly commemorate this historic "site of slavery," that in turn generated the interest in commissioning Jonathan Green to craft a work specifically for this occasion. Green worked on-site and began his process by visit-ing the gravesite and rendering a drawing from his earliest experi-ences. Many people who view the "Seeking" painting may not be aware of the fact that an African American slave burial became an inspiration for the work, and, of course, this insight is in no way nec-essary to the enjoyment or the experience that viewers will have with the work. "Seeking" sports lush vivid colors, most strikingly visible in the brilliant coloring of the trees suggestive of the bloodlines and the African Ancestry underwriting the ritual of seeking as well as the burial ground at Mepkin Abbey. The painting is focalized via a figure in a hat that might be interpreted as a seeker. In fact the wearing of a hat or sometimes a string tied around the head and the white clothing are visual indications that this figure is seeking. The visual depth of "Seeking" is rendered through Green's use of focalization and per-spective and it is punctuated by another figure off in the distance. This figure (also in white, also wearing a hat), might be the spiritual elder or a vision of a spiritual ancestor or it might be some spiritual or existential reflection of the seeker him/herself.

Jonathan Green himself experienced the seeking ritual as a young boy in the Low Country. He relates anecdotes of the ritual in a docu-mentary film, *Jonathan Green's Seeking*, directed by Charles Allan Smith and filmed throughout the creative process. Green does not reveal too much about his process but in the film he has clearly invested in an African American historical storytelling tradition. The film documents Green "as he brings to life on canvas the African American ritual of seeking. Pulling from his very own memories as a young man, he journeys back through his ancestry to paint 'Seeking,' honoring the African American slaves that lived and were buried at Clermont Cemetery on the grounds of the Mepkin Abbey in South Carolina" (Earthbeat Productions/Smith). One suggestion/argument that emerges from this deeper understanding of Jonathan Green's inspiration for the "Seeking," is that the Black visual underground is reflected in the artwork itself—most especially through an in-depth understanding of the ritual of "Seeking," its various stages and its central status within the Gullah communities of the Low Country. But the Black visual underground also works in the pre-craft stages where Green draws inspiration from an actual burial ground, a grave site that serves as a visual (and for Green, autobiographical, spiritual, historical, and political) portal to/through a particularly poignant "site of slavery."[13]

One reason why I have chosen to merge the concepts of seeing and seeking in order to wrestle with the complexities of a Black visual underground is because they speak directly to issues of enlightenment and consciousness present at the philosophical roots of the concepts of the underground (consider Plato's Parable of the Cave), but this search for a Black visual underground—initiated with my discussion of Thelonious Monk's 1968 album cover for—*Underground*—in another chapter of this book—requires both the visualization of certain "sites of slavery" such as those found in the Gravediggaz's "The Night the Earth Cried" music video, as well as the propensity to seek Black visual connections beneath the surface of artistic production. The intertextual examples that follow also help to inform the ritualistic nature of these Black visual discourses, all of which harken back to an assertion proven in Creel's research of socioreligious practices in Gullah communities. That "the ontological category of traditional African societies which also formed the basis of the Gullah world view, was the fusion of spirituality with human activity and the impact of a sacred presence in all areas of life" (59). This fusion of spirituality with human activity and the "impact" or the consequences of a sacred presence in "all areas of life" speak to the tenets of the Five-Percent Nation, the seeking rituals in the Gullah/Sea Island communities, and the urban landscapes beneath the surface and on the *Blocks* above ground in the forthcoming examples.

The music video for Scarface's "My Block," a standout single from his 2002 album, *The Fix*, visually narrates a panoramic snapshot of Scarface's subjective emergence within his south side, inner-city neighborhood of Houston, Texas. The album was acclaimed critically, earning a rare five-mic rating from *The Source* and the music video for "My Block" was directed by Marc Klasfield.[14] "My Block" was produced by the Hitmen, and it features a sample from the opening piano riff in the 1971 Roberta Flack and Donny Hathaway duet, "Be Real Black for Me." The duet is a love song that illuminates the interiority and the intimacy of romantic and sexual love between two Black subjects. The aura of intimacy is articulated through discrete descriptions of Black bodies: "soft and crinkly" hair, "strong and stately" bodies, and/or "warm and luscious" lips. "My Block's" sampling of the opening piano riff from "Be Real Black" has the capacity to recall the duet's interior perspective and intimate themes. This perspective and the themes of intimacy are underlying visual cues for Scarface's narration in both the song and the video for "My Block."

"My Block," the video, begins and ends with a young Black man throwing a pair of sneakers up into the air and over a power/ telephone line. This ritualistic practice has been the subject of much speculation and (mis)definition particularly across online media. Shoe slinging or "shoefiti," a term coined by Ed Kohler, has been defined as an urban practice that marks gang territory; as makeshift memorials for murdered gang members; as underground communication that drugs are sold on that block; as an indicator that the shoe-slinger has just lost his virginity; as a celebratory act done by school-aged youth at the end of an academic year; and/or as a way for bullies to taunt their victims. The term "shoefiti" suggests the communicative significance of the act itself even as it situates the ritualistic practice within the context of hip-hop's elemental practices of reclaiming public spaces through the visual aesthetics of graffiti art. Interestingly enough, so much of the urban mythology around "shoefiti" trucks in the imagery of coming-of-age, urban youth events and practices, that the presence of it as bookends in the "My Block" video potentially engenders meanings connected to and/or reflective of all of them (or possibly none of them). In *The Mystery of Flying Kicks*, a 14-minute documentary film written and directed by Matthew Bate, all of the aforementioned definitions of "shoe-flinging" are explored and detailed via a crowd-sourced survey featuring participants from around the world. In the film, University of Toronto (linguistics and anthropology) professor Marcel Danesi wonders: "Why we search for meaning and why must we leave our mark? It is connected to memory, a kind of communal long-lasting memory, as if we live on through memory. Just the fact that...you leave a shoe somewhere, you have proven that you exist. What an interesting feature of humanity even though its kind of an illusion...We do disappear from communal memory." The shoe-slinging bookends of the "My Block" video signal the desire in the Black visual underground for "communal memory" that leaves a mark. The notion that "My Block" features scenes that directly engage in an existential search, a seeking of sorts, reflects the video's capacity to wrestle with the questions of communal memory and an underground perspective on African American culture. That said, a recorded music video, particularly "My Block," because it features a panoramic visualized history of its subject, has much greater potential to attach to communal memory and history than an anonymous act of throwing a pair of sneakers over a public power line.

The video also features interior bookends of scenes where the subject of "My Block," as well as the viewing audience, watches a television clip. The viewing audience watches the subject of "My Block" first watching a clip of Stokely Carmichael delivering a speech—near the very beginning of the video—and then watching the subject, possibly the subject of the video, watching Rodney King on television when he famously quipped, "Can't we all just get along?" These clips, and the scenes wherein we watch the video's subject watching them, serve multiple purposes within the narrative arc of "My Block." The first marks an early childhood time period for the protagonist/subject/Scarface. His grandmother holds him (as a toddler) in her lap and points to the television screen where Stokely Carmichael (also known was Kwame Toure) is delivering a speech. The second scene takes place in a drug house as a much older version of the protagonist watches Rodney King give his statement. These "watching" scenes mark time in the narrative of the video's subject/protagonist but each also indicates some of the political discourse in the American public sphere. Together, like the shots of the young men slinging shoes up onto the power lines, the scenes where we watch someone else watching television history help "My Block" to instantiate itself in both communal and cultural memory.

"My Block" is a visual coming-of-age narrative. It features scenes of birth (presumably of Scarface, née Brad Jordan), death, riots, brutality, hustling, love, talking, teaching—living. It is a panoramic motion snapshot of the interior of Scarface's world—his block. "From the perspective of the artist, then, his neighborhood, figured adequately as a block, takes on the qualities of a corporeal, three-dimensional square: one both confining and small. The impression of the artist...allows the careful listener to envision an insider's representation of an urban, African American neighborhood."[15] The scenes featuring him (not played by younger actors but as himself) are telling as they conclude the video and directly embrace underground themes. One scene shows Scarface selling CDs out of the trunk of a Cadillac. In the very next scene, he is getting out of a Rolls Royce Bentley. These two scenes visually narrate Scarface's ascension from the underground of hip-hop—selling his own CDs out of the trunk of his car—to the successful station he achieved as a more mainstream artist on Def Jam Records (a major label). The video also features several scenes of unrest between the community and the police who are charged with protecting them. In an early scene the community is engaged in violent unrest presumably as a result of police misconduct and physical surveillance. In the closing scene of the video, Scarface approaches a crime scene where the crime is apparently the murder of a young Black man at the hands of the police. Scenes featuring resistance to police/state violence or the Do-It-Yourself (DIY) distribution of one's own rap records are the hallmarks of Black underground visual culture within the "My Block" music video. Yet the video features certain rituals: dice games, a minister admonishing a group of children, or watching television with family at key moments in history. These rituals construct a deliberately Black southern, urban hip-hop cultural context. And in these contexts, a Black visual underground sensibility organically thrives.

In addition to the rituals within the video's narrative arc, "My Block" also engages in the ritual of Black repetition with a signifying difference. The video's subject matter and visual/artistic structure riff on (or sample) Romare Bearden's classic collage—*The Block*. Bearden's "Block" is a six-panel collage created in 1971, the same year that the duet "Be Real Black for Me" was released. That Scarface's "My Block" samples visually and aurally from signal Black texts produced in 1971 gives some sense of the ways in which the Black Power/Black Arts aesthetics of the 1970s deeply influenced artistic production within hip-hop culture. According to Bill Cosby, "we experience 'The Block' through a series of events, almost as though we are watching a movie. In a sequence of scenes, people congregate at the barbershop, at the grocery store, a church, and even at a funeral parlor, and life in all of its myriad forms is paraded before us."[16] Bearden's *The Block* is an artistic source for Scarface's "My Block." Intentionality is not a factor in this ritualized intertextual relationship between Black visual texts. Each, by design, focalizes the interiority of Black life, a snapshot of the urban landscape replete with specific visual details to which only initiates of the culture—those who have access to what lies beneath the surface of the culture—have access. If the first pairing in this chapter centers on the seeking ritual that takes its initiates to physical sites of Black underground culture—either in the form of visual allusions to Middle Passage or a visual depiction of a burial ground of enslaved Africans—then this second pair constructs visual metaphors of urban space that are designed to invite viewers into the interiority of Black life—the intimate, triumphant, and painful experiences of African Americans beneath the surface of the mainstream world's cursory interface with Black culture.

In a third pairing, featuring a line from Mos Def's "hip-hop" and a striking photograph produced by Jeff Wall, both making direct allusions to Ralph Ellison's *Invisible Man*, the Black visual underground shifts from its seeing/seeking attributes toward a sense of watching and the phonic possibilities of visual culture. In *In Search of the Black Fantastic*, Richard Iton argues: "At the most superficial level, the visual surplus associated with the emergence of hip-hop—the work of graffiti artists starting in the 1970s; the advent of videos and music video channels, videocassettes in the next decade; and later, video games, digital videodiscs (DVDs), dual discs (combining CD and DVD content), and the internet—simply overflowed the previously existing networks of intercommunity discourse."[17] In many ways Mos Def (now known as Yasiin Bey) marks this "visual surplus" and points to the overflow (and in some ways the undermining) of "existing networks" throughout his lyrics in "hip-hop." One striking aspect of the song, released in 1999, from the album *Black on Both Sides*, is that it accomplishes the critique of the fraught relationship between hip-hop, (hyper)visibility, and the forces of neoliberalism most significantly through a bevy of allusions to Black literary culture. He opens his first verse with a metaphor where he equates his speech with a hammer with which he will shape the world. In the first verse, as he continues to lyrically draw attention to his own writing process, Mos Def poetically argues that speech, especially AAVE, literature, and writing are the authenticating and authenticated arts of hip-hop (N.B. that these are linguistic forms not necessarily visual forms). The music industry, represented here by chart positions, cell blocks, court rooms, advertisements, guns, and drugs represents the worst of what hip-hop, especially its superficial visual surplus of pathological imagery, has to offer to artists of the culture as well as their young constituents. He portends a larger, more significant set of allusions later in the song when he makes direct reference to Richard Wright's *Native Son* in what he refers to as his "native tongue." The "native" allusions are an intersection of the hip-hop underground and African American literary culture. According to Yvonne Bynoe, The Native Tongues were "an informal group of artists united by a sense that rap music had grown stale with materialism and ghetto stylings. Beginning in 1988 with A Tribe Called Quest, De La Soul, and The Jungle Brothers, [and eventually Queen Latifah and Monie Love], the Native Tongues movement did away with macho posturing in rap and instead embraced Afrohumanism and social issues with humor and creativity."[18] The Native Tongues represented an important thematic ethos within constructions of the underground in hip-hop culture: that mainstream rap music was, in Imani Perry's terms, detached from the organic roots of the community that generated it; and therefore less authentic as it became more and more formulaic and reductive in its representations of Black masculinity and Black life generally. The Native Tongues, especially De La Soul, were instrumental in providing Mos Def, an underground emcee (still) by most standards discussed in this book, with a more mainstream platform for him as a hip-hop artist. This important allusion to being a part of The Native Tongues collective also intersects with Richard Wright's well-known 1940 novel, *Native Son*. Based upon my interpretation of Mos Def's themes in "hip-hop," he is not associating himself neatly with Bigger Thomas, Wright's main character in *Native Son*, and one of the most critiqued and discussed characters in African American literature. The *Native Son* allusion almost naturally invokes James Baldwin's *Notes of a Native Son*, a collection of essays featuring the title-essay that challenges the flat nature of Wright's most popular character. In some ways Mos Def is using Black literary discourse—Baldwin critiquing Wright's reductive characterizations of Black male identity—to mirror and inform hip-hop discourse. The comparison works best with an understanding of the mission of the Native Tongue's collective as well as Mos Def's membership in that collective. Mos Def's artistry at that time (and since) has often been directed at other emcees/rappers whose representations or characterizations of Black male identity are more like Wright's Bigger Thomas than Ellison's Invisible Man. That is, the appeal of the pathological Black male menace is one that finds great purchase among mainstream audiences for African American literature and mainstream hip-hop culture.

In the center of Mos Def's "hip-hop" are allusive juxtapositions of slave labor, chain gangs, Bebop, hip-hop, the Blues, Amiri Baraka's *Blues People* and Ellison's *Invisible Man*. According to Mos Def's narrator, the hip-hop generation's "Invisible Man" actually has the whole world watching him. These lines articulate the intersections between the hip-hop underground and African American culture. Moving from slave labor to chain gangs, from Bebop to hip-hop, Mos Def traces the origins of the African American experience from its beginnings in chattel slavery to origins of Black music (in slavery and in the formulation of the modern prison system via chain gangs, convict leasing, etc.). The suggestion that "we went from" Bebop to hip-hop posits the underground connections between Bebop and certain aspects of hip-hop music—especially those aspects that communicate the conceptual structures, cultural moves, and the allusions to sites of slavery that (I argue elsewhere) formulate the most significant components of the hip-hop underground. Mos Def's allusion to Amiri Baraka's *Blues People* summons the warnings about mainstream appropriations of Black musical culture—a challenge for hip-hop that is eerily reminiscent of the very same challenges that Baraka is working through in *Blues People*. That said, Iton argues for a distinction between these connections, arguing that "with regard to music specifically, the densification of the visual realm triggered a challenge to the performative norms that marked late 1960s and early 1970s black politics and popular culture."[19] My emphasis on the *Invisible Man* reference in "hip-hop" reflects Iton's sense that the densification of the visual in hip-hop culture alters the terrain for relationships between politics and Black popular culture and in some ways it obscures the kinds of intersections (between African American cultural history and the hip-hop underground) upon which this book is based. Again, Iton is instructive: "Visual communication, in this sense, is detached from daily existence, in that it cannot be easily combined with other activities; it is distracting. The visual in this context is almost antisocial."[20] If hip-hop has created a space or a public sphere within which Invisible Man (a stand in for socially invisible people) now has the whole world "watching," the logical question is what is that world—a mainstream, aboveground world—actually seeing? For Iton, the hegemony inherent in the densification of the visual in hip-hop culture suggests that the "antisocial" distracting effects of these visuals might result in consequential social invisibility or more aptly, the inability to see (or seek) the full humanity of the Black subject in the eras of the hip-hop generation. There is some evidence that Iton is right; that Mos Def's lyrical inversion of Invisible Man's (in)visibility calls into question what the world sees (now that they are watching) when they look at hip-hop youth, especially young Black men who can be easily and visually associated with hip-hop culture. We need only to look at modes of dress and racial profiling (consider Stop and Frisk policies, or tragic cases such as the trial of George Zimmerman and the role of the hoodie) to understand that popular Black visual culture can function in the service of the state as well as in the service of elements of White supremacy and White privilege. The proliferation of dense images of hyper-masculine Black male subjects in music videos, television, and on film feed into the physical surveillance, harassment, profiling, and sometimes the murder of young Black people in reality.

Mos Def's allusion to *Invisible Man* and his lyrical inversion of the signal trope operating within the novel may not actually be an inversion. It might best be described as a mutation of the social invisibility and the socially challenged subjectivity of Ellison's protagonist. At issue here is the role of the Black visual (underground) in sociocultural contexts where the hegemony of dense visual imagery emerges in tandem with hip-hop culture. So, for example, if the lyrical and thematic work of the Native Tongues collective lost the battle (if you will) with the dense visual imagery of gangsta rap—and this is certainly true when one considers mainstream hip-hop right now—where/how then can the Black visual underground operate on or against the densification of the visual, or the overwhelming capacity for the visual to dominate Black performance and Black subjectivity? One way to consider how the Black visual underground might proffer some response to this conundrum is to consider Jeff Wall's photographic interpolation of one of the most visually dense scenes in *Invisible Man*: in the prologue to the novel, sitting in his underground dwelling, listening to Louis Armstrong.

In "Invisible Music (Ellison)," Copenhafer (2004) argues that the prologue to *Invisible Man* functions like a "hypertext," suggesting that there are links in the text to realizable audible experiences (179). In a sense, Copenhafer theorizes that sound, or at least some sense of sound, might be derived from a text or more importantly here, from an image. "In a beautiful photograph, 'After Invisible Man, by Ralph Ellison, The Preface,'" Jeff Wall imagines the narrator listening to music in his underground dwelling."[21] The Wall photograph recreates a scene from the novel (discussed earlier in this volume) that images an intersection between the undergrounds of Invisible Man's story world and hip-hop culture. Invisible Man is smoking weed in his underground dwelling, illuminated by 1,369 light bulbs and he is listening to a Louis Armstrong recording of "(What did I Do to Be So) Black and Blue?" As he listens, he imagines the possibility of being able to hear the song on multiple turntables at the same time, which I interpret as a prophetic imagination of a hip-hop listening experience where turntables can be used as instruments and as tools to manipulate records in order to produce new sounds. Copenhafer also marks this scene as being a distinct visual for the novel on the whole and for the ways in which readers experience Invisible Man's voice. "If we follow the narrator's lead in trying to understand Armstong's singing, is it not necessary to see-him-not-seeing that he is invisible? Is it not necessary, in other words, to see blackness, and to see the invisibility of blackness in order to comprehend the performance?" (184) Copenhafer is suggesting that a cross-pollination of sensory perceptions—in this case sight and sound—seeing blackness, seeing the invisibility of blackness in order to comprehend the aural performance—presents itself at this pivotal moment in Invisible Man's underground. Alex Weheliye reads the same scene as follows: "The corporeal viscerality of the protagonist's ideal listening scenario manifests an intense longing to experience his body in sound in ways that he cannot do visually."[22] Again, the tensions and potential interface between distinct sensory perceptions—listening and seeing, or feeling and listening destabilize any neat readings of the scene in question or viewings of the photographic image of the same scene, rendered by Jeff Wall. "'After Invisible Man' has the aspect ratio of a cinematic film still, and much about it seems intended to evoke the experience of cinema, not least the absent or 'implied' music."[23] The music implied in the scene and in this photographed example of the Black visual underground suggests an interesting counterpoint to the tyranny of images in hip-hop and contemporary Black popular culture. That is, if images might imply sound, especially those images associated with the Black visual underground, then there may be some antidote to the hegemony of dense visual images circulated by and through a mainstream culture that watches but still does not see the full range of black humanity and hip-hop subjectivity. "[The] 'interstitial' quality [of "After Invisible Man"] reinforces its evocation of a moment of intense listening, for listening always occurs in the interval between an event and its cognition" (202). A photograph that evokes intense listening is an image that encounters and counters Iton's assessment of antisocial, detached visual communication. Cultural theorist Fred Moten argues for the interstitial quality of the photograph in his discussion of the gruesome image of Emmett Till after his mutilated body is discovered. I will excerpt Moten at length here in order to preserve his theoretical maneuvering.

> In positing that...photographs in general bear a phonic substance, I want to challenge not only the ocularcentrism that generally...shapes theories of the nature of photography and our experience of photography but that mode of semiotic objectification and inquiry that

privileges the analytic-interpretative reduction of phonic materiality and/or nonmeaning over something like a mimetic improvisation of and with that materiality that moves in excess of meaning. This second challenge assumes that the critical-mimetic experience of the photograph takes place most properly within a field structured by theories of (black) spectatorship, audition, and performance.[24]

Here Moten challenges the interpretive principles of photographic analysis. He is arguing against the elision of "phonic substance" or "phonic materiality" in comprehensive understandings of the photographic text. His example is that of the infamous Emmett Till photo—a photo that contributed to the galvanization of the Civil Rights Movement in the mid-late 1950s. For Moten, experiencing that photo almost requires that one understands the contexts of Black mourning practices and the soundings of Black moans and cries in those home-going/funeral/memorial services. In this sense, Black visual underground imagery features a soundtrack whether that soundtrack is physically audible at the site of the viewing experience or not. Black visual underground culture invites viewers to be listeners and feelers—it compels viewers to be *experiencers*. We hear the sounds and smell the smells of Romare Bearden's *The Block*, just as we can feel the high and hear Louis Armstrong's bluesy query when we read the prologue to *Invisible Man* or see Jeff Wall's brilliant photographic rendition of the very same literary scene. The Black visual underground then invites viewers to take affective turns towards cross-referencing their perceptual experiences as they engage texts instantiated in a vast cultural genealogy of blackness that practices ritualistic intertextuality and signification.

These suggestions (and insights) about how we might discern a Black visual underground at the intersections of hip-hop and African American cultures are also informed by Gen Doy's definition of Black visual culture at the intersections of modernity and postmodernity. According to Doy, "many black artists and theorists have been more reluctant than their white counterparts to abandon [modernist] notions of history, truth, reality and conscious subjectivity." If postmodernism attempts to dispense with all of the master/grand narratives, artisans of Black visual culture(s) will confront an absence of sociopolitical and (possibly) racial moorings for some of their artistry, especially art that wrestles with Black subjectivity, social invisibility, and the interiority of Black life. Doy is not interested in tethering Black visual artists to race narratives or histories of discrimination and oppression. He is appreciative of wide-ranging diverse expressions of Black visual art-istry. But according to him, "there remain specific themes and issues which are embodied in the works of black artists and black visual culture...for example, history, memory, belonging and identity."[25] The embodiment of these themes and issues is an important reminder of the visceral effects of and inputs into Black visual culture. And Black visual underground culture reminds us of this in the iterations of underground imagery discussed in this chapter, including images of middle passage, slave burial grounds, the interiority of urban blocks, and the audible imagery of Invisible Man's underground dwelling.

In his 2011 children's book, *Underground: Finding the Light to Freedom*, Shane W. Evans writes few words to complement his stunning visual artistry depicting a story that has become the staple of African American narratives—the movement from bondage to freedom, from slavery to liberation. Evans's characters escape slavery via the Underground Railroad, a story so similar to others, so familiar to students of American history that no narration seems to be required. And in the case of Evan's Black visual *Underground*, the visage of his figures—their eyes, communicate the narrative almost in its entirety. But the words with which he closes the children's book articulate the rationale, the impetus that underwrites Doy's sense of Black visual culture and the collection of arguments and examples briefly discussed in this chapter: "Freedom. I am free. He is Free. She is Free. We are free."[26]

CHAPTER 7

THE DEPTH OF THE HOLE: INTERTEXTUALITY
AND TOM WAITS'S "WAY DOWN IN THE HOLE"

The opening theme music for HBO's series *The Wire* is a song
written by Tom Waits titled "Way Down in the Hole" (1987).
Each year, during the series' five-season run, the producers selected or
solicited a different version of the song. As a series, *The Wire* is often
interpreted as lacking a space for representations of Black spirituality.
Each of the five seasons features complex institutional characterizations and explorations of the Street, the Port, the Law, the Hall (i.e.,
politics), the School, and/or the Paper (i.e., media). Through these
institutional characters and the individual characters that inhabit,
construct, and confront them, *The Wire* depicts urban America, writ
large across the canvas of cultural and existential identity. For all of
its institutional complexity, *The Wire* then serially marginalizes Black
spirituality in favor of realism, naturalism, and some may argue,
nihilism.[1] "Way Down in the Hole" is a paratextual narrative that
embodies this marginalization and creates a potential space for viewers (and listeners) of the show, one that frames each episode and the
entire run, through literary and spiritual Black musical contexts. The
multiple versions of "Way Down in the Hole" ultimately function
as a marginalized repository for the literary and spiritual narratives
that are connected to the series—narratives that become legible via
intertextual analyses and in turn render visible *The Wire's* least visible
entities: Black spirituality and the Black Church.[2]

In an attempt to engage this marginality and its attendant space for
Black literary and spiritual content, I critically engage various versions of "Way Down in the Hole," the numerous artists who perform
the song, and the spiritual aesthetics central to each version of the

song. Moreover, each artist's interpretation or treatment of this song constitutes an intertextual relationship with developments in African American music.[3] Thus, "Way Down in the Hole" is an African American musical text—an Afro-American spiritual-blues text, to be precise. In several instances, specific lyrics function as *intertext* with and to multiple narratives within African American culture, including sociolinguistic phenomena, spirituality, and African American literary history. Generally speaking, intertextuality, a term coined by Julia Kristeva, refers to the ways in which language almost universally refers to itself. However, there are limited forms of intertextuality that include quotations, deliberate allusions, and various other linguistic connections and relationships.[4] The analysis in this chapter employs a limited type of narrative intertextuality as opposed to the universal intertextuality favored by various scholars such as Kristeva, Roland Barthes, and Jacques Derrida. This limited, critically deliberate intertextuality includes the cinematic variety found in the opening montages of *The Wire*, only briefly glossed in this chapter; the relationship among the various "Way Down(s)"; developments in African American music; and certain lyrics of the song that engender connections to African American literary history and spirituality. This limited intertextual model challenges viewers and listeners to consider how lyrical language, artistic experience, and musical genre function integrally to produce thematic suggestions not readily apparent in the narratives of the series itself. As a result of its apparent absence from the show, or at least its deliberately backgrounded or marginalized presence within the show, the Black Church, particularly manifestations of Black spirituality, exists in the spiritual narrativity of the various versions of the show's theme song. The legibility of the Black Church (in *The Wire*) then, a central institution in the Black American experience, relies on the audibility of multiple intertextual connections between versions of "Way Down in the Hole" and the artistic tools of African American cultural production. These multiple instances of intertextuality suggest a thematically grounded *Afro-blues spiritual* sensibility operating within and among the narratives of this critically acclaimed dramatic series.

Intertextuality is but one element upon which *The Wire*'s interpretability as a novel or work of literary significance might be established. At least one other narrative element, the paratextual nature or positioning of the series' theme song, lends additional plausibility to novelistic and/or narrative-oriented interpretations of *The Wire*.

"Paratextuality" is a term defined by narratologist Gerard Genette, who states that "peritext" and "epitext" together constitute the "paratextuality" of a novel or collection of texts. Paratextuality is defined as "those liminal devices and conventions both within the book (peritext) and outside it (epitext), that mediate the book to the reader: titles and subtitles, pseudonyms, forewords, dedications, epigraphs, prefaces, intertitles, notes, epilogues, and afterwords."[5] Here, paratextuality refers to *The Wire*'s opening visual sequences accompanied by various versions of the series's theme song, "Way Down in the Hole." Part of my argument is that "Way Down in the Hole" has an epitextual relationship to the series. It mediates *The Wire* (to the viewer) through the lyrics of the song, the various versions of the song, and the particularities of genre peculiar to each version. One by-product of this mediation is the way in which "Way Down in the Hole" reflects some semblance of Black spirituality not directly presented within the dramatic narratives of the show. "Way Down in the Hole" is a marginalized repository of musical narratives featuring spiritual themes rendered through expansive intertextuality within African American cultural production.

Each season of *The Wire* contains a cinematic montage, a visual epitext that corresponds with each version of the opening theme song, "Way Down in the Hole." Each montage features a collection of clips that point to, foreshadow, and/or underscore some element, character, or scene in the season or, in some cases, in the series. The montage is a visual precursor to the show, and its intertextual nature symbolizes an aspect of the argument of this chapter because it reflects the intertextual qualities of the songs that function as the soundtrack to the opening sequence. In season 1, "the sequence shows the series' fondness for counterintelligence and misdirection while setting the stage for a battle of wills in which neither side is inclined to lay down and die."[6] Season 1's montage introduces the audience to one clip that remains in subsequent montages/sequences that play at the opening of each episode of *The Wire*. This particular clip (again, found in each season's sequence) features two dealers (or denizens of the Street) throwing rocks at and cracking the lens of a video surveillance camera. The clip signals the dramatic ongoing tension between the Street and the Law, the central subject matter of the series. It is also "a display of defiance and a reminder that both sides are aware of the other's tactics."[7]

Season 4's cinematic montage is a reflective and intertextual opening sequence of the series. Since Andrew Dignan has crafted an astute gloss of each season's opening sequence, it is worth quoting him at length here:

> There's a procession of shots near the end of the credits that encapsu-lates everything *The Wire* has been working to establish over the years. A local shopkeeper spins open a countertop security window, sending through a pack of smokes; a hand spins a pair of expensive-looking designer rims; a piece of playground equipment spins anonymous at night; a child rolls a large tire around in an empty alley; bundles of narcotics are packed around a spare tire in the back of a car with a piece of carpeting pulled up to conceal them. And then a similar cut of fabric—this time a body being carried from an abandoned row house. The same motions are repeated throughout, and the eye is drawn to how these shots flow seamlessly into one another: The bodega is a front for drug distribution; the rims represent wealth and status among street youth; the playground equipment, an image of youthful inno-cence, is corrupted by the sight of an adult perched upon it, holding an alcoholic beverage; the child with the tire, left unsupervised, is forced to amuse himself with whatever is available; the drugs are another form of self-amusement; and of course there's the corpse, where all this is destined to lead.[8]

Dignan's attention to the circular motions "repeated throughout" the montage reflects the multiple ways in which the sequence(s) constructs intertextual relationships between certain visual clips and the plot and themes of the show. The show underscores the cycles of institutional progress; as the seasons accrue, new criminals emerge as old ones are killed or imprisoned, new politicos take power as old ones are voted out of office, and officers of the law rise up in the ranks. The cyclical nature of the real world that *The Wire* suggestively reflects is ulti-mately borne out in the series' conclusion as various new characters replace dead, or rehabilitated, old characters (e.g., Michael is posi-tioned to become Omar Little, and Duquan is positioned to become Bubbles). This intertextuality and repetition is also reflected in the versioning of the theme song, "Way Down in the Hole."

David Simon has often been quoted as describing *The Wire* as a series of conflicts and encounters between the institution and the individual. According to Simon, "*The Wire* depicts a world in which capital has triumphed completely, labor has been marginalized and monied interests have purchased enough political infrastructure to prevent reform. It is a world in which the rules and values of the free market and maximized profit have been mistaken for a social framework, a world where institutions themselves are paramount and every day human beings matter less."[9]

Various characters who populate the story world of *The Wire* often confront and are conflicted by the strictures of certain institutions.[10] These individual-institutional conflicts help to formulate the seasonal and serial narratives of *The Wire*. Simon's vision for the series always lent itself to serial narrativity and literary interpretation. In interviews during the series' inaugural year (2002), Simon "began referring to the work as a 'visual novel,' explaining that the first episodes of the show had to be considered much as the first chapters of any book of even moderate length."[11] Simon's sense of *The Wire* as a "novel for television" invites certain literary analyses of the series and underscores my narratological approach that features intertextual readings of the paratextual matter of the show (i.e., the various versions of "Way Down in the Hole").

Youthful Musings

Season 4 of *The Wire* features four Black male youth who are rocked by the institutional-individual nexus in inner-city Baltimore: Michael Lee, Namond Brice, Duquan Weems, and Randy Wagstaff are the season's main characters. Each of these middle school-aged African American boys faces the institutional-individual confrontation along at least two axes: the Individual versus the School and the Individual versus the Street. To underscore these conflicts and the youthful themes of the season, and to localize the thematic entrance to the show, DoMaJe, an underground Baltimore group, performs "Way Down 4" (2005). DoMaJe consists of five Baltimore teenagers: Tariq Al-Sabir, Markel Steele, Ivan Ashford, Cameron Brown, and Avery Bargasse. DoMaJe's version of "Way Down in the Hole" was arranged and recorded specifically for the show. Its rhythm and blues aesthetic features a more distinctly digital and synthesized vocal and musical production of all of the versions used for the series (see table 7.1). One contributing element of that advancement is the female lead voice, which makes it unique among all of the versions as well. Considering the somewhat limited presence of women's voices in the series itself, this version of "Way Down in the Hole" again creates space and place—here for a woman's vocalization—in the paratextual margins of the series.

Table 7.1   The various versions of "Way Down in the Hole"

Version	Performing artist	Musical genre(s)	Broad seasonal theme
Way Down 1	5 Blind Boys of Alabama	Gospel/blues	Inside the mind of a spiritually and emotionally reflective criminal
Way Down 2	Tom Waits	Delta blues	Hustlers'/cops'/working-class blues
Way Down 3	The Neville Brothers	New Orleans blues/go-go	Fusion and amalgamation: Consider the experimental nature of the "Hamsterdam" neighborhood, where drugs are temporarily not criminalized.
Way Down 4	DoMaJe	Rhythm and blues/Soul	Call-and-response and youth who came (always already) of age
Way Down 5	Steve Earle	Country blues	A full circle of sorts and the fiction/nonfiction continuum in media and in reality
Way Down X	M.I.A., Chateauhaag, Spirit & Blues, BlueTouch	Hip-Hop/ jazz/ blues/rock (respectively)	Not Applicable

Steve Earle, an actor who plays Walon in the series and records "Way Down 5," claims that DoMaJe "took the most unique approach" and that their version "proved the universality of the song."[12] Although other versions ("Way Down 1" and "Way Down 3," especially) of Waits's song feature various forms of call-and-response, sometimes between the instruments and other times between the vocals and the instruments, DoMaJe's "Way Down in the Hole" features a series of call-and-response improvisations that serve to distinguish it further from all of the other versions. Call-and-response is a staple form of African American spiritual and artistic expression. The call-and-response vocals gesture to the spiritual coordinates of developments in African American music even as they suggest multiple meanings of "the hole" in Waits' original lyrics. The call-and-response exchanges occur while the lead vocals repeat "Deeper in the hole / Down in the hole." The lyrics of the refrain function as the call. Members of DoMaJe respond to this call by referring to and/or lexically exchanging the original meaning of hole with *the gutter, the trash,* and/or *the sewer* in responsive phrases such as "keep him down in the gutter, right in the sewer yo" or "keep him in the trash, yo." Through this call-and-response, DoMaJe suggest a sociolinguistic intervention and innovation commensurate with the modern rhythm and blues stylings and universal interpretation of their performance. This intervention adds an interpretive layer to the meaning of the hole and pivots around the symbolic and intertextual nature of "the hole" in African American culture.

In the sense that it is used in the various versions of "Way Down...," the hole is another example of the conceptual structures that I have been referring to as the concepts of the underground in hip-hop and African American literary cultures. In hip-hop culture and in African American literary history, the hole engenders a surplus of meanings related to and reflective of identity, subversive action, addiction, and loss, among many other concepts, ideas, and emotions. Nat Turner digs a hole in the woods and hides for nearly a month after his rebellion is brutally put down.[13] How he hides out and survives in a hole in 1831 as the most wanted man in America (and maybe the most wanted Black man ever) is still one of Black History's unasked and unanswered queries. The ability to hide oneself in/on the earth became a central practicality of the Underground Railroad in the nineteenth century. *The Hole* in this sense was an underground, but the underground was the pathway to freedom and self-identification. Ellison, Wright, Baraka, and many others discussed in this book wrestle with various conceptualizations of the underground as a (w)hole space and these ruminations, are essential for the Black expressive urban realism that, in time, captures the imagination of the hip-hop Generation and certainly finds a "home" in intertextual connections to season 4 of *The Wire*.

(In)sight

Season 1 of *The Wire* features a version of "Way Down in the Hole" performed by the Five Blind Boys of Alabama (FBBA). Although this version of the song is not the original version, it is this interpretation that launches the series and elucidates several important initiate points. In addition, this song introduces an afro-blues spiritual impulse to *The Wire*. According to Cornel West, the "Afro-American spiritual-blues-impulse" consists of "polyphonic, rhythmic effects and antiphonal vocal techniques, of kinetic orality and affective physicality."[14] The *Afro-blues spiritual* modifier is an intertextual, originating reference point from which each version of "Way Down" might be categorized and considered. The *spiritual* component of the term underscores the content of the lyrics, which are fairly consistent across versions (glossed in greater detail below) and reflective upon archetypal Christian narratives in so much of African American music. The *blues* component of the term suggests both the laborious origins of the African American experience and the musical tenets articulated by and through that experience. The "antiphonal" (i.e., sung or chanted in alternation) vocal techniques, "kinetic orality," and "affective physicality"—that is, emotionally moving physical movement—also corroborate the ways in which blues performances are defined and described.[15] The "afro" descriptor constitutes a more complex aspect of the term. It refers to the "West African Roots" organized in Portia Maultsby's model, "African American music: its development." The "afro" designation also distinctly captures and/or refers to the percussive underpinnings of Black music.[16] Various forms of percussion, especially the drumbeat, pulsate at the core of spiritual and ritualistic practices throughout the continent of Africa. The "polyphonic, rhythmic effects" described by West thus point to an important conflation of the sacred in African percussive traditions with the secular in African American percussive and musical traditions. The "Afro-blues spiritual impulse" then enables us to articulate a starting point that captures the trajectories and coordinates through which various interpretations of "Way Down" might be organized and contextualized. Beginning the series of *The Wire* and the "Way Down(s)" with the FBBA thus makes musicological sense because, even though they are not the original writers or performers of the song, they represent the genre and a region from which the afro-blues spiritual expression of the African American experience emerges.

The Five Blind Boys of Alabama are gospel vocalists and musicians who, through the initial part of their career, sang only gospel music and performed for all-Black segregated audiences.[17] The group, and by extension their gospel-inflected or spiritually inflected performance, marks "Way Down 1." The tonal aspects of the Negro Spiritual infused in FBBA's gospel or spiritually based performance is a point of origin for African American music and the African American experience. The FBBA, who began performing in 1939, have remained true to their gospel roots but did eventually branch out as Black musical forms developed and fused and as gospel or spiritual themes and tonalities continued to inform various types of musical production.

Consider the 1930s and 1940s on Maultsby's model. The FBBA would have been considered a traditional gospel group since they formed in the late 1930s. Throughout the 1940s, the gospel quintet shared cross influences with rhythm and blues and urban blues, each serving to eventually spawn rock and roll, soul, and, by extension, various other forms and genres of African American music.

The FBBA made numerous conscious decisions to develop their recording and performative repertoire beyond their musical genre of origin. One such career-defining moment was the 1988 Broadway production of *The Gospel at Colonus*, which features Lee Breuer's lyrical reworking of Sophocles's *Oedipus Rex* and stars Morgan Freeman as the Preacher and Messenger, whose sermonic narrative is the rubric through which this intertextual version of the Oedipal narrative is rendered. In "*The Gospel at Colonus* (And Other Black Morality Plays)," Mimi D'Aponte refers to the play as a "gripping ritual drama" and "the interface between fifth-century B.C. Athenian text and twentieth-century Afro-American performance."[18] At one nexus of this intertextual interface, the FBBA perform the role of Oedipus's alter ego as a modern Greek chorus. According to D'Aponte, Breuer deliberately conflates and juxtaposes the Greek mythos of blindness with the poignant cultural significance of blindness in the African American musical tradition in jazz and the blues.[19] For the FBBA, this paradigm takes shape as their blindness allows them to ascribe to a mythological authenticity among Black musicians (consider Ray Charles and Stevie Wonder as more popular and recent examples of this), exemplified brilliantly when they portrayed a blind-men blues version of the Greek chorus in *The Gospel at Colonus*.

The intertextual significance of FBBA's version of "Way Down in the Hole" resides in the bluesy gospel delivery of the lyrics. The recorded vocals of Way Down 1 feature the diction, nuances in annunciation, and textured vibrato that listeners have come to associate with African American spiritual and gospel music. Yet the intertextual meaning of the lyrics (especially in certain lines) resonates with Christian narratives and themes of crime and street life in *The Wire,* and even draws from the African American literary canon. The opening line of "Way Down in the Hole" warns listeners who walk through "the garden" to watch their backs. This opening lyric engenders multiple meanings hinging on the pragmatic context of watching one's back and the biblical/mundane oppositional contexts of the word "garden."[20] A definitive meaning of garden is a space designated for growing plants, flowers, and vegetables. This mundane meaning of the term underscores the virtual absence of gardens across the urban landscape of Baltimore, but it is not this meaning that produces/yields the intertextuality within this line.

The biblical meaning of the garden as the site of the Fall in Genesis is a foundational intertext through which flow themes from the series and a telling example from Black literary history. Surely the "garden" of inner-city Baltimore is not the utopian garden of Genesis. It is a site, however, that is a backdrop of the fall of many characters within the storyworld of *The Wire*. In season 1, viewers are most privy to D'Angelo's near-Christian conflicted consciousness, but we should not lose sight of other instances of temptation throughout the season (or series, for that matter), such as Sergeant Ellis Carver and Officer Thomas "Herc" Hauk's desire to steal cash from criminals after an arrest and seizure or Officer James "Jimmy" McNulty's decision to manufacture homicide crime scenes in season 5. The complexity of moral conflict that the series tends to wrestle with throughout its five seasons is emblematized in D'Angelo Barksdale's narrative. Still, the power of the garden allusion to inform D'Angelo's character and other moral conflicts in the series stems from its recurring presence in African American literature as an allusive intertextual reference.

One such allusion is the "garden" episode in Frederick Douglass's classic slave narrative, *Narrative of the Life of Frederick Douglass, an American Slave*. In Chapter 3, Douglass briefly details an episode on Colonel Lloyd's plantation where slaves cultivate a beautiful garden: "This garden was probably the greatest attraction of the place. During the summer months, people came from far and near—from Baltimore, Easton, and Annapolis—to see it. It abounded in fruits of almost every description.... This garden was not the least source of trouble on the plantation."[21] The garden was a constant "source of trouble" because the slaves on the plantation were forbidden from eating any of its fruits. They were literally denied the fruits of their own labor. Moreover, the Christian narrative of temptation is also thematically present in Douglass's tone and word choice. The temptation of the abundant fruit in the garden on the plantation mirrors the material reality to which the denizens of the Street in the story world of *The Wire* do not have opportune access.[22] The temptation to steal that fruit then slips the viewing audience's moral judgment via the circumstantial social conditions of the slaves or, in the case of *The Wire*, some of the inhabitants of inner-city Baltimore. On Colonel Lloyd's plantation (coincidentally near Baltimore), Douglass is struck by the "master's" resourcefulness with respect to policing the garden that continues to tempt his slaves. Lloyd ultimately decides to tar the fence around the garden and instructs his chief gardener to whip any slave with the mark of tar on his or her person. According to Douglass, "this plan worked well; the slaves became as fearful of tar as of the lash. They seemed to realize the impossibility of touching *tar* without being defiled."[23]

Baltimore in *The Wire* is a "garden" rife with material temptation, depleted sociocultural resources, and utter lack of opportunity. In this environment, watching your back is an essential survival practice. Of course, "watching your back" is a colloquial phrase that figuratively signals a warning to look out for yourself. In the garden analogy/metaphor, the subject of the phrase is implored to be vigilant with respect to the devil's various temptations. In the more mundane sense in which the phrase operates in the storyworld of *The Wire*, the garden/Baltimore is an environment where one's social, economic, civic, and/or political life depends on the vigilant surveillance of one's surroundings, often peopled by enemies and allies who would do you harm. Those slaves unlucky enough to, in any way, get/have tar on them were summarily whipped—that is, lashed across the back, lending more critical credence to the admonition to watch it. For Larry Gilliard Jr.'s tragic Barksdale character, this lyrical warning ultimately proves its most critical sense when he is attacked from behind and strangled while in prison serving 20 years for his role in the family business.[24]

The FBBA's inability to watch their backs (at least not literally) reveals the potentially tragic irony facing even those who are the most vigilantly aware, those who watch their backs most studiously (consider Stringer Bell's fate at the conclusion of season 3 and/or the fate of Omar Little towards the end of season 5).[25] The vigilant watching of your back does not ultimately protect anyone in the storyworld of *The Wire*. This important thematic kernel is present in the first lines of the opening theme song of the series, and FBBA's performance of "Way Down 1" underscores it. After experiencing *The Gospel at Colonus*, poet Lucille Clifton authored a poem titled "Eyes" dedicated to "Clarence Fountain and The Five Blind Boys of Alabama after seeing *The Gospel at Colonus*."[26] Clifton lyrically ponders the performance of the FBBA and situates her rumination within a spiritual context that gestures toward the garden motif: "the fields of Alabama / sparkle in

the sun on broadway / five old men / sparkle in white suits / their
fingers light / on one another's back lights / proclaim The Five Blind
Boys / of Alabama five old men / black and blind / who have no
names save one / what ground is this / what god."[27]

The Original

"Way Down 2," opens each episode in season 2 of *The Wire*. Waits
wrote and recorded the song in 1986, and it appeared in 1987 as a
part of a dramatic production titled *Frank's Wild Years*.[28] This lyrical precursor tells the story of Frank, a used furniture salesman, who
is almost happily married but experiences the situational trap of his
modern working-class/middle-class station in life.[29] The play, *Frank's
Wild Years*, generally reflects the aesthetics of most of Tom Waits's
musical productions and songwriting.[30] Waits evidently is not interested in restaging the play, and because little or no video recording
of it exists, it is worth quoting him at some length to understand his
sense of the production. In a 1986 interview with *Spin* magazine,
Waits says:

> It actually starts out with Frank at the end of his rope, despondent,
> penniless, on a park bench in East St. Louis in a snowstorm, having
> a going-out-of-business sale on the whole last ten years of his life.
> Like the guys around here on Houston Street with a little towel on
> the sidewalk, some books, some silverware, a radio that doesn't work,
> maybe a Julie London album. Then he falls asleep and dreams his way
> back home. I've been saying that it's a cross between Eraserhead and
> *It's a Wonderful Life*.[31]

Both the lyrical Frank and the dramatic Frank are important characteristic touchstones for the narrator in *The Wire's* theme song. Frank is
an existentially challenged (blues) musician who must burn down the
material accouterments of his life in order to proceed into an afterlife or other life that, though rife with pain and socioeconomic challenges, still provides him with some hope and redemptive possibility
in the end. Given the bifurcated origins of the original version of the
tune, it makes sense that for the series it functions much like a standard that can and will be performed by multiple groups from multiple
nuanced perspectives.

Waits's "Way Down in the Hole" sports his potent working-
class blues delivery. This is a natural fit for the season that features

dockworkers in Baltimore struggling with (second-class) citizenship, crime, political invisibility, and general working-class warfare: "Mr. Waits is obsessed with America's low-life—the bars, the broads, the booze, the touts, the sleaze. His voice is variations on a gargle, half-conversational mutterings about life's disappointments and dreams. His songs are cast in a folkish, bluesy idiom."[32] Waits's "bluesy idiom" is readily audible in his recording of the song. Although it is the original, or sui generis, version of the tune, its position as the second version in the series is chronologically consistent with Maultsby's model for developments in African American music and West's sense of the afro-blues spiritual impulse. That is, the blues follows gospel in the development of the African American experience and developments in African American music (and oral/folk expression more generally). This proximity, of the blues to the spiritual, underscores the ways in which secular expression in African American musical forms functions along the continuum of an afro-blues spiritual impulse and thus the narratives of the Black experience; even those that appear to be consumed by socially institutionalized subject matter, such as that of *The Wire*, always already have Black spirituality as an inherent predicate.

Waits's vocal performance and the accompanying musical production reflect the Delta blues aesthetics: "The Delta blues of the 1920s and 1930s are the most homogeneous blues products associated with any of the pre-war, regionally defined blues traditions. It was usually a solo music which was dominated by rhythmic (and at its best polyrhythmic) repetition, deep gravely vocals and bottleneck guitar playing."[33] The vocalized form of Waits's "gravely" or "gargle"-like delivery both suggests an authentic folk style and underscores a spiritual longing that suits the lyrical content of the tune. Tom Waits's bluesy, spiritually inflected singing voice might (to many listeners) sound like the archetypal Black blues singer. In his essay "Why Do Whites Sing Black?" Mike Daley explores this phenomenon and qualifies this trace of authenticity: "The discourse of folk authenticity can be traced back at least as far as the nineteenth-century Romantics, inasmuch as it articulates a longing for a fantasized lost innocence—as if the folk society is a reflection of the modern culture 'before the fall,' as it were."[34] Waits is not Black, but his voice is, according to nearly all critical consensus, authentic in its articulation of a folk ethos.

One laudatory essay on the music and vocal styles of Tom Waits is titled "The Flying Slaves." This title alludes to a foundational African American folktale and its various attendant African mythologies. In the most common version of the folktale "The People Could Fly," a mysterious old man approaches various field slaves who have been brutalized by a vicious overseer. He whispers something in the ear of each, and they are subsequently able to fly away.[35] The folktale is related to myths of flying Africans, the concept of death as liberation or transcendence, and a mass suicide committed by a group of Igbo captives who refused to be slaves. According to the author of the essay, Stephan Wackwitz, "Tom Waits gets close to the archaic experience of liberation—the experience of flying away from death."[36] The "flying slaves" essay attempts to explicate the work of Waits by generating an intertextual relationship between Waits's music and one of the earliest African American folktale narratives. The intertext that connects Waits to certain African American cultural foundations is, in this case, not the blues—not the "Negro spiritual" or other forms of Black music along the afro-blues spiritual impulse to which Waits pays artistic homage. The intertextual relationship rests on the liberation themes that anchor the spiritualized folk aesthetics in Waits's music. Waits celebrates this intertextuality in his oeuvre, in his music, in a variety of ways (and means): H e articulates the style(s) of the folk: "Stylization, sweeping gestures, grandiosity, mannerisms, as emblems of a weakness that can't be expressed any other way: these are the formal gestures Tom Waits has inscribed into his figures and songs. They are the big gestures of the small people."[37] Waits also often combines blues aesthetics with spiritual or religious reflection: "Blues musicians themselves, as well as scholars, have noted the affinity of the blues and religion. The resemblance between blues performance and ritual has led Black theologian James Cone to refer to blues as 'secular spirituals.'"[38] The sacred and the profane regularly intersect in his lyrics: "The cities through which Tom Waits' figures move might be Heaven and Hell."[39] Lastly, through his music Waits is invested in both sociopolitical and spiritual liberation. Wackwitz is, again, incisive: "The aesthetic of the escape in the face of death and power is at the center of Tom Waits' songs."[40]

In Waits's music, "Jesus and the Devil pass by us in regular beats—as does death."[41] In fact, the refrain for all versions of "Way Down in the Hole" instructs listeners to keep the devil way down in the hole. Not unlike the "garden" in the first lines of the song, the "devil" in the refrain engenders multiple meanings and a distinct intertextuality with African American spirituality and cultural history. The literal or standard meaning of the devil is Satan, Lucifer, or the ruler of Hell. The standard devil certainly holds its meaning in "Way Down 2" based upon its existential origins in the song and play, "Frank's Wild Years." The traditional meaning of devil here also underscores the religious or spiritual aspect of the afro-blues spiritual impulse within which each version of "Way Down" is artistically rendered. But at least two other meanings of devil should be considered here. Historically, the founders and several leaders of the Nation of Islam (NOI), including Elijah Muhammed, a young, pre-Mecca Malcolm X and retired minister Louis Farrakhan, have often referred to the White man as the devil.[42] Although an elaborate mythos, NOI religious narrative and Black sociopolitical history accompany this meaning of devil, it is not nearly as conventional within the Black community as it was at the zenith of the NOI during the civil rights movement. The NOI meaning of the devil as the White man is not necessarily maintained (or does not necessarily emerge) in *The Wire* series. Instead, the meaning of the devil in *The Wire* that is most relevant is actually a tertiary meaning in most dictionaries: something that is unruly or difficult to control. In the series, this could take on many meanings across various episodes and seasons, but the devil that is most pervasive (and often backgrounded) is the devil of addiction. Characters in the series were addicted to money and power (Avon Barksdale, Marlo Stanfield, Mayors Royce, and Carcetti), and alcohol (Jimmy McNulty and various other police). However, drug addiction centers the narrative on the underground economy of the illegal drug trade throughout much of the series. Drug addiction is the devil that must be kept in the hole or at bay for too many folk in the storyworld of *The Wire*, but this struggle is most readily apparent in the narrative of Bubbles.

In many ways, Tom Waits's music and the song "Way Down in the Hole" are aesthetically suited to the themes of the series—no surprise there. The creators of maybe the best show ever written and produced for television picked an apropos opening theme song. Each version sheds some light on how the lyrical nuances of the original song construct a powerful cultural valence with the show and sometimes with particular seasons and or characters. Waits's ability both musically and in his performative persona, to represent and reflect fugitive culture then helps to seal the sociocultural and spiritual intertextualities within the show, as well as between the show and numerous forms of African American cultural production: "The term, fugitive culture, designates less a rigid cultural formation than it does a conflicting

and dynamic set of experiences rooted in a working-class youth culture marked by flows and uncertain interventions into daily life."[43]
Fugitive culture includes the folk of the criminal underground ruled
first by the Barksdales and eventually by Marlo Stanfield, the workers at the Port, the children in the school system, and the citizens of
inner-city Baltimore. Within the storyworld of *The Wire*, the writers/
creators are able to express the trauma of those "uncertain interventions" that dog the existence of their characters.

Musical Fusion

"Way Down 3" then lies at a center within the afro-blues spiritual mapping of the various seasonal versions of Tom Waits's tune. The Neville
Brothers (of New Orleans) recorded and perform a New Orleans jazz-
styled interpretation of "Way Down": "The New Orleans sound...is
actually based on a particular rhythmic feeling, a certain syncopation
or 'backbeat' that seems to have been infused into the city's collective unconscious and which no doubt can be traced beyond parade
music to slaves dancing in Congo Square."[44] The mapped connection
between the New Orleans percussive sound and the experience of
enslaved Africans in America interlocks Giroux's fugitive culture with
slave culture. The visual accouterments and reflections of the culture
include a variety of kinesthetic communal celebrations and rituals,
including the Mardi Gras celebration. The music encourages constant
movement in response to its syncopated rhythms. Thus, it embodies the
"affective physicality" component of the afro-blues spiritual impulse.
The afro-percussive roots of the New Orleans sound also serve as a
pool of musical resource for go-go music. Cultivated in the metropolitan Washington, DC, area by Chuck Brown in the middle to late
1970s, go-go music features a syncopated backbeat laden with both
hip-hop and funk-styled vocals and instrumentation: "Go-go's essential beat is characterized by a syncopated, dotted rhythm that consists
of a series of quarter and eighth notes...which is underscored most
dramatically by the bass drum and snare drum, and the hi-hat... [and]
is ornamented by the other percussion instruments, especially by the
conga drums, timbale, and hand-held cowbells."[45] Musically and per-
cussively, the sound of the Neville Brothers' version of "Way Down
in the Hole" is animated by its fusion-oriented form and its aesthetic
intertextuality between the New Orleans sound and go-go music.
Once again, when the lyrics are taken into account (i.e., considering

the song as a whole), "Way Down in the Hole" powerfully captures each signal component of the afro-blues spiritual impulse in African American music.

That the Neville Brothers contribute this selection (for this season of *The Wire*) is not completely coincidental or disconnected from the thematic underpinnings of the show. In George Lipsitz's essay on the Mardi Gras Indians, "Carnival and Counter-Narrative in Black New Orleans," he explicates the fusion of African and Native American culture in the form of music and the ritual (and rituals in) the parade. The Neville brothers are related to a tribe that performs regularly in New Orleans, and Lipsitz cites Art Neville as remembering "music as a viable alternative to gang fighting in the public housing project where he grew up in the 1940s and 1950s."[46] There is no indication that music is a viable alternative to violence in the storyworld of *The Wire*.[47] But Lipsitz suggests that Neville's recollection links various African American communal-musical practices across region, genre, and history.[48] He quotes Cyril Neville as saying, "The drum comes to me as a symbol of what I, or we, used to be. I can't speak on the drums, but I try to convey my feelings. . . . [M]y Africa is the drums 'cause when I feel like going back to Africa, I play my drums."[49] The syncopated percussion in the Neville Brothers' "Way Down in the Hole" links the afro-blues aesthetic to the New Orleans sound and to the region-specific sounds of go-go music and thus helps to center this version within the afro-blues spiritual trajectory or Black musical mapping of the show's theme.

"Way Down in the Hole" also subtly (re)connects the theme music to the themes inherent in season 3 of the series. The season's themes of innovation, transition, and collaboration or fusion are also present in the musical coordinates on Maultsby's model that designate the areas within which the New Orleans and go-go sounds exist in the developments of African American music.[50] As an additional point of fiction-nonfiction intertextuality, Slim Charles (a denizen of the Street) is played by Anwan Glover. Slim begins season 3 as an enforcer for the Barksdale organization. As the battle between the Barksdale organization and Marlo's insurgency continues, Slim attempts to organize and innovate the Barksdale crew but to little or no avail. Eventually Barksdale is arrested, and Slim fortuitously avoids incarceration and is almost immediately recruited into Joseph "Prop Joe" Stewart's organization. By the series' conclusion, Slim emerges as the head of New Day, the series' central criminal co-op. Anwan Glover is also known as

"Big G," a founding member and vocal front man for the go-go musical group Backyard Band. Because go-go music is generally regional, most viewers of *The Wire* outside of the metropolitan Washington, DC, area would not have recognized Slim as a go-go music star; that he is a local go-go sensation is only one example (among many) of where the creators of *The Wire* blur the boundaries between storyworld and reality in order to render an affective realism in the series. Slim/Big G's pivotal role in season 3 accentuates the intertextual relationship between "Way Down 3," the themes of season 3, and the various forms of music flowing through "Way Down 3" that are generated via the afro-blues spiritual impulse.

Full Circle

Steve Earle performs the fifth and final version of the theme. This version is a modern country version of the song, and Earle is an accomplished, award-winning country music singer and songwriter. Country music is a fusion of popular music forms emerging out of the Southern United States, including folk music and gospel music. Although it is technically not considered a part of the afro-blues spiritual impulse or documented or charted in the Maultsby model of African American musical development, country music and many of its subgenres—bluegrass, rock and roll, and Southern rock—are all influenced by the afro-blues spiritual aesthetic, and certainly some of the subgenres can claim space on the map of Black musical forms. Steve Earle's success as a musician and his recurring role on the series make his recording a natural fit for the final season of *The Wire*.

Steve Earle is also a recovering drug addict, and in *The Wire* he plays Walon, who is in recovery but lends his considerable skills as a drug reform/recovery coach to work with Bubbles, who is tragically addicted to heroin. As Bubbles's scruffy Narcotics Anonymous sponsor, Walon leverages his own painful past to help others clean up their lives. His gentle hand with Bubs has firmed up over the past year, though, and Walon is losing patience with his friend's treading water in the program. By the end of season 4, Bubbles is committed to a psychiatric institution after he attempts to hang himself while in police custody. He is distraught for many reasons, including losing the battle with his addiction, but in a failed attempt to poison a brutal bully in the neighborhood he mistakenly kills Sherrod, a close friend and street mentee of his, with whom he builds an intimate relationship over the course of the season. For viewers, Bubbles's narrative is the most personal reflection of "the hole" and/or "the devil" as signifiers of addiction and the perils of unabated substance abuse in the raw naturalistic environs of inner-city America. Knowing that Earle struggled in ways similar to Walon and Bubs is an important intertextual narrative connecting the series to lived realities of its actors.

In season 5, Bubbles becomes more committed to his recovery, and by extension he is more receptive to Walon's sponsorship and guidance. He gets a job selling newspapers and is able to convince his sister to allow him to stay at her home. She is very reluctant and only agrees to allow him to stay in the basement. He is thus restricted to the sublevel or "hole" of the home. Throughout season 5, Bubbles is able to stay clean and in some ways redeem himself in his own eyes. Eventually, Walon's efforts and his firm support results in Bubs's own recovery in the series finale. This recovery is signaled in the closing montage of the series when Bubbles emerges from the basement and joins his family at the dining-room table. That Bubs overcomes his devils and emerges from the hole are important signifiers of the themes in "Way Down 1–5" and subtle statements made in the finale.

The critically acclaimed historical novel by David Bradley, *The Chaneysville Incident*, features a professor of history as a protagonist who struggles with the complexities of race, region, and history as they relate to his family and the cultural lineage to which he is bound. In an early analysis of societal institutions, the protagonist states: "The Church justifies the actions of the State, the State the teachings of the School, the School the principles of the Economy, the Economy the pronouncements of the State."[51] According to the protagonist of the narrative, societal institutions tend to conceal any agendas so that they might more effectively control the populace. While much has been made of the institutional themes of *The Wire*, many have noted that one institution is obviously lacking from the creators' analysis and treatment: the institution of the Black Church. I contend that the series marginalizes Black spirituality within its paratextual matter. Sometimes this matter is presented through the title and credit sequences that unveil the real people behind the dramatic performances, and other times it rests in the versions of the theme song and each version's attendant genre distinctions and the aesthetic choices made by the artists performing the song. Through my intertextual analyses of Tom Waits's "Way Down in the Hole," certain spiritual and literary themes emerge in the atmosphere of the show.

The themes of insightfulness and working-class struggle are both spiritually rendered and regenerated through the dramatic intertextualities of "Way Down 1" and "Way Down 2" with the lyrics of the song
as well as the plays that function intertextually with the lives and artistic products of the FBBA and Tom Waits. The Black underground and
literary intertextuality of "Way Down 1–4" also underscores certain
spiritual narratives and themes within the show, such as the *garden*,
the *devil*, and the *hole*. The song then, through its ability to exist as an
interwoven pattern in the fabric of Black musical history, production,
and development, encroaches upon the institutional space that might
be normally reserved for the Church, at least in the storyworld of *The
Wire*. That is, the multiple versions of "Way Down in the Hole" provide a repository of spiritual and literary intertextuality that suggests
ways in which it might stand in for *The Wire's* missing institution: the
Church. This is in some ways cemented by the mimesis and intertex-
ted fictive and nonfictive elements of Walon (vis-à-vis Steve Earle),
Bubbles, and certain interpretations of "Way Down 5." Thus, what
many have referred to as (or crowned as) the best show on television
has/had in many ways the most textured and textual theme song that
a show of such vaunted praise might have. And although the Church
does not exist in the storyworld of *The Wire* to the extent that the
Street, the Law, the School or the Port do, it is subtly and powerfully
present in each version of Tom Waits's "Way Down in the Hole."

THE IRONIES UNDERGROUND: REVOLUTION, CRITICAL MEMORY, AND BLACK NOSTALGIA

The central concept of the underground is that of revolution. The Underground Railroad sought to subvert and ultimately overthrow the slaveocracy. The Black literary undergrounds of Richard Wright, Ralph Ellison, and Amiri Baraka, all sought to articulate and/ or depict the psyche of a Black revolutionary in the ultimate signifying space underground, a space that facilitates the subversion of White supremacy. The hip-hop underground signifies on much of this historical, political, and literary energy. Gil Scott Heron's "The Revolution Will Not Be Televised" is situated at the intersection of these intersections. This poem, a precursor to hip-hop culture and rap in many ways, provides the touchstone from which certain ironies of the underground unfold in the public sphere. "The Revolution Will Not Be Televised" employs commercial references to explore the lure of consumer culture on the collective conscious of Black folk. Television is the media that produces the imagery and celebrates the popular trinkets that distract people from their revolutionary objectives. In a prolific referential array of popular commercial products, Heron creates a timeless sense of advertising and marketing as the dominant modes of communication in capitalist culture. This germ finds its most frightening realization in the emphatically repeated lines: "There will be no pictures of pigs shooting down brothers on the instant replay." Images of "pigs shooting down brothers" is in the center of Heron's list of commercial products (e.g., mouthwash, makeup, or diet supplements) advertising themselves in television-style commercial barrage. This particular image in the list of ads suggests the destructive inclinations of capitalist media. In addition to the poetic irony of Heron's instant replay of this line, the mimetic reflections with the FOX TV show, *Cops*, which featured an endless barrage of police officers arresting Black and latino men, resonate with us now as much as his direct references to media-slanted images of urban riots, circa 1970.[1] "There will be no pictures of you and Willie Mae pushing that shopping cart down the block on the dead run or trying to slide that color t.v. in a stolen ambulance." Heron brilliantly interweaves revolution, with his critique of the ill-affects of the television, with his discursive erasure (there will be none) of the image of rioters stealing televisions. Unfortunately there have been images of rioters stealing televisions. The media coverage of the 1992 LA riots, much of the political discourses in the Obama era, as well as some of the coverage of the George Zimmerman and Michael Dunn trials reflects the marketing potential in racial divisiveness.[2] Part of the potential of Heron's political masterpiece is that it references time-sensitive commercial images, but its intent to incite action and think-ing produces prophetic images of late(r) urban America. Reading/ Hearing of his poem in 2014 is as relevant an experience as hearing in 1970. The mainstream release of "The Revolution…" is merely five years before the seeds of hip-hop culture are sprouting. Its form (spoken word with musical accompaniment) is the progenitor for rap music. Its content utterly embodies the discursive subjects of hip-hop culture. Rap music (which vocalizes much of the discourse in hip-hop culture) has struggled with its television-like ability to promote and disseminate images, ideas, and commercial products in the public sphere. Because Heron effectively targets commercial culture he estab-lishes the archetypal struggle between the mainstream and the under-ground, between conscious or enlightened content versus Dionysian, violent, sexist content in the lyrics of rap music. The "underground" in hip-hop culture is allegedly wedded to consciousness and enlighten-ment while the mainstream conspicuously consumes shallow content in rap music. "The Revolution Will Not Be Televised" anticipates and expresses the lyrical content in Grand Master Flash and the Furious Five, Kurtis Blow, KRS One (BDP era), Public Enemy, Wu-Tang, Blackalicious, and Dead Prez. This poem initiates discursive content in rap music at the same time that it figuratively predicts the form's inherent engagement with popular commercial culture and the willful resistance to that culture, the mainstream versus the underground in and through the public sphere.

In the opening essay of a collection of articles about the Black Public Sphere (titled *The Black Public Sphere*), Houston A. Baker Jr. defines crit-ical memory as "the very faculty of revolution. Its operation implies a continuous arrival at turning points. Decisive change, usually attended by considerable risk, peril or suspense, always seems imminent."[3] Baker contrasts critical memory with nostalgia, which is a "purposive construction of a past filled with golden virtues, golden men and sterling events. [Nostalgia] writes the revolution as a well passed aberration [and] it actively substitutes allegory for history."[4] He posits this paradigm as a productive means to evaluate the public sphere. In this epilogue I briefly extend this evaluation and focus it on the intersections between hip-hop culture and certain aspects of basketball culture. I have not paired these realms of the public sphere arbitrarily. From an ethnographic, cultural studies perspective, hip-hop culture is basketball and vice versa. The writers (McCall, Wideman, etc.) and the artists (Gil Scott Heron and Snoop Dogg) referenced herein, all either indirectly or directly attest to the inextricable connections between basketball and hip-hop culture. It is within the discourse about hip-hop culture and basketball that a critical memory of history can be exercised. Ultimately this juxtaposition yields insights concerning the confusion created by nostalgia and nostalgic memories of "the Revolution."

Basketball is currently enjoying the benefits of thriving in (and spurring) the fast pace of our information age—the right now, slam dunk immediacy that has infiltrated America's collective psyche. In the last decade or more, basketball icons have enjoyed dominant status in sports media. Even beyond the 1990s throwback jersey trends, Basketball does not need nostalgia yet. The sense of "home," integral to Dr. Baker's suggestion that "homesickness" is the conceptual core of nostalgia, is globally dispersed across countries, continents, classes, cultures, and gender.[5] The worldwide popularity of basketball and America's (relatively) recent infatuation with it mirror a general American shift (especially with respect to economics) toward global perspectives.[6]

Hip-hop culture has enjoyed a similar global development. If economic globalization refers to an erasure of regulations in trade and commerce between nations then the globalization of hip-hop refers to the unfettered cultural exchange and hip-hop commerce between nations. Similar to the recent trends in globalization, the spread of hip-hop around the world appears very healthy for hip-hop in many ways, but beneath the surface of these developments the identity of Black Americans has been commodified. Ronin Ro's ethnographic account of his experiences on tour with Luther Campbell in Japan has already underscored this phenomenon. According to him Luke's Japanese interpreter, Itomi, claims: "They (japanese b-boys) are catching on... They're goin in for the fashion, wearing those caps, sneakers, T-shirts, long shorts. Many kids think hip-hop is a very Black culture so they tan themselves; they go to tanning salons and perm their hair very strong to look like a brother. The language barrier is the only thing that gets in the way. They learn some words but they can't really understand... Youth sought their identities in a Black American music culture, clinging to hip-hop's more superficial aspects and consciously overlooking its political intentions."[7] Of course, this account does not describe the complete picture of hip-hop in Japan, but it presents a perception of hip-hop that explains its commercial outgrowth and underscores its potential for globalization.

Critical memory is the tool through which commercial and revolutionary tensions in hip-hop culture or baskeball (i.e., young Black male culture) can be defined and explored. Critical memory is not simply a sense of homelessness or a globally oriented perspective. As the inherent power of revolution, critical memory is the point guard for consciousness in the postmodern hip-hop world. "It judges severely, censures righteously, renders hard ethical evaluations of the past that it never defines as well-passed."[8] In order to accurately determine what role young Black male culture can have in a post–civil rights revolution in America (or any other postcolonial revolutionary directive), the discourse on young Black male culture must resist nostalgic tendencies and confused notions of revolution. The pitfalls of these tendencies will bare themselves out below. An important employment of critical memory is the use and understanding of the vernacular and a working knowledge of the difference between standard and vernacular contexts (i.e., an underground understanding). I use the term vernacular here, as I have throughout this book, to attempt to describe the languages (or dialects) and cultures that vary from American Standard English and mainstream culture. More importantly though, vernaculars vary more rapidly and more widely than Standards; Standard language forms are protected against too much variance by numerous forces, including mainstream media and education, especially textbooks. A standard requires nostalgia whereas a vernacular thrives on critical memory.

In a collection of essays titled *Yo' Mama's Disfunktional...*, historian, Robin D. G. Kelley explicates this tension:

> When we compare graffiti with basketball, it is interesting to note that the latter does not lose its street credentials once individuals take their

skills into more bourgeois, institutionalized contexts. . . . The different
responses to sports and graffiti, I believe, are linked to the very nature
of sports as a spectacle of performing bodies.[9]

Kelley's observation suggests that performing bodies communicate the
vernacular in ways that art (graffiti), music (rap), or language (African
American English—AAE) cannot, outside of some semblance of their
vernacular contexts.[10] Most languages (vernaculars included) do not
directly translate into other languages. This effect can be exacerbated
by changes in context. Vernacular basketball may be resistant to these
contextual shifts because athletic bodies convey a distinctly spectacular
representation of African American Culture, a vernacular slam dunk,
if you will. Regardless of this assured authenticity, the *discourse* on
basketball is susceptible to the aforementioned problems of translation.
In some basketball-related sports writing, and in certain documentary
films, this susceptibility to lose one's street credentials upon entering
"more bourgeois, institutionalized contexts" (i.e., the Academy and
its mainstream presses) plays itself out in concert with the rhetorical
dynamic between nostalgia and critical memory.

Nathan McCall details his personal experience of witnessing a group
of nonathletic White men beat some "supercool brothers" on a public
court. McCall's essay titled "The Revolution Is About Basketball"
blasts various ad campaigns that trap African American men into plac-
ing too much emphasis on the importance of basketball.

> When I was a teen, my buddies and I often listened to a popular
> rap called "The Revolution Will Not be Televised." Back then, that
> record filled us with the hope that one day we'd rise up from life's
> sewer and kick whitey's ass. Little did we know that our long awaited
> revolution would one day be reduced to commercial breaks. . . . It's
> no wonder they walked around believing that. . . BASKETBALL IS
> LIFE! It's no wonder you hear so many folks humming the tune to
> the hoops theme song, popularized by the Penny Hardaway doll:
> "They're playin' baaskettbaalll!/We love that baa-sket-baal!"[11]

Note the nostalgic tone in McCall's recollection of the Gil Scott
Heron tune (re)popularized by the public backlash following Nike's
commercial adaptation of "The Revolution Will Not Be Televised."
McCall's nostalgic recollection of he and his buddies listening to Gil
Scott Heron and eagerly awaiting revolution cannot be rectified with
the gun-toting gangsters who gang-rape girls in his autobiography,

Makes Me Wanna Holler.[12] He compliments this inconsistency with the allegorical figure of Lil' Penny who may have popularized the aforementioned basketball theme, but the credit for that tune belongs to Kurtis Blow. McCall is simply not critical enough in the presentation of his revolutionary remembrances. And ultimately, he does not offer any productive insight into the problems that he sees in how we view basketball. He does not show that he has a grasp on the mentalities of the young Black men he is so quick to indict as mindless television-entranced cronies who think they can jump just because Mike can.

Kelley, on the other hand, works to demonstrate how the standard concept of play permutates into work. "The pursuit of leisure, pleasure, and creative expression is labor, and...some African American youth have tried to turn that labor into cold hard cash."[13] Through a highly accurate vernacular lens, Kelley reveals an overlap of the deep structural meanings of play and work for some African American youth. This type of vernacular accuracy speaks to the importance of linguistic proficiency in the critical discourse that deals with a sport that has been and continues to be shaped by young Black people.

John Edgar Wideman's use of the vernacular in writing about basketball has also produced an interesting interpretation of one of the most visible former players in the NBA, Dennis Rodman. "'Taint'...was their way of contracting 'it ain't' to one emphatic beat, a sound for saying 'it is not' in African American Vernacular, but also for saying much more depending on tone, timing, and inflection...[Dennis] Rodman embodies 'taint'" (Wideman 94).[14] Wideman informs his perspective with a vernacularity and style matched only by the subjects with whom he is concerned. And unlike McCall's observatory stance, Wideman is an ethnographer who speaks from within the frame of study. "On the playgrounds of Pittsburgh, where I learned the game, we had a word for gawkish, all elbows and knees, one-dimensional-game, raw-boned hurry-with-no-finesse chumps who must be somebody's country cousin wetbacked into our sleek city run...'cockstrong.'" According to Wideman, Rodman is "cockstrong" and "cocksure." He plays with our notions about gender as readily as he challenges our cultural investment in the game of basketball. "Maybe that's what really scares, outrages, and entertains us about Dennis Rodman. He dons the uniform, takes the paycheck, but doesn't exactly go to work. He enters a zone where play is not reducible to anything else" (Wideman 95).

Kelley's suggestive analysis (in tandem with John Wideman's analysis of Dennis Rodman) almost obscures the extraordinary development of basketball and hip-hop culture to mainstream culture. "Hip-hop's appeal to white youth extends the refashioning of mainstream America by black popular culture. From sports to fashion, from music to film, innovations in American art owe a debt to the creativity of black culture. For example, 25 years ago, it was unimaginable that black basketball stars would make television commercials or have sneakers named after them."[15] Certainly NBA stars of the likes of LeBron James or Kevin Durant make this assertion by Michael Eric Dyson all the more poignant. He relates his experience testifying before the United States Senate Judiciary Committee's Subcommittee on Juvenile Justice as a heroic defense of hip-hop culture's gangsta rap at the time embodied by rapper Snoop Dogg. "Snoop was made to appear like Hiphop's Mephistopheles, seducing...children to trade their souls for the corrupt delights of 'G-Funk.'" Since then, Snoop has continued to thrive in entertainment by reinventing his image as a conveyor of the nostalgic impulse in hip-hop and popular culture toward the 1970s represented by the music or presence of funk icons George Clinton and Bootsy Collins. Co-starring with Pam Grier in *Bones* and with Dr. Dre in *The Wash* (which signifies on the 1970s' cult classic *Car Wash*) provide some of the imagery to go along with the funkadelic-inflected sound tracks. A key step in Snoop's career extending process toward nostalgia is his Nike basketball commercial featuring himself, George Clinton, and Bootsy Collins, all in Parliament-funkadelic gear and flanked by partying NBA and WNBA stars dressed in full 1970s' fashionable attire. Snoop's staying power derives from his connection to the nostalgia for the 1970s; most recently he changed his name to Snoop Lion and recorded an album in homage to Bob Marley. Ironically, Michael Eric Dyson's snapshot of Snoop finds him on the "short end" of the Black nostalgic stick, as after he defends Snoop before congress ("the music and its artists are complex...they must be understood in both their cultural and racial settings...") he is accused of being a "dumb ass." Dyson reads this personal assault on himself as a manifestation of the misunderstanding inherent in Black nostalgia. Some of these misunderstandings include remembering Black communities as idyllic utopias prior to the hip-hop generation. "Nostalgia is colored memory. It is romantic remembering. It recreates as much as it recalls."[16] Snoop's turn toward the 1970s reflects his artistic roots, but it also makes him more palatable to the public than his gang-banging Crip-Image. His 1970s' image is inherently romantic and in it he can couch his sexually exploitive narratives without drawing as much attention to himself as he did with narratives like "murder was the case that they gave me." According to Dyson, the prominence of hip-hop culture inspires a deep-seeded Black nostalgia for an indeterminable time when Black communities were more conscious and community-motivated.

There is a range of discourses that inform this epilogue's out-take. Many of them can be situated within the practical and theoretical connections among various formations of the concept of the underground throughout African American cultural history. In the 1990s there was some discussion in the Black Public Sphere regarding KRS's voiceover for the (in)famous 1996 Nike commercial, in which he performs an arguably capitalistic revision of Gil Scott Heron's "The Revolution Will Not Be Televised." Some argued that KRS One disrespected the politically charged content of the original, authentic Heron version. The sense of nostalgia for the "revolutionary '60s" resides in these responses: "How could KRS One, in cahoots with Nike, suggest that the revolution will be televised or that the revolution is about basketball?!" Others argued that perhaps we aren't critical enough in our understanding of Black History. Perhaps we have to challenge the authenticity and/or revolutionary praxis in the publishing, production, sale and distribution of the original recording. Both arguments were important to the discussion so I went through the normal journalistic routes to secure an interview with Gil Scott Heron about the commercial, the revolution, and basketball. The following are excerpts from our conversation recorded on July 7, 1998.

JP: Can I tell you a little bit about myself and about the project?
GSH: Yeah. If you feel that that would enhance it.
JP: Yeah. I think it will. My name is James Peterson. I'm from Newark, New Jersey, and I'm at the University of Pennsylvania. I'm working on a PhD.
GSH: Okay.
JP: My project is about the concept of the underground; from the underground railroad in slavery to the underground of hip-hop. [I was asked] to do piece on basketball and hip-hop. And I immediately thought of KRS One and the Nike commercial and I wanted to talk to you about that Nike commercial, about your work, and about what you think about hip-hop culture and basketball and how those

things are starting to come together in some ways today. So, I just wanted you to talk freely about any of those things. My main, specific question is have you spoken to KRS One at all about the commercial or what your thoughts are about that Nike commercial.

GSH: I worked with him on it.

JP: Can you tell me about that process?

GSH: We were in the studio on Green Street.

JP: Okay.

GSH: I was called and made aware of the fact that the music from that tune was gonna be used for a Nike commercial that would be produced down there and that I would be involved with it. People thought I should be involved with it since they were rewriting the words.

JP: [Laughter]

GSH: See that particular tune does not belong to my publishing company. So I did not have an option one way or the other in terms of whether or not it was used. But since it was gonna be used, I had an option as to whether or not I should be involved to see how it was gonna be used. A copy of the script was sent to me. I went over it. Took a look at it. And [I] played basketball both in High School and College.

JP: Oh! Okay.

GSH: And followed the people (particularly in the Washington area) because I lived there for so long and taught at Federal City College and at Johns Hopkins before I left there. And [I] knew Coach [John] Thompson and some of the other people down there. And [I] saw how it was being put together and really admired the cats they were puttin' on the commercial.

JP: That's right.

GSH: As Young... as a whole new squad [that] I believed they would develop to be with Jason Kidd, Joe Smith...

JP: I think Kevin Garnett was on there.

GSH: Right. That's going to be the all-star five in a couple of years.

JP: No question.

GSH: Kris (KRS ONE) is not that familiar with basketball. And he does not keep up with it like that and so what he needed more than anything else was some way to work the names and the attitude that they were trying to put together to syncopate the shit. And that's what I tried to help with.

JP: So you actually worked on the commercial. You know a lot of people don't know that. So when you first saw the script, what was your response to it. You were positive about it?

GSH: I was positive they were going to do it because it was not my publishing.

But it was nice of the people who published it to call me.

JP: No question.

GSH: And tell me that it was going to be done.

JP: Did you get a chance to meet KRS One?

GSH: We worked with them in the studio. We were there and [we] saw how it was done and tried to help shape it. Since it wasn't my words, I didn't have that much of an attitude towards it at all other than the fact that I enjoy basketball and I like the cats that they were talking about and [I] like KRS.

JP: Let me reproduce for you some of the conversations that have happened in response to the commercial. Some people (who may not know that you were involved with the production) think KRS One was out of control using those words to talk about basketball. They say the revolution is not about basketball.

GSH: Well...young folks are about revolution and basketball is a part of their culture. And a lot of the people that they admire and will admire and have admired were basketball players...from the time Kareem Jabar was the best man at my wedding. [Laughter] He introduced me to my wife. There's nothing alien as far as I'm concerned about basketball at all. Its ours. We let them play every once in a while [laughter].

JP: Another question: is basketball more like hip-hop or more like Jazz?

GSH: Basketball is a separate thing altogether. My father was a professional soccer player. I don't consider soccer as a part of the culture he was livin' in. He played for Celtics and was the first Black player to play in Scotland.

JP: Wow.

GSH: I think that we have to learn to separate our art and our athletics and our disciplines because we go different ways. That's what freedom is. Having the choices to go and...

JP: ...do different things.

GSH: You know they wasn't lettin' nobody like us in the University of Pennsylvania not too long ago [laughter].

JP: That's right.

GSH: So now we can jam on it together if we want to, but if we do it negates the things that a lot of folks did to make those things possible. We ignore the sacrifices that were made to make certain things possible if we do not acknowledge them as such. So what we're doing with our academic potential, athletic potential, and artistic potential, all of that is owed to various people who made certain sacrifices to make it possible, but they're not the same thing.

JP: Okay. Who are some of your favorite basketball players?

GSH: Oh. I got a bunch of them [laughter].

JP: Go ahead and name them all.

GSH: Now that I'm living in New York—I've been in New York for 3 or 4 years. I'm a Knicks fan now so just put down the Knicks and roll with that.

JP: [Laughter] Okay.

GSH: Before I came back here, wherever I lived, that's the team that I check out. Now I was born in Chicago, but I ain't goin' back that far to get a team to root for [laughter]. When the Knicks were eliminated I started to root for Chicago 'cause I'm from Chicago and it goes like that when they play Utah [laughter] I was definitely for Chicago.

JP: Everybody is against Utah.

GSH: I don't guess everybody is. I was not against Utah I was for Chicago.

People can look at it that way if they want to—that they're against somebody. But I don't look at it as an "against" I look at it as a "for." And I was for Chicago and I'm glad I was for them [laughter].

JP: To see them win?

GSH: Yeah. I'm glad to see that cause I like the effort that they put forth.

JP: No question. Just a couple more NBA-type questions. What's your take on the lock out?

GSH: It's business strategy. If you see it coming then it ain't no shock. And they announced in terms of what they was going to do and the players union knows what they're trying to do. It is a union-management thing. I'm a union member myself, so I'll speak on it like that. I belong to a union. That's what I'm tryin' to say.

The most intriguing information that I learned from this interview was that Mr. Scott-Heron did not own the publishing to arguably, his most famous tune, "The Revolution Will Not Be Televised." For whatever reasons, "The Revolution..." had to be sold. I am not interested in this irony because I think that it undermines revolutionary thought or action in the 1960s and 1970s. It doesn't. For all intents and purposes this commercial was an unauthorized remake. Mr. Scott-Heron *consulted*, but he couldn't halt the reproduction of his previously owned work. For that matter, KRS ONE could not have done this either. His voice certainly confounds the issue because he is considered by many to be a seminal voice for sociopolitical awareness by and in hip-hop culture, an old-school underground artist, if you will. But I don't think that this commercial fooled anyone either. The revolution is not about basketball when we are 80 percent of the players and less than 2 percent of the owners. The revolution is not about basketball when players don't invest time and resources in their (former) communities. At best, the Nike-produced re(tele)vision of Mr. Scott-Heron's work provides all of us with the opportunity to be critical in our memories of African American activism in the 1960s and right now. The revolution is about basketball when its commercials force us to rethink our history and challenge those who would misrepresent it. The revolution is about basketball (or hip-hop for that matter) when young Black men and women earn wealth and resources and reinvest in their own communities.[17] Critical memory in the Black Public Sphere does not allow for a comfortably nostalgic remembrance of the revolutionary 1960s. Instead it challenges us to rethink and intensely evaluate homely notions of the past in conjunction with the dynamic elements of the present and the future.

Finally, we are left to contemplate the meaning of revolution. The simplest definition of revolution is "the overthrow and replacement of a government."[18] African Americans have not ever overthrown the American government. We have engaged in revolutionary struggles (slave revolts, the Underground Railroad, boycotts, sit-ins, etc.). We have written and performed many revolutionary lyrics (Ellison, Sanchez, Baraka, Giovanni, and KRS One). We have had many revolutionaries (i.e., people who have seriously challenged the American government with the intent to overthrow, replace, or reform—Nat Turner, Frederick Douglass, MLK and Malcolm X, Dead Prez, etc.). Reformation now appears to be the struggle in which most "revolutionary" activists are engaged. Mr. Scott-Heron suggested to me that "we learn to separate our art and our athletics and our disciplines because we go different ways. We can jam on [these things] together if we want to, but if we do it negates the things that a lot of folks did to make those things possible." Contrary to Heron's admonitions this book has jammed on the concepts of the underground. This book begins by talking about revolutionary struggles through slavery and ends speaking about the discursive and economic ironies of revolution and revolutionary language. It is a cipher of sorts as it revolves around and rifts on several of the concepts of the underground in hip-hop and African American (literary) culture. Moreover, the subversion of White supremacy in life, language, and letters is a consistent mission borne out in the various disciplines and writing styles that proliferate in this book. I'll therefore close with my response to Gil Scott Heron's interview and a quote on the meanings of Revolution. If we are invested in reforming America, then we will need revolutionary reformers in all of our "disciplines."

> Revolutionary struggle and resistance always involve multileveled transformation. We can speak of the individual's role in changing his or her particular political commitments.... We can also focus on the historical record of the resistance movement: key factions and splinter groups, strategies, political maneuvering and so on. Another perspective is ideological. As people are forced to resist the imposition of "foreign leadership," they are also made to shift, transmute and transform how they see, what they see, and how they organize in response to what (and who) surrounds them.[19]

How we organize in the twenty-first century, in the face of less visible/tangible threats—particularly in the ways that racial biases inform social structures such as the criminal justice system and public schools—has become the critical question for those invested in social justice in these United States. *The hip-hop Underground and African American Culture* offers little in terms of answering this searing question, but my hope is that the work here has laid some compelling blueprints for the work ahead.

APPENDIX: THE TIMEPIECE HIP-HOP TIMELINE

1967 Clive Campbell aka DJ Kool Herc (hip-hop's first DJ) immigrates to the West Bronx in New York City from Jamaica.

1968 Rucker Park is a must stop for top college and pro-basketball stars eager to prove themselves. Julius Erving, Wilt Chamberlain, and Kareem Abdul Jabar establish the legacy maintained by the likes of Allen Iverson, Stephon Marbury, Ron Artest, and Elton Brand. The Rucker Tournament, the Rucker Pro League, and the Entertainer's Basketball Classic are legendary touchstones for hip-hop's love affair with athletics.

1968–9 James Brown records and releases "Funky Drummer" (one of the most sampled drum tracks in hip-hop history) and "Say It Loud (I'm Black and I'm Proud)."

1969 Greek-born Demetrius from 183 Street in the Bronx makes himself famous by "tagging" Taki 183 throughout the five boroughs of New York City.

1973 DJ Kool Herc DJs his first party.

1974 Afrika Bambaataa leaves the Black Spades (one of the largest and most violent gangs in New York) to form hip-hop's first organization, the ZULU Nation.

1974 Busy Bee Starski, DJ Hollywood, and/or Afrika Bambaataa coin the term "hip-hop."

1975 Grand Wizard Theodore discovers the scratch.

1976 The first pieces (i.e., graf-like murals) appear on New York City subway trains.

1977 Bronx B. Boys, Jimmy D., and Jojo establish the legendary Rock Steady Crew (joined by Crazy Legs and Lenny Len in 1979).

1979 Sugarhill Gang's "Rapper's Delight" spends 12 weeks on the Billboard pop chart, ushering in the era of the emcee with all of its lyrical battles and authorial challenges.

1980   The Times Square Graffiti Show indicates the mainstream's brief love affair with hip-hop's visual art.

1980   The High Times Crew is arrested for break dancing. The first photos of break dancing enter mainstream circulation.

1980   The first rap radio show debuts on WHBI, Mr. Magic's Rap Attack.

The Golden Age (A Stopwatch Timepiece)

1983   Run DMC's "Sucka MC's" signals the end of the Old School Era and the dawn of hip-hop's first "pop" stars.

1984   "Roxanne, Roxanne" released by UTFO spawning hundreds of response "dis" records. KDAY becomes Los Angeles's and United States' first rap-formatted radio station.

1984   Rick Rubin and Russell Simmons form Def Jam in a dorm room.

1986   Run DMC's "Walk this Way" enters heavy rotation on MTV.

1988   NWA's first album, *Straight Outta Compton*, introduces Gangsta Rap to the mainstream (ICE-T, Schoolly D, and BDP have defined the genre earlier for hip-hop culture).

1988   Basquiat (the first hip-hop visual artist to be recognized by "high culture" art circles) dies from a heroin overdose at the age of 27.

1989   Public Enemy scores Spike Lee's film, *Do the Right Thing* (the single is titled "Fight the Power") positioning political rap and the director at the center of urban culture.

1990   2 Live Crew is arrested for performing songs from *As Nasty as They Wanna Be*. First Amendment advocates testify on their behalf and they are released, but explicit lyrics labeling is born.

1990   September *The Fresh Prince of Bel-Air* debuts on NBC, marking the first sitcom starring a rapper.

1991   Soundscan technology becomes widespread and rap music usurps pop/rock as America's most eagerly consumed music.

1991   Rapper/actor Ice Cube, actors Cuba Gooding Jr., Lawrence Fishburne, and Morris Chestnut star in the film *Boyz N the Hood*, directed by John Singleton.

1991   Lyricist Lounge in New York City starts its open mic sessions.

1991	Sway, King Tech, and DJ Joe Quixx broadcast the "Wake Up Show" in the Bay area on KMEL.
1992	FUBU Clothing is launched.
1992	Karl Kani begins production of his distinctively logoed, loose-fitting, street-chic sportswear. Within two years, aided by ads that feature artists like Snoop Doggy Dogg and Tupac Shakur, the company will earn between $30 million and $40 million.

The NOW Age (a Platinum Timepiece)

1993	Hip-hop's greatest producer releases his first masterpiece (*The Chronic* featuring Snoop Dogg and Tha Doggpound). Dr. Dre also produced NWA's first two albums as well as various R&B artists', prior to this release.
1993	VIBE magazine is launched with Snoop Doggy Dogg on the cover. Snoop subsequently appears on the cover of *Rolling Stone* dated September 30 (with Dr. Dre), even though his highly anticipated Doggy style debut hasn't come out yet.
1994	Sean Puffy Combs establishes Bad Boy Records. The notorious B.I.G. releases *Ready to Die* (Bad Boy).
1994 February	Wu Tang Clan releases their debut album *Enter the Wu Tang (36 Chambers)* (Loud/RCA).
1994	Snoop Dogg releases his debut album *Doggy Style* (Death Row/Interscope).
1995	The Roots album *Do You Want More* brings live instruments back into hip-hop popularity.
1996 September 13	Tupac Shakur dies after being shot at while driving through Las Vegas with Death Row CEO Suge Knight.
1997 March	Rapper Notorious B.I.G. dies of gunshot wounds while sitting in his car after attending a *Vibe* magazine industry party.
1998	Dre discovers Eminem and produces Em's debut album, on Interscope Records, *The Slim Shady LP* (1999).

2000–present   Popular hip-hop artists reduce lyrics to Dionysian exploits and experiences. Jay-Z and other artists supplant Biggie and Tupac as "the emcees" of hip-hop culture. The well-recorded battle between Nas and Jay-Z, coupled with the popularity of Hollywood's version of Eminem's life story (*8 Mile*), reinvigorate the dominance of emcees in hip-hop and popular culture.

NOTES

1 Roots, Rhymes, and Rhizomes: An Introduction to Concepts of the Underground in Black Culture

1. Deleuze and Guattari, *A Thousand Plateaus: Capitalism and Schizophrenia*, translated by Brian Masumi (Minneapolis: University of Minnesota Press, 1987). Originally published as *Mille Plateaux: Capitalisme et schizophreni II* (Paris: Minuit, 1980).
2. James Baldwin, "A Review of Roots," in *The Price of the Ticket* (New York: St. Martin's Press, 1985), p. 553.
3. James Baldwin, "Alas, Poor Richard," in *The Price of the Ticket*, p. 273.
4. Ibid., p. 278.
5. Ibid., p. 556.
6. Kevin Young, *The Grey Album: On the Blackness of Blackness.* Minneapolis: Graywolf Press, 2012, p. 36.
7. William Andrews, ed., *The Oxford Frederick Douglass Reader* (New York, Oxford University Press, 1996), p. 67.
8. Ibid., p. 69.
9. Young, *The Grey Album*, p. 38.
10. It must be noted here that Charles Chesnutt's *Conjure Woman* collection enters here through the story of Po' Sandy, a conjure-man/root worker. Chesnutt's *Conjure Woman* is taken up directly in the sociolinguistic identity chapter of this book.
11. Kimberly Bentson, "The Topos of (Un)naming," in *Black Literature and Literary Theory*, ed. Henry Louis Gates (New York: Routledge, 1990), p. 164.
12. My critical discussion of nostalgia in African American culture (chapter 7) is informed by Houston Baker's notions of the Black Public Sphere in The Black Public Sphere Collective, eds., *The Black Public Sphere* (Chicago: University of Chicago Press, 1995), and Michael Eric Dyson's discussion of nostalgia in *Race Rules: Navigating the Color Line* (New York: Vintage Books, 1996).
13. Ralph Ellison, *Invisible Man* (New York: Vintage International, 1995), pp. 264–7.
14. Ibid., p. 266.

15. Please review the comprehensive Timepiece Time-Line in the appendix (with accompanying images) in order to grasp the chronological trajectory of the development of hip-hop culture.

16. Mark Anthony Neal, *What the Music Said: Black Popular Music and Black Public Culture* (New York: Routledge, 1999), p. 131.

17. I spend much more time with definitions of hip-hop culture and the concept of the underground in hip-hop later in this book and in various aspects of the appendices. For more information on hip-hop culture's predisposition to the postindustrial urban landscape, please see Tricia Rose, *Black Noise: Rap Music and Black Culture in Contemporary America* (Hanover: University Press of New England, 1994).

18. Cornel West, *Prophetic Fragments* (Trenton, NJ: Africa World Press, 1988), p. 185–6.

19. "Tip the Scale," *Undun*, The Roots.

2   Verbal and Spatial Masks of the Underground

1. Sadly, Gangstarr's front man, GURU (Gifted Unlimited Rhymes Universal) nee Keith Edward Elam, passed away in April of 2010.

2. For more detail on repetition in Black Culture, please see James Snead, "Repetition as a Figure of Black Culture," in *Black Literature and Theories*, ed. Henry Louis Gates Jr. (New York: Routledge Press, 1990).

3. Schloss, Joseph. *Making Beats: The Art of Sample-Based Hip-Hop.* Middletown: Wesleyan University Press, 2004, p. 138.

4. Murray Forman, *The 'Hood Comes First: Race, Space, and Place in Rap and Hip Hop* (Middletown, CT: Wesleyan University Press, 2002), p. 17.

5. Houston Baker, *Black Studies, Rap and the Academy* (Chicago: University of Chicago Press, 1993), p. 33.

6. Henry Louis Gates, *Figures in Black: Words, Signs, and the Racial Self* (New York: Oxford University Press, 1987), p 172.

7. This point puts into bold relief one of the most interesting connections between hip-hop and Bebop cultures: "In Bebop we see the rise of Black musicians creating publishing companies to protect their 'compositions' which are, in many instances, simply the improvised chord progressions of jazz standards where the harmonic emphasis produces a 'new' song, but which is always already the old song made over." Herman Beavers (personal communication).

8. Tricia Rose, *Black Noise: Rap Music and Black Culture in Contemporary America* (Hanover: University Press of New England, 1994). Rose is the first scholar to refer to rap as a transcript in her explanation and analysis of various lyrics (see pp. 100–10).

9. For a more in-depth discussion and analysis of "wilding" please see Stephen J. Mexal's "The Roots of 'Wilding': Black Literary Naturalism, the Language of Wilderness, and Hip Hop in the

Central Park Jogger Rape," *African American Review* 46(1), (Spring 2013): 101–15, Johns Hopkins University Press.

10. Rose, *Black Noise*, pp. 132–3.
11. Baker, *Black Studies, Rap and the Academy*, p. 42.
12. Trisha Meili made her story public with a book titled *I Am the Central Park Jogger: A Story of Hope and Possibility* in early spring 2003. According to her, she has absolutely no recognition of the events of that night, leading up to and through time of the crime.
13. Baker, *Black Studies, Rap and the Academy*, p. 46.
14. Frederick Douglass's quote and biographical information on Paul Laurence Dunbar taken from University of Dayton Website on Paul Laurence Dunbar (www.plethoreum.org/dunbar).
15. Paul Laurence Dunbar, *Lyrics of Lowly Life* (with an introduction by W. D. Howells) (New York: Dodd, Mead, 1896).
16. Ibid., "Introduction."
17. Gates, *Figures in Black*, pp. 179–80.
18. Robin D. G. Kelley, *Race Rebels: Culture, Politics, and the Black Working Class* (New York: Free Press, 1996).
19. Ben Sidran, *Black Talk* (New York: Holt, Rinehart and Winston, 1971). Sidran coins this term on page 79 of Chapter Four titled "The Evolution of the Black Underground 1930–1947."
20. Leroi Jones, *Black Music* (New York: William Morrow, 1967), p. 23.
21. Eric Lott, "Bebop's Politics of Style," in *Jazz Among the Discourses*, ed. Krin Gabbard. (Durham, NC: Duke University Press, 1995), p. 246.
22. Henrietta Buckmaster, *Let My People Go: The Story of the Underground Railroad and the Growth of the Abolition Movement* (Columbia: University of South Carolina Press, 1992), p. 59.
23. Ibid., p. 13.
24. Ibid., p. 59.
25. Charles Blockson, *Hippocrene Guide to The Underground Railroad* (New York: Hippocrene Books, 1994), pp. 11–12.
26. Taken from Underground Railroad Website, http://www.nps.gov/undergroundrr/ugsum.htm.
27. For a chronological history of graffiti in hip-hop, please see the timelines in the appendix.
28. Michael P. Jeffries, *Thuglife: Race, Gender, and the Meaning of Hip-Hop* (Chicago: University of Chicago Press, 2011), p. 146. The terms "flow" and "layered meaning" or "layering" are applied by Tricia Rose in her discussion of hip-hop aesthetics in *Black Noise*.
29. As a scholar I occasionally attempt to grapple with notions of authenticity in my work. This is a losing effort because of a desire to situate Black authenticity conceptually in the underground. That is, I want to posit authenticity as intrinsic to the underground.

30. Imani Perry, *Prophets of the Hood: Politics and Poetics in Hip Hop* (Durham, NC: Duke University Press, 2004), p. 87.

31. Jeffries, *Thuglife*, p. 132.

32. Farah Jasmine Griffin's *Who Set You Flowin'* is the standard bearer on migration studies and African American literature.

33. Christopher Holmes Smith, "Method in the Madness: Exploring the Boundaries of Identity in Hip-Hop Performativity," *Social Identities* 3(3) (1997): 350.

34. Ibid., p. 353.

35. Anthony K. Harrison (2009) deals with the ways in which racial identity becomes even more fluid in the Do-It-Yourself underground hip-hop communities of the Bay Area in California. I will briefly engage his work in chapter 3.

36. Jeffries, *Thuglife*, p. 75.

37. An interesting example of "those who can bend class and geography to their own purposes have the power to shape what race is" reside in Danny Hoch's film *White Boys*. The first third of the film is a study of Hip-Hop Culture's notions of Black authenticity. The first scene is a cipher (the foundation of rhyming rituals in hip-hop, and Flip is the best amongst his boys). The next scene shows Flip and his boys writing graffiti on the walls of a barn, a complex play on the reclamation of public spaces in the ghetto suggested by Baker. In the next scene, Flip and his friends meet his girlfriend at the mall where he gives a poem to her showcasing his expertise in the Black traditional notion of "rapping" to woo a woman. Flip's father loses his job in an industrial factory alluding to the advent of the postindustrial effects on middle America. The film juxtaposes Flip's Black-aspiring reality (he literally believes that his whiteness is an epidermic nonfactor) and several dream/fantasy sequences where he lives out his desires as a White-Black rapper, gangster, and pimp.

38. William L. Andrews, ed., *The Oxford Frederick Douglass Reader* (New York: Oxford University Press, 1996), p. 84.

3 The Hip-Hop Underground and African American Culture: The Deep Structure of Black Identity in American Literature

1. For a much more thorough discussion of these phenomena please see Geneva Smitherman's "The Forms of Things Unknown: Black Modes of Discourse" in *Talkin' and Testifyin': The Language of Black America*. Boston: Houghton Mifflin, 1977, pp. 101–66.

2. My deductive reasoning here stems from the exchange of reviews between Hurston and Wright that reveal Wright's self-conscious

attempts to represent black speech in a manner distinct from Hurston and other folk-loric authors.

3. Elijah Wald, *The Dozens: A History of Rap's Mama* (New York: Oxford University Press, 2012), p. 3.

4. Geneva Smitherman, *Talkin and Testifyin* (Boston, MA: Houghton and Mifflin, 1977), p. 192.

5. William Labov, *Language in the Inner City: Studies in the Black English Vernacular* (Philadelphia: University of Pennsylvania Press, 1972), p. 201.

6. See Martin Deutsch, Irwin Katz, and Arthur Jensen, eds., *Social Class, Race and Psychological Development* (New York: Holt, Rinehart and Winston, 1968); Carl Bereiter and Siegfried Englemann, *Teaching Disadvantaged Children in the Pre-school* (Englewood Cliffs, NJ: Prentice Hall, 1966); Arthur Jensen, "How Much Can We Boost IQ and Scholastic Achievement?" *Harvard Educational Review* 39 (1969).

7. Chapter 9 of Labov's *Language in the Inner City* provides many examples of the conversational, narrative-inducing formats of the sociolinguistic interview (pp. 354–55).

8. Labov, *Language in the Inner City*, pp. 205–207. In my masters thesis I complicate certain ideas concerning symmetry in sociolinguistic interview situations where symmetrical interviewers tend to accommodate perceived vernacular features of their informants. I should also note here that the interviews for this book are all conducted in the conversational, sociolinguistic style in which I was trained by Dr. Walt Wolfram.

9. Smitherman, *Talkin and Testifyin*, p. 193.

10. Ibid., p. 194.

11. For a thorough consideration of Deep Structure, see Noam Chomsky, *Aspects of a Theory of Syntax* (Cambridge, MA: MIT Press, 1965). For an extraordinary analysis of the history of the field of linguistics, see Randy Allen Harris, *The Linguistic Wars* (New York: Oxford University Press, 1993). My ideas in this section of the text are thoroughly influenced by these works.

12. Harris, *The Linguistic Wars*, p. 81.

13. This idea is taken up fully in the "cipher" chapter of this book concerned with other underground moments in African American culture.

14. Michael Awkward, *Inspiriting Influences: Tradition, Revision, and Afro-American Women's Novels* (New York: Columbia University Press, 1989), p. xiv.

15. Zora Neale Hurston, *Their Eyes Were Watching God* (New York: Harper Perennial Classics, 1998 [first published 1937]), p. 78.

16. Ibid., p. 79.

17. Claudia Tate, *Psychoanalysis and Black Novels: Desire and the Protocols of Race* (New York: Oxford University Press, 1998), p. 150.
18. Ibid.
19. Yvonne Bynoe, ed., *Encyclopedia of Rap and Hip-Hop Culture* (Westport, CT: Greenwood Press, 2006), p. 326.
20. Catherine Clinton, *Harriet Tubman: The Road to Freedom* (Boston, MA: Back Bay Books, 2004), p. 78.
21. Ann Petry, *Harriet Tubman: Conductor on the Underground Railroad* (New York: HarperCollins Children's Books, 1983 [1955]).
22. Bynoe, *Encyclopedia of Rap and Hip-Hop Culture*, p. 326.

4   Defining an Underground at the Intersections of Hip-Hop and African American Cultures

1. As I am reviewing the page proofs for this book, Saul Williams is completing a (very short) six-week run starring in "Holler If You Hear Me," a dramatic adaptation of Tupac's rap lyrics performed at the Palace Theatre on Broadway.
2. Eargasms: Crucialpoetics Vol. 1., Rha Goddess, Jessica Care More, Mos Def, Mike Ladd, Saul Williams, et al. New York: Ozone Music, 1997.
3. Williams's two written collections of poetry represent two distinct styles of expression and a host of social, political, spiritual, and personal content. In *The Seventh Octave*, Saul makes plain his allegiance to hip-hop culture by connecting the corners of the 'hood to ancient cultural artifacts. His ability to defamiliarize the oppressive but somehow trite conditions of the inner city mark his voice as prophetic and necessary to the postindustrial/Information age(s). In *She*, Williams attempts to explore the more sensitive aspects of his narrative persona here engaged in various personal relationships. In a personal communication, he explained to me that he wanted to tap into all aspects of his emotional perceptions, responses, and senses in this book. He believes that we often shut out certain aspects of our creative and communicative abilities according to socially constructed gender roles. In *She*, Williams explores these roles and expresses the pain, joy, and addiction of intimate relationships.
4. Saul Williams exploded onto a Black Expressive stage through which he negotiates the various artistic contributions made by people of African descent in America. His creative presence in various genres and media (film, record, and text) provides us with multiple opportunities to experience his unique genius. In the introduction to The Seventh Octave: "The Early Writings of Saul Williams," Jessica Care Moore claims that Saul Williams's voice is "a weapon against hypocrisy, a celebrated new addition to the literary tradition. A son

of Larry Neal, Amiri Baraka, Ben Okri, Bob Kaufman, The Last Poets, Gil Scott Heron, Sonia Sanchez, Audre Lorde, and Ntozake Shange, Saul is easily one of the most noted unique writers of his generation."

5. Depending upon who is doing the reporting, the underground homeless are referred to as mole people, tunnel people, or other monikers.

6. It is also worth noting here that *Business as Usual* is also the album featuring the very first major label appearance of Redman—an emcee whose entire career thrived on the border between underground and mainstream styles of hip-hop music.

7. I am thinking here specifically of Richard Iton's discussion (in *In Search of the Black Fantastic*) of black aesthetics and modernity where conceptual trajectories of movement or progress from darker, that is, less-enlightened places to lighter, more enlightened places/spaces entraps black subjectivity in a bind constructed by traditional discourses on enlightenment, race, and modernity. For rap duo EPMD, "coming from the underground" suggests an ongoing connection to that darker, more authentic, space.

8. In the interest of full disclosure, Professor Morgan was on my dissertation committee. Although I trained at the University of Pennsylvania, Professor Morgan (Harvard University) graciously agreed to provide outstanding support, critique, and advice on my dissertation writing and research. My dissertation, "Concepts of the Underground in Black Culture" (UPENN 2003) is an early precursor to this book.

9. Marcyliena Morgan, *The Real Hiphop: Battling for Knowledge, Power, and Respect in the LA Underground* (Durham, NC: Duke University Press, 2009), p. 16.

10. Ibid.

11. James G. Spady, Stefan Dupree, and Charles G. Lee. *Twisted Tales in the Hip Hop Streets of Philadelphia*. Philadelphia, PA: UMUM LOH, 1995.

5 A Cipher of the Underground in Black Literary Culture

1. Kim Bentson discusses the genealogical relationship among Black authors in Henry Louis Gates (ed.), *Black Literature and Literary Theory* (New York: Routledge Press, 1990).

2. Webster's New World Dictionary, p. 254.

3. The five percent Nation of Gods and Earths founded by Clarence 13X in the early 1970s. A philosophical offshoot of the Nation of Islam, 5 percenters believe that 85 percent of the human population is "dumb, deaf, and blind." Ten percent is enlightened but they tend to

exploit the 85 percent, and 5 percent are the poor righteous teachers who work to enlighten and liberate the 85 percent.

4. Houston A. Baker Jr., *Blues, Ideology, and Afro-American Literature: A Vernacular Theory* (Chicago: University of Chicago Press, 1984), p. 172.
5. Ibid., pp. 151–2.
6. Please see the introduction to this book for more information on Baldwin's reads on Wright. For more on Ellison's position with respect to Wright, see "The World and the Jug" in *Shadow and Act*.
7. Ibid., p. 172.
8. The name/character Big Boy appears throughout the genealogical inter-course between African American Literature and culture. Big Boy is the character/subject of Sterling Brown's work as well as the nickname of Jean Toomer's "Tom Burwell" from "Blood Burning Moon" in the modernist classic, Cane. Toomer's big Boy is tortured and lynched after he slashes the throat of his love interest's (the sirenesque Louisa) White "boyfriend." The (cross) references alone suggest that the figure (and by extension the figurative literary and lyrical voice) of Big Boy resonates in underground culturally expressive formats.
9. *The American Heritage College Dictionary*, 3rd ed. (Boston, MA: Houghton Mifflin, 1993).
10. A cursory, comparative reading the following texts will illustrate my point here: "Big Boy Leaves Home," in Richard Wright's *Uncle Tom's Children* [first published in 1938] (New York: First Harper Perennial, 1991); *Black Boy* [first published in 1945] (New York: HarperCollins, 2007); Richard Wright, "How Bigger Was Born," in *Native Son* [first published in 1940] (New York: Harper Perennial Modern Classics, 2008).
11. Richard Wright, "The Man Who Lived Underground" in *Norton Anthology of African American Literature*, edited by Henry Louis Gates Jr. and Nellie Y. McKay (New York: W. W. Norton, 1997), p. 1431.
12. See Henry Louis Gates's Signifying Monkey.
13. Houston A Baker Jr., *Blues, Ideology*, p. 157.
14. Wright, "The Man Who Lived Underground," p. 1433.
15. Ralph Ellison, *Invisible Man* New York: Vintage International, 1995, p. 13.
16. Baker, *Blues Ideology*, p. 152.
17. This is the most appropriate moment to note that I am fully aware of the role that Fyodor Dostoyevky plays in the genesis of both Wright's work and Ellison's *Invisible Man*. I always teach *Notes from Underground* as a part of my course "The Concepts of the Underground." I am also aware of the 1940s' race scientist, L. Stoddard who published the very popular *Revolt against Civilizations*, which was not only a best seller

(in the midst of Wright's and Ellison's genesis as writers), but it also proffered the concept of the "under man" as ethnic minority always already beneath the white standard of "civilized" humanity. I have turned down the volume on both of these figures for time constraints and because I want to.

18. Ellison, *Invisible Man*, p. 8.

19. DJ Kool Herc is the founding DJ of hip-hop culture by historical and ethnographic consensus. The connection between IM's aural aesthetic coupled with the kinesthetic reaction and the aesthetics of hip-hop culture (esp. DJ-ing and Hiphop dance/movement here) is one of many anticipations of hip-hop culture in *Invisible Man*. This one is noted for its underground locale and the interactive cultural valence between Louis Armstrong's moment in Jazz and Kool Herc's role in hip-hop culture. Louis Armstrong could sing and play (MC and DJ in hip-hop), and Kool Herc initially was a breaker/B-boy and he eventually became Hiphop's first DJ.

20. I venture into a more complete discussion of this scene from IM, which also serves as the scene of inspiration for this book's cover art, in the next chapter.

21. Shirley Anne Williams, "The Search for Identity in Baraka's Dutchman," in *Imamu Amiri Baraka (Leroi Jones): A Collection of Critical Essays* (New Jersey: Prentice Hall, 1978), p. 136.

22. Paul Gilroy, *The Black Atlantic: Modernity and Double Consciousness* (Cambridge, MA: Harvard University Press, 1993).

23. Leslie C. Sanders, *The Development of Black Theater in America: From Shadows to Selves* (Baton Rouge: Louisiana State University Press, 1988), p. 139.

24. My use of the term "treatise" reflects both its obsolete meaning—a tale or narrative—and its current meaning—a systematic discourse on a topic. The imagery (the idea) of Bessie Smith or Charlie Parker killing White people as a means of expressing the regular frustration of Black existence in America outshines and obscures the violent conclusion of the play itself. Since these words are told in Clay's monologue/narrative, Clay's violent, incendiary voice is disconnected (i.e., disembodied) from his stuffy middle-class body. Clay's voice is an underground call to arms, a revealing of the potentially murderous encoding of Black vernacular forms. The movement on and of the subway symbolizes the interplay and the mobility of these discursive interactions in the underground.

25. I stated earlier in this chapter that the underground is a space where dominant culture's representations are squeezed to zero volume.

26. Gilroy, *Black Atlantic*, p. 174.

27. William J. Harris, *The Poetry and Poetics of Amiri Baraka: The Jazz Aesthetic* (Missouri: University of Missouri Press, 1985), p. 100.

28. Ibid., p. 93.

29. Greg Tate, "Vicious Modernism," a foreword to *The Fiction of Leroi Jones/Amiri Baraka* (Chicago: Lawrence Hill Books, 2000), p. vii.

30. I'm considering it a well-known fact that emcees like Grandmaster Flash and the Furious Five, KRS One, Rakim, Will Smith, Black Thought, Common, Erykah Badu, Lauryn Hill, and Jill Scott are the artistic lineage of the aforementioned poets before spoken word.

31. Harris, *The Poetry and Poetics of Amiri Baraka*, p. 93.

32. Shirley Anne Williams, "The Search for Identity in Baraka's Dutchman," p. 136.

33. The murder narrative is a term that I have coined to describe my analysis of the trajectory of the violent murder of hip-hop figures from Scott La Rock to Jam Master Jay, from Malcolm X and Martin Luther King to Tupac and Biggie.

34. Amiri Baraka, "Sound and Image," in *The Fiction of LeRoi Jones/Amiri Baraka* (Chicago: Lawrence Hill Books, 2000), p. 125. "Sound and Image" is Baraka's insightful analysis of the creation of The System of Dante's Hell.

35. Amiri Baraka, "The System of Dante's Hell," in *The Fiction of LeRoi Jones/Amiri Baraka*, p. 18.

36. Notions of the veil are derived directly from Du Bois, and my ideas about modernity and blackness come from *The Black Atlantic*.

37. Baraka has pointed to the System of Dante's Hell as a "coming out" party for his definitive signature, artistic voice, but through the process he exorcises his eurocentric anxieties of influence. The clarity of his rich lyrical prose (as compared to the encoded fragments that constitute much of the novel) reflects an artistic achievement of a distinctly Black voice.

38. Amiri Baraka, "The System of Dante's Hell," p. 107.

39. Ibid., p. 122.

40. One of the thugs crouches down on all fours behind the narrator and one of the other two pushes him down. This mode of confronting and jumping individuals was a regular occurrence in my Newark neighborhood.

41. Amiri Baraka has regularly suggested that his work and the work of poets in the Black Arts Movement serve as the very foundation for rap music and hip-hop culture.

42. *Underground* was recorded at Columbia Studios in New York City on December 14 and December 27, 1967, and February 14 and December 14, 1968. It was released in late 1968 and re-released in 1987. It was the last album compiled from the recordings of his 1960's quartet featuring Charlie Rouse, Ben Riley, and Larry Gales.

43. Thelonious Monk, "Liner Notes for *Underground*, Columbia Records, 1968.

44. The Harlem Slide style is a by-product of the BeBop movement of which Monk was an integral part. Track one of Underground, the self-titled "Thelonious" is an earlier composition that features his innovative underground style and suggests his overall inventive/innovative consistency.
45. Robin Kelley, Thelonious Monk: The Life and Times of an American Original (New York: Free Press, 2010), p. 394.
46. Ibid., p. 394.
47. Ibid.
48. This list includes in no specific chronological order: Gangstarr, OC, The Roots, Underground Kings, Lords of the Underground, Das EFX, The Cella Dwellas, The Grave Diggas, The Nappy Roots, and many others whose underground identities would be largely unrecognizable (e.g., The Last Emperor from Philadelphia, Pennsylvania).
49. KRS ONE is an acronym for Knowledge Reigns Supreme Over Nearly Everyone. My diacritic/parenthetical notation on the title will be explained in detail. "Hold" is on KRS ONE's self-titled album released on Jive Records in 1995.
50. In the prologue, Invisible Man bumps into someone who refuses to see him and he beats him. Dostoyevsky's narrator orchestrates a similar encounter with a soldier from whom he seeks revenge, but the soldier does not acknowledge him.
51. Kimberly W. Bentson, "I yam what I am: the topos of un(naming) in Afro-American literature," in Black Literature and Literary Theory, ed. Henry Louis Gates (New York: Routledge, 1990), p. 152.

6   Tears for the Departed: See(k)ing a Black Visual Underground in Hip-Hop and African American Cultures

1. Marita Sturken and Lisa Cartwright, eds., Practices of Looking: An Introduction to Visual Culture (New York: Oxford University Press, 2001), p. 2.
2. Ibid., p. 2.
3. Dambe is a traditional fighting game practiced by the Hausa of West Africa, especially Nigeria. For more information on Dambe, please see Edward Powe's Combat Games of Northern Nigeria, Madison: Dan Aiki, 1994.
4. Ghost Dog is a good example of this.
5. Monica R. Miller, Religion and Hip Hop (New York: Routledge, 2013), p. 81.
6. It's worth noting here that the Middle Passage had by some estimates a 30–40 percent mortality rate. Some enslaved Africans resisted by

simply diving overboard, others died from disease and sickness exacerbated by conditions of Middle Passage itself. Historical records have also occasionally referred to the fact that schools of Sharks sometimes followed slave ships for miles in order to feed on the corpses of those who were discarded upon death.

7. The 5 percent of the Five Percenters doctrine refers to an initiate and/or enlightment taxonomy within which 85 percent of the world's population is dumb, deaf, and blind; 10 percent of the world's population are the sinister group of people who exploit the 85 percent; and the five percenters are the poor righteous teachers who work to enlighten and liberate the 85 percent.

8. Felicia Miyakawa, *Five Percenter Rap: God's Music, Message, and Black Muslim Mission* (Bloomington: Indiana University Press, 2005), p. 11.

9. Emory S. Campbell, *Gullah Cultural Legacies: A Synopsis of Gullah Traditions, Customary Beliefs, Art Forms and Speech on Hilton Head Island and vicinal Sea Islands in South Carolina and Georgia* (South Carolina: Gullah Heritage Consulting Services, 2008).

10. According to Margaret Washington Creel in her landmark study, *A Peculiar People: Slave Religion and Community-Culture Among the Gullahs* (New York: New York University Press, 1988), pp. 286–88.

11. Creel, *A Peculiar People*, p. 287.

12. Elizabeth McNeil, "The Gullah Seeker's Journey in Paule Marshall's Praisesong for the Widow," *MELUS: Multi-Ethnic Literature of the U.S.*, 34(1) (Spring 2009): 187.

13. One scene in the documentary reveals a Rosa Lee Green tombstone in the slave burial ground. Although I have met Jonathan Green once, I have not had an opportunity to interview him directly about this work. That said, I am curious about whether or not this Rosa Lee Green was in any way related to his own family.

14. Marc Klasfield has directed scores of music videos and commercial television ads. He is also the director of the viral video "Scarface School Play," a comedic interpretation of *Scarface*, the film starring Al Pacino.

15. Scott Crossley, "Metaphorical Conceptions in Hip-Hop Music," *African American Review*, 39(4) (2005): 501.

16. Bill Cosby, "Introduction," in *The Block: Collage by Romare Bearden, Poems by Langston Hughes* (New York: The Metropolitan Museum of Museum of Art/Viking, 1995), p. 6.

17. Richard Iton, *In Search of the Black Fantastic: Politics and Popular Culture in the Post Civil Rights Era* (New York: Oxford University Press, 2008), p. 104.

18. Yvonne Bynoe, ed., *Encyclopedia of Rap and Hip-Hop Culture* (Westport, CT: Greenwood Press, 2006), pp. 281–2.

19. Iton, *In Search of the Black Fantastic*, p. 105.

20. Ibid., p. 107.

21. David Copenhafer, "Invisible Music (Ellison)," *Qui Parle*, 14(2) (Spring 2004): 200.

22. Alexander Weheliye, "I am I Be: The Subject of Sonic Afro-Modernity," *Boundary 2* 30(2) (Summer 2002): 109.

23. David Copenhafer, "Invisible Music (Ellison)" *Qui Parle*, vol. 14, No. 2 Spring 2004, p. 201.

24. Fred Moten, *In the Break: The Aesthetics of the Black Radical Tradition* (Minneapolis: University of Minnesota Press, 2003), p. 198.

25. Gen Doy, *Black Visual Culture: Modernity and Postmodernity* (London: I. B. Tauris, 2000), p. 3.

26. Shane W. Evans, *Underground: Finding the Light to Freedom* (New York: Roaring Book Press, 2011).

7 The Depth of the Hole: Intertextuality and Tom Waits's "Way Down in the Hole"

1. Spirituality and realism or naturalism are not necessarily parallel categories (e.g., spiritualism is not readily deployed as a literary descriptor). My point here is that the show's sense of realism and its naturalistic depiction of the individual versus the institution marginalizes Black spirituality. Nihilistic interpretations of the show have been proffered by Mark Chou in his 2010 article "When the Towers Fell: Mourning and Nostalgia after 9/11 in HBO's *The Wire*" (http://www.e-ir .info/?p=4217 [accessed October 30, 2010]) and in Rev. Eugene Rivers's fall 2010 study group at Harvard University—"Obama in the Age of the Wire"—where he reads the series, especially the figure of Marlo Stansfield, through the lens of Cornel West's well-known essay, "Nihilism in Black America" from *Race Matters* (New York: Vintage Books, 1994).

2. The African American church (used interchangeably with "Black Church" throughout) is one of the formative institutional entities in the Black experience in America. It has served all of the traditional spiritualistic and redemptive functionality of the church in general, but the African American church historically has been also charged with political progress and organization. Black spirituality emerged in and thrived through the African American church; its near absence in the show is thus striking. When the African American church does "appear" in *The Wire,* it is generally relegated to the realm of the political via the oft-referenced "ministers" who represent a valuable political voting bloc.

3. Occasionally, I refer to specific versions as "Way Down 1," "Way Down 2," "Way Down 3," etc. See table 7.1 for a taxonomic breakdown.

4. According to Christian Moraru, "intertextuality refers to the presence of a text A in a text B. A is the intertext if one stresses the textual precursor, the pretext absorbed by a later text. Or one could call B the intertext if one lays emphasis on the text incorporating a previous text thereby becoming intertextual (*Routledge Encyclopedia of Narrative Theory*, ed. David Herman, Manfred Jahn, and Marie-Laure Ryan [New York: Routledge, 2005], s.v. "intertextuality," pp. 256–57).

5. Gerard Genette, *Paratexts: Thresholds of Interpretation,* Literature, Culture, Theory series (Cambridge: Cambridge University Press, 2001), p. xviii.

6. Andrew Dignan, Kevin B. Lee, and Matt Zoller Seitz, "*The Wire*: A Close Analysis of the Season 1 Title Sequence," video essay, Moving Image Source: Extra Credit, Part 1, http://www.movingimage source.us/articles/extra-credit-part-1-20080728 (accessed September 18, 2009).

7. Ibid.

8. Andrew Dignan, Kevin B. Lee, and Matt Zoller Seitz, "*The Wire*: A Close Analysis of the Season 4 Title Sequence," video essay, Moving Image Source: Extra Credit, Part 1, http://www.movingimage source.us/articles/extra-credit-part-1-20080728 (accessed September 20, 2009).

9. David Simon, "Introduction" to *"The Wire": Truth Be Told,* ed. Rafael Alvarez (New York: Grove Press, 2009), pp. 2–34, quotation on 30.

10. For example, in season 1, D'Angelo Barksdale was often at odds and sometimes in direct conflict with the institution of the Street represented by his own family: the Barksdales. In season 2, we see Jimmy McNulty against the Law and the workers (especially union secretary treasurer Frank Sobotka) against the Port. Season 3 features Omar Little versus the Barksdale organization/the Street and Major Colvin, oddly enough, against the Law.

11. David Simon, "Introduction," p. 23.

12. Rafael Alvarez, "Way Down in the Hole: The Music of *The Wire*," in Alvarez, *The Wire* (see note 9), pp. 246–50, quotation on 247.

13. Kenneth S. Greenberg, ed., *The Confessions of Nat Turner and Related Documents,* Bedford Series in History and Culture (Boston, MA: Bedford/St. Martin's Press, 1996).

14. Cornel West, "On Afro-American Popular Music: From Bebop to Rap," in *Prophetic Fragments: Illuminations of the Crisis in American Religion and Culture* (Trenton, NJ: Africa World Press, 1983), 177–87, quotation on 177.

15. Giles Oakley, *The Devil's Music: A History of the Blues,* updated edition (New York: Da Capo Press, 1997).

16. Portia K. Maultsby, "Africanisms in African American Music," in *Africanisms in American Culture*, ed. Joseph E. Holloway (Bloomington: University of Indiana Press, 1991), pp. 185–210, quotation on 186.

17. Ben Sandmel, "The Blind Boys of Alabama," http://www.npacf.org /uploads/BlindBoys_bio.doc (accessed September 15, 2009).

18. Mimi Gisolfi D'Aponte, "*The Gospel at Colonus* (And Other Black Morality Plays)," *Black American Literature Forum* 25(1) (1991): pp. 101–11, quotation on 106.

19. The intertextual connections of blindness and tragedy serve to highlight important thematic touchstones between "Way Down 1" and season 1 of *The Wire*. While Oedipal blindness functions both as the metaphorical inability of the protagonist to "see" his tragic circumstances and the retributive response to his familial tragedy, the literal blindness of the FBBA serves to authenticate them as Black musical practitioners and make powerful suggestions about how viewers might engage *The Wire* as a narrative series generally and the character D'Angelo Barksdale in particular. *The Wire* depicts an urban (under)world that features (in season 1) the Barksdales, an organized Black crime family, whose prodigal son, D'Angelo Barksdale, played by Larry Gilliard Jr., is prone to deep reflection about the criminal activities with which he and his family are engaged. D'Angelo's general consternation throughout season 1 subtly suggests and foreshadows his tragic assassination while in prison in season 2. In many ways, D'Angelo reverses the trope of Oedipal blindness. He is painfully aware of his tragic circumstances. He knows who his mother is (which does not necessarily erase all Oedipal traces in the mother-son relationship) and knows who his father was. He is a brooding, insightful character who, in the narrative world of *The Wire*, simply thinks too much.

20. Tom Waits, "Way Down in the Hole," *Frank's Wild Years* Island Records, 1987.

21. Frederick Douglass, *Narrative of the Life of Frederick Douglass, an American Slave* (New York: Penguin Classics, 1986), 59 (originally published 1845).

22. On the HBO website for the series, the characters are assigned to distinct categorical designations, including the Street, the Law, the Hall, the Port, the Paper, and the School.

23. Douglass, *Narrative*, 59.

24. D'Angelo Barksdale is an enigmatic character in the storyworld of *The Wire*. My truncated reference to him here is an attempt to situate him as a "garden" figure in the sense that his consternation about his role in the illegal family business ironically does not prevent him from being assassinated in prison. The scene of his murder puts into

bold relief the significance of the theme song's warning to "watch your back."

25. Stringer Bell is murdered by Brother Mouzone and Omar Little at the end of season 3. He is essentially set up by his longtime partner in crime, Avon Barksdale. Omar Little is murdered by Kenard near the end of season 5.

26. Lucille Clifton, "Eyes: For Clarence Fountain and The Five Blind Boys of Alabama after seeing *The Gospel at Colonus*," *Callaloo* 39 (1989): 379–81.

27. Ibid., pp. 379–80.

28. Waits, "Way Down in the Hole."

29. *Frank's Wild Years* (see note 24) was cowritten by Tom Waits and Kathleen Brennan and directed by actor Gary Sinise. The play ran for two months at Chicago's Steppenwolf Theatre. The general thematic narrative of the play derives from a song penned by Waits in 1983. That song, also titled "Frank's Wild Years" was recorded on the album *Swordfishtrombones*.

30. In response to his unnarrated alienation from a white-picket-fence existence, Frank drinks some beer, Mickey's Big Mouths, to be exact; purchases a gallon of gasoline; goes home; and douses his home and sets it ablaze as he watches from across the street. After murdering his wife and burning his house and his wife's dog that he "never could stand," Frank turns on a top-40 station and heads north on the Hollywood Freeway. Although this foundational narrative for the play is both tragic and transcendent, Waits's original Frank also exhibits signs of the emotional nihilism present in certain characters in *The Wire* (especially Marlo Stanfield and his murderous henchman, Chris Partlow). The humor built into the closing line of the song, "Never could stand that dog," does not alleviate the horrors of murdering his wife by driving a nail through her forehead or burning his house down as he watches, but the conflation of the horror, the humor, and the existential angst is a generally classic recipe of the blues oeuvre and of *The Wire's* thematic underpinnings.

31. Glenn O'Brien, "Tom Waits for No Man," *Spin*, November 1985.

32. John Rockwell, "Tom Waits Stars in 'Frank's Wild Years,'" *New York Times*, July 10, 1986.

33. Fred J. Hay, "The Sacred/Profane Dialectic in Delta Blues: The Life and Lyrics of Sonny Boy Williamson," *Phylon* 48(4) (2005): 317–26.

34. Mike Daley, "'Why Do Whites Sing Black?': The Blues Whiteness, and Early Histories of Rock," *Popular Music and Society* 26(2) (2003): 161–67, quotation on 162.

35. This is the Virginia Hamilton version published as a children's book with an audio companion narrated by James Earl Jones.

36. Stephan Wackwitz and Nina Sonenberg, "The Flying Slaves: An Essay on Tom Waits," *Threepenny Review* 40 (1990): 30–32, quotation on 32.
37. Ibid., p. 30.
38. Hay, "Sacred/Profane Dialectic," 319.
39. Wackwitz and Sonenberg, "Flying Slaves," 30.
40. Ibid., p. 31.
41. Ibid., p. 32.
42. Although many viewers of *The Wire* and even some of its characters might associate Brother Mouzone with the Nation of Islam, there is not enough conclusive evidence to prove this (or it has not been conclusively proven) in the storyworld of the series.
43. Henry A. Giroux, *Fugitive Cultures: Race, Violence, and Youth* (New York: Routledge, 1996), p. 8.
44. Mark McKnight, "Researching New Orleans Rhythm and Blues," in *Black Music Research Journal* 8(1) (1988): 113–34, quotation on 115.
45. Kip Lornell and Charles C. Stephenson Jr., "The Roots and Emergence of Go-Go," in *Beat: Go-Go's Fusion of Funk and hip-hop* (New York: Billboard Books, 2001), pp. 11–44, quotation on 12.
46. George Lipsitz, "Mardi Gras Indians: Carnival and Counter-Narrative in Black New Orleans," *Cultural Critique* 10 (1988): 99–121, quotation on 101.
47. In fact, Chris and Snoop, Marlo's murderous henchmen, use a musical litmus test to murder a low-level New York drug dealer randomly in season 4. After asking the victim if he has heard of certain local Baltimore performers/songs, they immediately conclude that he is from New York City and shoot him in the head.
48. Lipsitz, "Mardi Gras Indians."
49. Ibid., pp. 118–19.
50. Portia K. Maultsby, "Africanisms in African American Music," in *Africanisms in American Culture*, ed. Joseph E. Holloway (Bloomington: University of Indiana Press, 1991), p. 185.
51. David Bradley, *The Chaneysville Incident* (New York: Harpers & Rowling, 1981), p. 6.

Epilogue   The Ironies Underground: Revolution, Critical Memory, and Black Nostalgia

1. Amadou Diallo's life and horrific murder come directly to mind here, as do the murders of Sean Bell, Oscar Grant, and the brutal beating of Rodney King. But the recent cases of justifiable homicides or more aptly stated—"Stand Your Ground" murders—of Renisha McBride, Trayvon Martin, and Jordan Davis are also relevant to Heron's themes.

2. Michael Dunn stood trial for the first degree murder of Jordan Davis. The trial was referred to in the media as the "Loud Music Trial," referencing the fact that the conflict arose over Davis and his friends playing hip-hop music loudly in a car. Dunn was convicted of attempted murder for shooting into the vehicle as it was driving away but the jury was "hung" on the murder of Jordan Davis.

3. The Black Public Sphere Collective, eds., *The Black Public Sphere* (Chicago: University of Chicago Press, 1995), p. 7.

4. Ibid.

5. Ibid. Dr. Baker's definition of nostalgia also suggests "heimweh or homesickness."

6. Consider the popularity of the NBA's international b-ball stars, Tony Parker, Steve Nash, Dirk Nowitzki, and Yao Ming.

7. Ronin Ro, *Gangsta: Merchandising the Rhymes of Violence* (New York: St. Martins Press, 1996), pp. 81–2.

8. Ibid.

9. Robin D. G. Kelley, *Yo' Mama's Disfunktional: Fighting the Culture Wars in Urban America* (Boston, MA: Beacon Press, 1997), pp. 64–5.

10. Ibid.

11. Nathan McCall, *What's Going On: Personal Essays* (New York: Random House, 1997), p. 13.

12. See Nathan McCall's *Makes Me Wanna Holler: A Young Black Man in America* (New York: Vintage Books, 1995).

13. Kelley, *Yo' Mama's Disfunktional*, pp. 44–6.

14. This essay was published in the 1996 special edition of The New Yorker focusing on black culture.

15. Michael Eric Dyson, *Race Rules: Navigating the Color Line* (New York, Vintage Books, 1996), p. 115.

16. Ibid.

17. A nearly identical argument can be directed at the artisans of hip-hop culture.

18. *The American Heritage College Dictionary*, 3rd ed. (Boston, MA: Houghton Mifflin, 1993), p. 1169.

19. Renee T. White, "Revolutionary Theory: Sociological Dimensions of Fanon's Sociologie d'une revolution," in *Fanon: A Critical Reader*, ed. Lewis R. Gordon, T. Denean Sharpley-Whiting, and Renee T. White by (Cambridge, MA: Blackwell, 1996), p. 100.

BIBLIOGRAPHY

Alim, H. Samy. *Roc the Mic Right: The Language of Hip Hop Culture*. New York: Routledge, 2006.

The American Heritage College Dictionary. 3rd ed. Boston, MA: Houghton Mifflin, 1993.

Andrews, William, ed. *The Oxford Frederick Douglass Reader*. New York: Oxford University Press, 1996.

Augenbraum, Harold, and Margarite Fernandez Olmos, eds. *U.S. Latino Literature: A Critical Guide for Students and Teachers*. New York: Greenwood, 2000.

Baker Houston, Jr. *Blues, Ideology, and Afro-American Literature: A Vernacular Theory*. Chicago: University of Chicago Press, 1983.

Baker, Houston. *Black Studies, Rap and the Academy*. Chicago: University of Chicago Press, 1993.

Baldwin, James. *The Price of the Ticket*. New York: St. Martin's Press, 1985.

Baraka, Amiri. *The Fiction of LeRoi Jones/Amiri Baraka*. Chicago: Lawrence Hill Books, 2000.

Bentson, Kimberly, ed. *Imamu Amiri Baraka (Leroi Jones): A Collection of Critical Essays*. Upper Saddle River, NJ: Prentice Hall, 1978.

The Black Public Sphere Collective, eds. *The Black Public Sphere*. Chicago: University of Chicago Press, 1995.

Blockson, Charles. *Hippocrene Guide to the Underground Railroad*. New York: Hippocrene Books, 1994.

Buckmaster, Henrietta. *Let My People Go: The Story of the Underground Railroad and the Growth of the Abolition Movement*. Columbia: University of South Carolina Press, 1992.

Chesnutt, Charles. [first published 1899]. *The Conjure Woman*. Ann Arbor: University of Michigan Press, 1969.

Deleuze and Guattari. *A Thousand Plateaus: Capitalism and Schizophrenia*. Translated by Brian Masumi. Minneapolis: University of Minnesota Press, 1987. Originally published as *Mille Plateaux: Capitalisme et Schizophreni II* (Paris: Minuit, 1980).

Deutsch, Martin, Irwin Katz, and Arthur Jensen, eds. *Social Class, Race and Psychological Development*. New York: Holt, Rinehart and Winston, 1968.

Dunbar, Paul Laurence. *Lyrics of Lowly Life* (with an introduction by W. D. Howells). New York: Dodd, Mead, 1896.

Dyson Michael Eric. *Race Rules: Navigating the Color Line.* New York: Vintage Books, 1996.

Ellison, Ralph. [first published 1952]. *Invisible Man.* New York: Vintage International, 1995.

Ellison, Ralph. *Shadow and Act.* New York: Vintage Books, (Reissue edition) 1995.

Essien-Udom, E. U. *Black Nationalism: A Search for an Identity in America.* Chicago: University of Chicago Press, 1962.

Fabian, Johannes. "Ethnographic Misunderstanding and the Perils of Context." *American Anthropologist* 97(1) (1995).

Favor, J. Martin. *Authentic Blackness: The Folk in the New Negro Renaissance.* Durham: Duke University Press, 1999.

Forman, Murray. *The 'Hood Comes First: Race, Space, and Place in Rap and Hip-Hop.* Middletown, CT: Wesleyan University Press, 2002.

Gabbard, Krin, ed. *Jazz among the Discourses.* Durham, NC: Duke University Press, 1995.

Gates, Henry Louis. *Figures in Black: Words, Signs, and the Racial Self.* New York: Oxford University Press, 1987.

Gates, Henry Louis, ed. *Black Literature and Literary Theory.* New York: Routledge Press, 1990.

Gates, Henry Louis. 1998. "Foreword." In Hurston, *Their Eyes Were Watching God.*

Gates, Henry Louis. *The Signifying Monkey: A Theory of African American Literary Criticism.* New York: Oxford University Press, 1989.

Gilroy, Paul. *The Black Atlantic: Modernity and Double Consciousness.* Cambridge, MA: Harvard University Press, 1993.

Glover, Suresh. "Stephen Lawrence Inquiry: A Turning Point." *London Monitor* 2 (Autumn 1998).

Gordon, Lewis R., T. Denean Sharpley-Whiting, and Renee T. White, eds. *Fanon: A Critical Reader.* Cambridge, MA: Blackwell, 1996.

Gray, Herman. *African Americans and the Politics of Representation.* Oakland: University of California Press, 2005.

Green, Charles, ed. *Globalization and Survival in the Black Diaspora: The New Urban Challenge.* Albany: State University of New York Press, 1997.

Harris, Randy Allen. *The Linguistic Wars.* New York: Oxford University Press, 1993.

Harrison, Anthony Kwame. *The Hip Hop Underground: Intergrity and Ethics of Racial Identification.* Philadelphia: Temple University Press, 2009.

Hurston, Zora Neale. [first published 1937]. *Their Eyes Were Watching God.* New York: Harper Perennial Classics, 1998.

Jackendoff, Ray S. *Language, Consciousness, Culture: Essays on Mental Structure.* Cambridge: A Bradford Book/MIT Press, 2009.

Jackson, John L. *Real Black: Adventures in Racial Sincerity*. Chicago: University of Chicago Press, 2005.

Jeffries, Michael. *Thug Life: Race, Gender, and the Meaning of Hip Hop*. Chicago: University of Chicago Press, 2011.

Jones, Leroi. *Black Music.*, New York: William Morrow, 1967.

Kelley, Robin D. G. *Race Rebels: Culture, Politics, and the Black Working Class*. New York: Free Press, 1996.

Kelley, Robin D. G. *Yo' Mama's Disfunktional: Fighting the Culture Wars in Urban America*. Boston, MA: Beacon Press, 1997.

Kohn, Hans. *Nationalism: Its Meaning and History*. New York: Van Nostrand Reinhold, 1965.

Labov, William. *Language in the Inner City: Studies in the Black English Vernacular*. Philadelphia: University of Pennsylvania Press, 1972.

McCall, Nathan. *What's Going On: Personal Essays*. New York: Random House, 1997.

Neal, Mark Anthony. *What the Music Said: Black Popular Music and Black Public Culture*. New York: Routledge, 1999.

Neate, Patrick. *Where You're At: Notes from the Frontlines of a Hip Hop Planet*. New York: Riverhead Press, 2004.

Oumano, Elena. "British Hip-Hop Scene Bounds Back." *Billboard.*, June 26, 1999.

Perry, Imani. *Prophets from the Hood: Politics and Poetics in Hip Hop*. Durham: Duke University Press, 2004.

Perry, Theresa, and Lisa Delpit, eds. *The Real Ebonics Debate: Power, Language, and the Education of African American Children*. Boston, MA: Beacon Press, 1998.

Peterson, James B. "The Revenge of Emmett Till: Impudent Aesthetics and the Swagger Narratives of Hip Hop Culture." *African American Review* 44.4, (Winter 2012): pp. 617–631.

Rose, Tricia. *Black Noise: Rap Music and Black Culture in Contemporary America*. Hanover: University Press of New England, 1994.

Rose, Tricia. *The Hip Hop Wars: What We Talk About When We Talk About Hip Hop – and Why It Matters*. New York: Basic Civitas Books, 2008.

Sanders, Leslie C. *The Development of Black Theater in America: From Shadows to Selves*. Baton Rouge: Louisiana State University Press, 1988.

Schloss, Joseph. *Making Beats: The Art of Sample-Based Hip-Hop*. Middletown: Wesleyan University Press, 2004.

Sidran, Ben. *Black Talk*. New York: Holt, Rinehart and Winston, 1971.

Slater, Ross, and Raymond Enisuoh. "Stephen's Best Pal Speaks Out: Brave Duwayne Brooks reveals all to the press for the first time." *New Nation*, February 8, 1999.

Smith, Charles Allan. *Jonathan Green's Seeking: A Documentary by Charles Allan Smith*. South Carolina: Earthbeat Productions/University of South Carolina Press, 2008.

Smith, Christopher Holmes. "Method in the Madness: Exploring the Boundaries of Identity in Hip-Hop Performativity." *Social Identities* 3(3) (1997).

Smitherman, Geneva. *Talkin and Testifyin*. Boston, MA: Houghton Mifflin, 1977.

Smitherman, Geneva. *Black Talk: Words and Phrases from the Hood to the Amen Corner*. Revised edition, Boston: Houghton Mifflin, 2000.

Tillet, Salamishah. *Sites of Slavery: Citizenship and Racial Democracy in the Post-Civil Rights Imagination*. Durham: Duke University Press, 2012.

Toth, Jennifer. *The Mole People: Life in the Tunnels Beneath New York City*. Chicago: Chicago Review Press, 1995.

Toure. "The Hip-Hop Nation: Whose Is It Anyway?" *New York Times*, August 22, 1999.

Ward, John William. "Afterword." Harriet Beecher Stowe. *Uncle Tom's Cabin*. New York: Signet Classics, 1966.

West, Cornel. *Prophetic Fragments*. Trenton, NJ: Africa World Press, 1988.

White, Renee T. "Revolutionary Theory: Sociological Dimensions of Fanon's Sociologie d'une revolution." In *Fanon: A Critical Reader*, edited by Gordon Lewis R., T. Denean Sharpley-Whiting, and Renee T. White. Cambridge, MA: Blackwell, 1996.

Wideman, John Edgar. "Taint." *New Yorker*. Special edition focusing on black culture. 1996.

Williams, Patricia. *The Alchemy of Race and Rights*. London: Virago Press, 1993.

Wright, Richard. [first published 1944] "The Man Who Lived Underground." In *Norton Anthology of African American Literature*, edited by Henry Louis Gates Jr. and Nellie Y. McKay. New York: W. W. Norton, 1997.

Wright, Richard. [first published 1938]. *Uncle Tom's Children*. New York: First Harper Perennial, 1991.

Young, Kevin. *The Grey Album: On the Blackness of Blackness*. Minneapolis: Graywolf Press, 2012.

INDEX

Page numbers in *italics* denote information in tables.